10 277
5

986
10

1. 30
3.00
8
3
7
9
31.3

1036.58
2075

98.6

67.3.

# Intermediate Russian

My needs:
cute

Written by

Constantine Muravnik

1036.58

**LIVING LANGUAGE**®

Content from this program has been modified and enhanced from Complete Course Russian: The Basics, published in 2008.

Living Language and colophon are registered trademarks of Random House, Inc.

Published in the United States by Living Language, an imprint of Random House, Inc.

www.livinglanguage.com

Editor: Erin Quirk
Production Editor: Ciara Robinson
Production Manager: Tom Marshall
Audio Producer: Ok Hee Kolwitz
Interior Design: Sophie Chin
Illustrations: Sophie Chin

First Edition

ISBN: 978-0-307-97210-1

This book is available at special discounts for bulk purchases for sales promotions or premiums. Special editions, including personalized covers, excerpts of existing books, and corporate imprints, can be created in large quantities for special needs. For more information, write to Special Markets/ Premium Sales, 1745 Broadway, MD 3-1, New York, New York 10019 or e-mail specialmarkets@ randomhouse.com.

PRINTED IN THE UNITED STATES OF AMERICA

10 9 8

## About the Author

Constantine Muravnik is a native of Moscow. He holds a Ph.D. from the Slavic Department of Yale University, where he has been teaching since 1995. Prior to this, he taught Russian in the Slavic Department of Georgetown University and at Moscow State University, where he earned his B.A.

## Acknowledgments

Thanks to the Living Language team: Amanda D'Acierno, Christopher Warnasch, Suzanne McQuade, Laura Riggio, Erin Quirk, Heather Dalton, Fabrizio LaRocca, Siobhan O'Hare, Sophie Chin, Ann McBride, Tina Malaney, Pat Stango, Sue Daulton, Alison Skrabek, Ciara Robinson, Andrea McLin, and Tom Marshall.

**UNIT 1:** Food 13

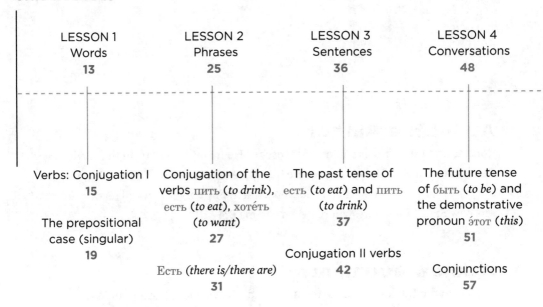

| LESSON 1 | LESSON 2 | LESSON 3 | LESSON 4 |
|---|---|---|---|
| Words | Phrases | Sentences | Conversations |
| 13 | 25 | 36 | 48 |

Verbs: Conjugation I
15

The prepositional
case (singular)
19

Conjugation of the
verbs пить (*to drink*),
есть (*to eat*), хотéть
(*to want*)
27

Есть (*there is/there are*)
31

The past tense of
есть (*to eat*) and пить
(*to drink*)
37

Conjugation II verbs
42

The future tense
of быть (*to be*) and
the demonstrative
pronoun э́тот (*this*)
51

Conjunctions
57

COURSE

**UNIT 2:** Family and the Home **66**

| LESSON 5 | LESSON 6 | LESSON 7 | LESSON 8 |
|---|---|---|---|
| Words | Phrases | Sentences | Conversations |
| **66** | **81** | **94** | **105** |

Singular possessive pronouns and the genitive case (singular)
**68**

The instrumental case and the verbs работать (*to work*) and жить (*to live*)
**83**

Personal pronouns in the genitive case
**96**

Reflexive verbs and the instrumental case of pronouns and adjectives
**110**

Prepositional phrases with the verb роди́ться and rooms of the house
**75**

The dative case
**90**

Negation
**100**

The genitive of origin
**117**

OUTLINE

**UNIT 3:** Everyday Life **127**

| LESSON 9<br>Words<br>**127** | LESSON 10<br>Phrases<br>**141** | LESSON 11<br>Sentences<br>**155** | LESSON 12<br>Conversations<br>**171** |
|---|---|---|---|
| Imperfective and perfective verbs<br>**129** | More imperfective-perfective verb pairs and the days of the week<br>**143** | The genitive plural case and telling time<br>**157** | Expressing likes and dislikes<br>**174** |
| The verbs покупа́ть — купи́ть (*to buy*)<br>**134** | More on verbs of motion<br>**148** | The accusative of duration, numbers 100—1,000, and ordinal numbers<br>**163** | The verbs занима́ться (*to study*) and игра́ть (*to play*)<br>**182** |

COURSE

**UNIT 4:** Health and the Human Body **192**

| LESSON 13 Words **192** | LESSON 14 Phrases **206** | LESSON 15 Sentences **217** | LESSON 16 Conversations **233** |
|---|---|---|---|
| Body parts and the plural of neuter nouns and the verb болéть (*to be sick*) **194** | The imperfective verbs казáться and чýвствовать and the modal verb мочь **208** | *Something* and *anything* and negative pronouns and adverbs **220** | Perfective aspect in negative sentences **236** |
| The verb болéть (*to hurt*) and expressing ailments **199** | Irregular genitive plurals **213** | The accusative of personal pronouns **226** | Imperatives and aspect **240** |

OUTLINE

**UNIT 5:** Talking on the Phone 253

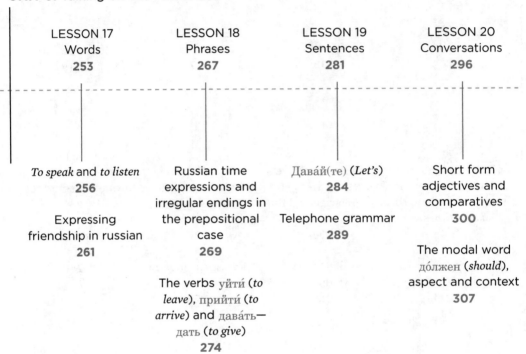

LESSON 17
Words
**253**

LESSON 18
Phrases
**267**

LESSON 19
Sentences
**281**

LESSON 20
Conversations
**296**

*To speak* and *to listen*
**256**

Expressing
friendship in russian
**261**

Russian time
expressions and
irregular endings in
the prepositional
case
**269**

The verbs уйти́ (*to
leave*), прийти́ (*to
arrive*) and дава́ть—
дать (*to give*)
**274**

Дава́й(те) (*Let's*)
**284**

Telephone grammar
**289**

Short form
adjectives and
comparatives
**300**

The modal word
до́лжен (*should*),
aspect and context
**307**

Pronunciation Guide 319
Grammar Summary 333

# How to Use This Course

Welcome to *Living Language Intermediate Russian*! Before we begin, let's take a quick look at what you'll see in this course.

## CONTENT

*Intermediate Russian* is a continuation of *Essential Russian*. It will review, expand on, and add to the foundation that you received in *Essential Russian*. In other words, this course contains an in-depth review of important vocabulary and grammar from *Essential Russian*; an expanded and more advanced look at some key vocabulary and grammar from *Essential Russian*; an introduction to idiomatic language and more challenging Russian grammar.

## UNITS

There are five units in this course. Each unit has four lessons arranged in a "building block" structure: the first lesson will present essential *words*, the second will introduce longer *phrases*, the third will teach *sentences*, and the fourth will show how everything works together in everyday *conversations*.

At the beginning of each unit is an introduction highlighting what you'll learn in that unit. At the end of each unit you'll find a self-graded Unit Quiz, which tests what you've learned.

## LESSONS

There are four lessons per unit for a total of 20 lessons in the course. Each lesson has the following components:

- **Introduction** outlining what you will cover in the lesson.

- **Word Builder 1** (first lesson of the unit) presenting key words and phrases.

- **Phrase Builder 1** (second lesson of the unit) introducing longer phrases and expressions.

- **Sentence Builder 1** (third lesson of the unit) teaching sentences.

- **Conversation 1** (fourth lesson of the unit) for a natural dialogue that brings together important vocabulary and grammar from the unit.

- **Word/Phrase/Sentence/Conversation Practice 1** practicing what you learned in Word Builder 1, Phrase Builder 1, Sentence Builder 1, or Conversation 1.

- **Grammar Builder 1** guiding you through important Russian grammar that you need to know.

- **Work Out 1** for a comprehensive practice of what you saw in Grammar Builder 1.

- **Word Builder 2/Phrase Builder 2/Sentence Builder 2/Conversation 2** for more key words, phrases, or sentences, or a second dialogue.

- **Word/Phrase/Sentence/Conversation Practice 2** practicing what you learned in Word Builder 2, Phrase Builder 2, Sentence Builder 2, or Conversation 2.

- **Grammar Builder 2** for more information on Russian grammar.

- **Work Out 2** for a comprehensive practice of what you saw in Grammar Builder 2.

- **Drive It Home** ingraining an important point of Russian grammar for the long term.

- **Tip** or **Culture Note** for a helpful language tip or useful cultural information related to the lesson or unit.

- **How Did You Do?** outlining what you learned in the lesson.

- **Word Recall** reviewing important vocabulary and grammar from the lesson.

- **Take It Further** sections appear throughout the lessons, providing extra information about new vocabulary, expanding on certain grammar points, or introducing additional words and phrases.

## UNIT QUIZ

- After each Unit, you'll see a **Unit Quiz.** The quizzes are self-graded so it's easy for you to test your progress and see if you should go back and review.

## PROGRESS BAR

You will see a **Progress Bar** on each page that has course material. It indicates your current position within the unit and lets you know how much progress you're making. Each line in the bar represents a Grammar Builder section.

## AUDIO

Look for the symbol ⊙ to help guide you through the audio as you're reading the book. It will tell you which track to listen to for each section that has audio. When you see the symbol, select the indicated track and start listening. If you don't see the symbol, then there isn't any audio for that section.

You can listen to the audio on its own, when you're on the go, to brush up on your pronunciation or review what you've learned in the book.

## PRONUNCIATION GUIDE, GRAMMAR SUMMARY, AND WRITING GUIDE

At the back of this book you will find a **Pronunciation Guide** and **Grammar Summary**. The Pronunciation Guide provides information on Russian pronunciation and spelling. The Grammar Summary contains an overview of key Russian grammar, some of which is covered *Essential* and *Intermediate Russian, and some of which you won't formally learn until Advanced Russian.*

# FREE ONLINE TOOLS

Go to **www.livinglanguage.com/languagelab** to access your free online tools. The tools are organized around the units in this course, with audiovisual flashcards and interactive games and quizzes. These tools will help you to review and practice the vocabulary and grammar that you've seen in the units, as well as provide some bonus words and phrases related to the unit's topic. The additional audio practice can be downloaded for use on the go.

# Unit 1:
## Food

Поздравля́ем с оконча́нием нача́льного у́ровня и нача́лом сре́днего! Добро́ пожа́ловать! *Congratulations on the completion of Essential Russian and the beginning of Intermediate Russian! Welcome!*

In this unit, you'll prepare yourself to plan meals and eat at a restaurant. You'll learn essential vocabulary about food and drink, more about the past tense and prepositions to express different locations, and how to talk about what you like and what you want.

## Lesson 1: Words

In this lesson, you'll learn:

- [ ] How to talk about food, eating, and drinking.
- [ ] The names of different food items and meals.
- [ ] How to use correct prepositions with different locations.
- [ ] More about verb conjugations.
- [ ] More about the prepositional case.

Гото́вы? Тогда́ начнём! *Ready? Then, let's begin!* Let's get started with some words and phrases.

## Word Builder 1

▶ 1A Word Builder 1 (CD: 4, Track: 2)

| | |
|---|---|
| зáвтрак | *breakfast* |
| зáвтракать | *to have breakfast* |
| обéд | *lunch* |
| обéдать | *to have lunch* |
| ýжин | *dinner* |
| ýжинать | *to have dinner* |
| омлéт | *omelet* |
| бутербрóд | *(open-faced) sandwich (lit., butter-bread)* |
| водá | *water* |
| кóфе | *coffee* |
| молокó | *milk* |
| мюсли | *cereal* |
| буфéт | *cafeteria* |
| ресторáн | *restaurant* |
| цéнтр | *downtown, center* |
| гостúница | *hotel* |
| фойé | *lobby (of a hotel or theater)* |

## Take It Further

Notice that the Russian word for *cereal*, мюсли, comes from the brand name of popular Swiss cereal, *Muesli*. This type of word is called "proprietary eponym"; compare it with the English usage of the word *Kleenex* for any facial tissue.

The Russian word for *hotel* or ~~theater lobby~~, фойé, comes from the French word *foyer*, also borrowed in English.

*proprietary eponym* фойé

## ✎ **Word Practice 1**

Match the following English words on the left with their Russian equivalents on the right.

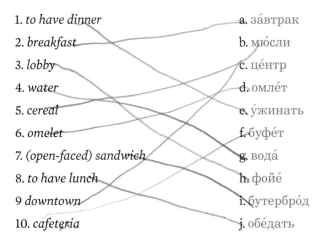

1. *to have dinner*          a. за́втрак

2. *breakfast*               b. мю́сли

3. *lobby*                   c. це́нтр

4. *water*                   d. омле́т

5. *cereal*                  e. у́жинать

6. *omelet*                  f. буфе́т

7. *(open-faced) sandwich*   g. вода́

8. *to have lunch*           h. фойе́

9 *downtown*                 i. бутербро́д

10. *cafeteria*              j. обе́дать

**ANSWER KEY**
1. e; 2. a; 3. h; 4. g; 5. b; 6. d; 7. i; 8. j; 9. c; 10. f

## **Grammar Builder 1**

▶ 1B Grammar Builder 1 (CD: 4, Track: 3)

### **VERBS: CONJUGATION I**

There are three daily meals in Russia: за́втрак (*breakfast*), обе́д (*lunch*), and у́жин (*dinner/supper*). The Russian verbs за́втракать (*to have breakfast*), обе́дать (*to have lunch*), and у́жинать (*to have dinner/supper*) are derived from the above nouns. Notice that their infinitive forms are marked by the Russian ending –ть, which corresponds to the English particle *to,* as in *to have.* In order to say *I have breakfast* rather than *to have breakfast*, you need to change the verb's ending. A verb's conjugation depends on the person and number of the subject performing an action (*I have breakfast, she has breakfast, etc.*) and on the time when the action takes place (*I have breakfast, I had breakfast, etc.*). There are two regular conjugation types in Russian along with a few exceptions, and some irregular verb conjugations. In this lesson, we'll review the first type of verb conjugation, which is called Conjugation I.

Let's take a look at the regular present tense conjugations. Memorize these forms; most Russian verbs will have the same or very similar endings when conjugated.

| CONJUGATION I | |
|---|---|
| я –ю/–у | мы –ем |
| ты –ешь | вы –ете |
| он/онá –ет | они́ –ют/–ут |

The –ю (first person singular) and –ют (third person plural) Conjugation I endings are actually a combination of the stem ending –й and the conjugation endings –у and –ут; we'll look at how and why this happens in Unit 3. Most of the Conjugation I verbs you'll see in the next few lessons will have –ю and –ют endings. Now let's look at how these endings work with the Conjugation I verb зáвтракать (*to have breakfast*). Notice that the –ть is dropped. The above endings are then attached to conjugate the verb—in this case зáвтракать—in the present tense.

| ЗÁВТРАКАТЬ *TO HAVE BREAKFAST* | |
|---|---|
| я зáвтракаю | мы зáвтракаем |
| ты зáвтракаешь | вы зáвтракаете |
| он/онá/онó зáвтракает | они́ зáвтракают |

# ✎ Work Out 1

A. Fill in the blank with the correct personal pronoun: я, ты, он/она́, мы, вы, они́.

1. _Я_ за́втракаю

2. _мы_ обе́даешь

3. _мы_ у́жинаем

4. _он_ обе́дает

5. _вы_ за́втракаете

6. _они_ у́жинают

B. Using the pronouns below as clues, conjugate the three different verbs for meals за́втракать, обе́дать, у́жинать in the present tense.

1. мы _за́втракаем_

2. вы _обе́даете_

3. я _обе́даю_

4. Ната́лья _обе́дает_

5. ты _у́жинаешь_

6. Ната́лья и Джон _у́жинают_

**ANSWER KEY**

A. 1. я; 2. ты; 3. мы; 4. он/она́; 5. вы; 6. они́

B. 1. за́втракаем, обе́даем, у́жинаем; 2. за́втракаете, обе́даете, у́жинаете; 3. за́втракаю, обе́даю, у́жинаю; 4. за́втракает, обе́дает, у́жинает; 5. за́втракаешь, обе́даешь, у́жинаешь; 6. за́втракают, обе́дают, у́жинают

## Word Builder 2

▶ 1C Word Builder 2 (CD: 4, Track: 4)

| | |
|---|---|
| супермáркет | *supermarket* |
| рыба | *fish* |
| мясо | *meat* |
| зелёный салáт | *lettuce (lit., green salad)* |
| лук *лук* | *onion (non-count)* |
| картóшка *картошка* | *potatoes (colloquial)* |
| макарóны, пáста *макероны* | *pasta (lit., macaroni; always plural)* |
| сыр *сыр* | *cheese* |
| чай *чай* | *tea* |
| сок *сок* | *juice* |
| сегóдня *сегодня* | *today* |
| кафé *кафе* | *café* |
| столóвая *столовая* | *dining hall, cafeteria* |
| дóма *дома* | *at home* |
| вмéсте *вместе* | *together* |
| купúть *купить* | *to buy* |
| едá *еда* | *food* |

## ✎ Word Practice 2

Write the following nouns in the correct category and translate them into English.

рыба, буфéт, мясо, зелёный салáт, ресторáн, чай, лук, картóшка, макарóны, сыр, сок, кафé

A. Places to Eat

1. _____

2. _____

3. _____

## B. Things to Eat

1. _____

2. _____

3. _____

4. _____

5. _____

6. _____

7. _____

## C. Things to Drink

1. _____

1. _____

**ANWER KEY**

A. 1. буфе́т (*cafeteria*); 2. рестора́н (*restaurant*); 3. кафе́ (*café*)
B. 1. ры́ба (*fish*); 2. мя́со (*meat*); 3. зелёный сала́т (*green salad*); 4. лук (*onion(s)*); 5. карто́шка (*potato(es)*); 6. макаро́ны (*pasta/macaroni*); 7. сыр (*cheese*)
C. 1. чай (*tea*); 2. сок (*juice*)

# Grammar Builder 2

▶ 1D Grammar Builder 2 (CD: 4, Track: 5)

## THE PREPOSITIONAL CASE (SINGULAR)

To denote where something is happening (*at a restaurant, in a cafeteria, in Moscow, in New York,* etc.), the preposition в (*in or at*) is used and the ending of a Russian singular noun typically changes to –e. This ending marks the prepositional case of the noun. Location (*at* or *in* a place) is one possible meaning of the prepositional case. Remember not to confuse location with direction in Russian. Direction (*to* a place) requires the accusative case. The prepositional ending –e replaces the masculine "zero" ending, the feminine –а/я endings and the neuter –о/e ending.

| PREPOSITIONAL SINGULAR: –E ENDING | EXAMPLES |
|---|---|
| *m.* | в Нью-Йóрке, в ресторáне |
| *f.* | в Москвé |
| *n* | в кафé |

Compare the following.

| NOMINATIVE | PREPOSITIONAL |
|---|---|
| Москвá (*f.*) <br> *Moscow* | в Москвé <br> *in Moscow* |
| Нью-Йóрк (*m.*) <br> *New York* | в Нью-Йóрке <br> *in New York* |
| ресторáн (*m.*) <br> *restaurant* | в ресторáне <br> *at/in the restaurant* |
| кафé (*n.*) <br> *café* | в кафé <br> *at/in the café* |

One exception to this pattern is дóма, which means *at home*. You don't need to use the prepositional case to say *at home* in Russian.

Я дóма.
*I'm home./I'm at home.*

Another locative preposition, the preposition на (*on* or *at*), usually refers to open locations, such as floors, streets, avenues, stadiums, fields, squares, islands, etc. It also refers to work or social gatherings, such as parties and picnics. На with a noun in the prepositional case means *on* rather than *in*, but there are exceptions, so it's best to learn which individual words in Russian take на or в as their preposition. Adjectives modifying masculine and neuter nouns in the prepositional case take –ом/–ем endings and those modifying feminine nouns in the prepositional case take –ой endings.

| PREPOSITIONAL CASE WITH НА AND В | *на первом этаже* |
|---|---|
| на пе́рвом этаже́ (*masc.*) | on the first floor |
| на Не́вском проспе́кте (*masc.*) | on Nevsky Prospect (Avenue) *на Невском* |
| на Садо́вой у́лице (*fem.*) | on Sadovaya Street *на Садовой улице* |
| на рабо́те *на работе* | at work *на работе* |
| на стадио́не *на стадионе* | at the stadium |
| на Мадагаска́ре | in Madagascar *на Мадагаскаре* |
| в университе́те | at the university *в университете* |

## ✎ Work Out 2

Say that the following people were in the following places. Remember to use the past tense of the verb *to be* (быть) in accordance with the person's gender: он был (*m.*), она́ была́ (*f.*), or они́ бы́ли (*pl.*).

1. я (*masc.*), буфе́т

   *Я был в буфете*

2. Джон, Москва́

   *в Москве*

3. Ири́на, рестора́н

   *в ресторане*

4. мы, центр

   *в центре*

The prepositional case
(singular)

5. вы, гости́ница

*в гостинице*

6. о́ля, Аме́рика

*в Америке*

7. она́, до́ма

*дома*

8. вы, Мадагаска́р

*на Мадагаскаре*

9. он, пе́рвый эта́ж

*на первом этаже*

10. она́, Садо́вая у́лица

*на Садовой улице*

**ANSWER KEY**

1. Я был в буфе́те. 2. Джон был в Москве́. 3. Ири́на была́ в рестора́не. 4. Мы бы́ли в це́нтре. 5. Вы бы́ли в гости́нице. 6. О́ля была́ в Аме́рике. 7. Она была́ до́ма. 8. Вы бы́ли на Мадагаска́ре. 9. Он был на пе́рвом этаже́. 10. Она́ была́ на Садо́вой у́лице.

## ✎ Drive It Home

Now that you've reviewed some familiar words and expressions and learned some new ones, let's see how they fit together. Fill in the missing Russian words and repeat the full Russian sentence aloud.

1. *Yesterday we were on Nevsky Prospect.*

Вчера́ мы бы́ли *на невском проспекте*

2. *My friends stayed/lived at a new hotel.*

Мои́ друзья́ жи́ли _в но́вой гости́нице_

3. *He usually has lunch at home.*

Он обы́чно _обе́дает до́ма_

4. *His wife worked in New York in the summer.*

Его́ жена́ рабо́тала _в Нью-Йо́рке_ ле́том.

5. *She was at the stadium in the morning.*

Она́ была́ _на стадио́не_ у́тром.

6. *We vacationed in Madagascar in the spring.*

Мы отдыха́ли _на Мадагаска́ре_ весно́й.

7. *You had breakfast at the cafeteria.*

Вы _за́втракали в буфе́те._

8. *My husband was at work in the afternoon.*

Мой муж был _на рабо́те_ днём.

9. *She lives on Sadovaya Street.*

Она́ живёт _на Садо́вой у́лице_

10. *His office is on the first floor.*

Его́ о́фис _на пе́рвом этаже́._

**ANSWER KEY**

1. на Не́вском проспе́кте; 2. в но́вой гости́нице; 3. обе́дает до́ма; 4. в Нью-Йо́рке; 5. на стадио́не; 6. на Мадагаска́ре; 7. за́втракали в буфе́те; 8. на рабо́те; 9. на Садо́вой у́лице; 10. на пе́рвом этаже́

The prepositional case
(singular)

Есть (*there is/there are*)

## How Did You Do?

Let's see how you did in this lesson. You should know:

☐ How to talk about food, eating, and drinking. (Still unsure? Go back to page 14.)

☐ More about verb conjugations. (Still unsure? Go back to page 15.)

☐ The names of different food items and meals. (Still unsure? Go back to page 18.)

☐ How to use correct prepositions with different locations. (Still unsure? Go back to page 19.)

☐ More about the prepositional case. (Still unsure? Go back to page 20.)

## ✎ Word Recall

And now you'll have a chance to review the vocabulary and structures we've worked on. Match the Russian words and expressions on the left with their English equivalents on the right.

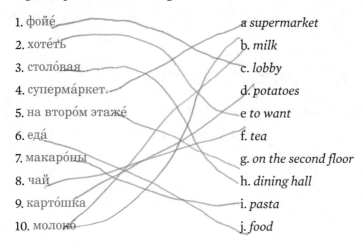

1. фойé                     a *supermarket*
2. хотéть                   b. *milk*
3. столóвая                 c. *lobby*
4. супермáркет              d. *potatoes*
5. на вторóм этажé          e *to want*
6. едá                      f. *tea*
7. макарóны                 g. *on the second floor*
8. чай                      h. *dining hall*
9. картóшка                 i. *pasta*
10. молокó                  j. *food*

**ANSWER KEY**

1. c; 2. e; 3. h; 4. a; 5. g; 6. j; 7. i; 8. f; 9. d; 10. b

# Lesson 2: Phrases

Добро́ пожа́ловать ещё раз! *Welcome, once again!*

In this lesson, you'll learn how to:

☐ Conjugate some irregular verbs related to food.

☐ Name different food items and meals.

☐ Express your wants.

Гото́вы? Тогда́ начнём! *Ready? Then, let's begin!*

Let's get started with some words and phrases.

## Phrase Builder 1

▶ 2A Phrase Builder 1 (CD: 4, Track: 6)

| | |
|---|---|
| Как у вас дела́? | *How are you doing? (form./pl.)* |
| на пе́рвом этаже́ | *on the first floor* |
| то́лько что | *just, recently* |
| на за́втрак | *for breakfast* |
| Что там (есть)? | *What is there?* |
| фру́кт(ы) | *fruit(s)* |
| бутербро́д с сы́ром | *open-faced cheese sandwich* |
| ко́фе с молоко́м | *coffee with milk* |
| есть | *to eat** |
| пить | *to drink* |
| хоте́ть | *to want* |

*Be aware that есть (*to eat*) is a homonym of the 3rd person form of the verb быть (*to be*).

The prepositional case
(singular)

| в цéнтре гóрода | in the center of the city, downtown |
| Прия́тного аппети́та! | *Bon appétit!* |
| уви́димся *увидимся* | *see you* |
| Спаси́бо за по́мощь! | *Thank you for (your) help!* |
| Не за что. *не за што* | *Not at all./Don't mention it.* |

*Be aware that есть (*to eat*) is a homonym of the 3rd person form of the verb быть (*to be*).

## ✎ Phrase Practice 1

Match the English phrases on the left to their Russian equivalents on the right.

1. *in the center of the city*

2. *Bon appétit!*

3. *Not at all (don't mention it)*

4. *just (recently)*

5. *What's there?*

6. *coffee with milk*

7. *for breakfast*

8. *on the first floor*

9. *see you*

10. *How are you doing?*

a. Что там есть?

b. на за́втрак

c. уви́димся

d. в цéнтре гóрода

e. Не за что.

f. Как у вас дела́?

g. Прия́тного аппети́та!

h. то́лько что

i. кóфе с молокóм

j. на пéрвом этажé

**ANSWER KEY**
1. d; 2. g; 3. e; 4. h; 5. a; 6. i; 7. b; 8. j; 9. c; 10. f

The past tense of есть (*to eat*) and пить (*to drink*) | The future tense of быть (*to be*) and the demonstrative pronoun этот (*this*)

Conjugation II verbs | Conjunctions

# Grammar Builder 1

▶ 2B Grammar Builder 1 (CD: 4, Track: 7)

## CONJUGATION OF THE VERBS ПИТЬ (*TO DRINK*), ЕСТЬ (*TO EAT*), ХОТЕ́ТЬ (*TO WANT*)

The verb пить (*to drink*) in the present tense follows the Conjugation I paradigm. Note that the letter –ё replaces –е when it is stressed.

| ПТЬ *TO DRINK* | |
|---|---|
| я пью | мы пьём |
| ты пьёшь | вы пьёте |
| он/она́/оно́ пьёт | они́ пьют |

Not all Russian verbs stick to the same pattern. There are several irregular verbs, and you will simply need to memorize their conjugation. The verb есть (*to eat*) is one of these irregular verbs. Let's review its conjugation table in the present tense.

| ЕСТЬ *TO EAT* | |
|---|---|
| я ем | мы еди́м |
| ты ешь | вы еди́те |
| он/она́/оно́ ест | они́ едя́т |

Another irregular verb is хоте́ть (*to want*). Let's review its present tense conjugation.

| ХОТЕ́ТЬ *TO WANT* | |
|---|---|
| я хочу́ | ы хоти́м |
| ты хо́чешь | вы хоти́те |
| он/она́/оно́ хо́чет | они́ хотя́т |

Note that it's uncommon to say *I would like* in Russian. Most people prefer a more direct expression: я хочу́ (*I want*).

The prepositional case
(singular)

Есть (*there is/there are*)

Что вы хотите?

Я хочу́ …

*What would you like (lit., What do you want)?*

*I would like … (lit., I want)*

This expression is perfectly polite and acceptable.

## ✎ Work Out 1

A. Write the correct forms of the verb есть (*to eat*) in the present tense next to the following pronouns. Repeat the phrase out loud.

1. ты *ешь*

2. я *ем*

3. она́ *еет*

4. мы *едим* они едят

5. они *едим* едят

6. вы *едите*

7. он *ед ест*

B. Write the correct forms of the verb пить (*to drink*) in the present tense next to the following subjects.

1. Ли́за и Ко́ля *пьют*

2. Ната́ша *пьёт*

3. я *пью*

4. Джон и я *пьём*

The past tense of есть (*to eat*)
and пить (*to drink*)

The future tense of быть (*to be*) and the
demonstrative pronoun э́тот (*this*)

Conjugation II verbs

Conjunctions

5. студе́нты _пьют_

6. моя́ жена́ _пьёт_

C. Insert the correct forms of the verb хоте́ть (*to want*) in the following sentences.

1. Я _хочу́_ за́втракать.

2. Мы _хоти́м_ вме́сте обе́дать в столо́вой.

3. Что вы _хоти́те_ купи́ть в суперма́ркете?

4. Они́ _хотя́т_ у́жинать в рестора́не.

5. Где ты _хо́чешь_ обе́дать?

**ANSWER KEY**

A. 1. ешь; 2. ем; 3. ест; 4. еди́м; 5. едя́т; 6. еди́те; 7. ест
B. 1. пьют; 2. пьёт; 3. пью; 4. пьём; 5. пьют; 6. пьёт
C. 1. хочу́; 2. хоти́м; 3. хоти́те; 4. хотя́т; 5. хо́чешь

# Phrase Builder 2

▶ 2C Phrase Builder 2 (CD: 4, Track: 8)

| | |
|---|---|
| что́-нибу́дь | something, anything |
| что́-нибу́дь на за́втрак | something, anything for breakfast |
| Что́-нибу́дь ещё? | Anything else? |
| У меня́ мно́го рабо́ты. | I have a lot of work (to do). |
| сего́дня | today |
| за́втра | tomorrow |
| за́втра ве́чером | tomorrow night |
| в столо́вой | in the dining hall/cafeteria |
| с друзья́ми | with friends |
| мо́жет быть | maybe, probably, perhaps |
| Я куплю́ сыр. | I will buy cheese. |

The prepositional case
(singular)

Есть (there is/there are)

*В холодильнике* (handwritten)

| в холоди́льнике | in the refrigerator |
|---|---|
| обы́чно *обычно* (handwritten) | usually, normally |

## ✎ Phrase Practice 2

Read the English sentence first and then fill in the blank in the Russian sentence. Repeat the entire Russian sentence out loud.

1. *She had dinner with friends in a restaurant.*

   Она́ у́жинала *с друзьями* в рестора́не.

2. *Tomorrow night I will have dinner at home.*

   *Завтра вечером* я бу́ду у́жинать до́ма.

3. *Would you like anything else?*

   Вы хоти́те *что-нибудь ещё*?

4. *I have a lot of work today.*

   У меня́ сего́дня _____.

5. *The food is in the refrigerator.*

   Еда́ *в холодильнике*

6. *He usually has lunch in a dining hall.*

   Он обы́чно обе́дает *в столовой*

7. *Maybe I'll buy cheese.*

   _____ я куплю́ сыр.

**ANSWER KEY**
1. с друзья́ми; 2. За́втра ве́чером; 3. что́-нибудь ещё; 4. мно́го рабо́ты; 5. в холоди́льнике; 6. в столо́вой; 7. Мо́жет быть

The past tense of есть (*to eat*)
and пить (*to drink*)

The future tense of быть (*to be*) and the
demonstrative pronoun э́тот (*this*)

Conjugation II verbs

Conjunctions

# Grammar Builder 2

▶ 2D Grammar Builder 2 (CD: 4, Track: 9)

## ЕСТЬ (*THERE IS/THERE ARE*)

Now let's learn how to say *there is/there are* and *I have* in Russian. Do you remember the expression Что там есть? (*What is there?*) from Phrase Builder 1? In modern Russian, the verb есть is the only possible form of the verb *to be* in the present tense and is often omitted in the present. In order to say that something is somewhere in Russian, you need to start with the location (там, в суперма́ркете, в холоди́льнике, etc.), then есть, and then the thing that *is* or the things that *are* at this location. This Russian construction corresponds to the English construction *there is/there are*.

В холоди́льнике есть молоко́.
*There is milk in the refrigerator. (lit., In the refrigerator is milk.)*

Notice that the subject молоко́ appears at the end of the sentence. Because the word order in Russian is not as strict as in English, the end of a sentence is usually reserved for new information and the beginning of the sentence restates something already familiar from the context. The subject of the sentence is normally in the nominative case and answers the questions кто? что? Instead of в холоди́льнике you can also say у меня́ (*lit., by me*) to express that you have milk (меня́ is the genitive case of the pronoun я; we will study it later).

У меня́ есть молоко́.
*I have milk. (lit., By me [there] is milk.)*

У меня́ мно́го рабо́ты.
*I have a lot of work (to do). (lit., By me [there is] a lot of work.)*

Notice the omission of есть in the second example. It is not necessary when the emphasis is on the quality or quantity of item in possession rather than on the fact of its possession. (Also note the noun рабóты, which is in the genitive singular case. Memorize it for now as it is.)

## ✎ Work Out 2

Что там есть? (*What is there?*) Answer this question by forming sentences with the following items and locations. Remember to keep the locations in the prepositional case and the available items in the nominative!

1. буфéт, бутербрóд с сы́ром

   _____

2. холодúльник, ры́ба и мя́со

   _____

3. супермáркет, лук, картóшка и помидóры

   _____

4. столóвая, омлéт и фрýкты

   _____

5. цéнтр, ресторáны и кафé

   _____

6. пéрвый этáж, óфисы

   _____

7. Нью-Йóрк, интерéсные музéи

   _____

The past tense of есть (*to eat*)
and пить (*to drink*)

The future tense of быть (*to be*) and the
demonstrative pronoun этот (*this*)

---

Conjugation II verbs

Conjunctions

8.  Москва, Кремль и Красная площадь

---

**ANSWER KEY**

1. В буфете есть бутерброд с сыром. 2. В холодильнике есть рыба и мясо. 3. В супермаркете есть лук, картошка и помидоры. 4. В столовой есть омлет и фрукты. 5. В центре есть рестораны и кафе. 6. На первом этаже есть офисы. 7. В Нью-Йорке есть интересные музеи. 8. В Москве есть Кремль и Красная площадь.

# ✎ Drive It Home

A.  Что у вас есть на завтрак, на обед, на ужин? (*What do you have (to eat) for breakfast, lunch, dinner?*) Use the construction у нас есть and the following prompts in your answers.

1.  на завтрак, омлёт и бутерброд с сыром

    *у нас*
    _____

2.  на завтрак, сок и кофе с молоком

    _____

3.  на обед, суп и мясо

    _____

4.  на обед, салат и сок

    _____

5.  на ужин, рыба и зелёный салат

    _____

6.  на ужин, макароны, салат и вино

    _____

The prepositional case
(singular)

Есть (*there is/there are*)

B. Fill in the blanks with the appropriate form of the verbs есть (*to eat*) and пить (*to drink*) in the present tense. Repeat the entire sentence out loud.

1. Я обычно _____ кофе на завтрак.

2. Ты обычно _____ зелёный чай на завтрак.

3. Он обычно _____ сок на завтрак.

4. Они обычно _____ вино на ужин.

5. Я обычно _____ зелёный салат и суп на обед.

6. Вы обычно _____ рыбу на обед.

7. Мы обычно _____ мясо и картошку на ужин.

8. Ты обычно _____ омлет на завтрак.

**ANSWER KEY**
A. 1. На завтрак у нас есть омлет и бутерброд с сыром. 2. На завтрак у нас есть сок и кофе с молоком. 3. На обед у нас есть суп и мясо. 4. На обед у нас есть салат и сок. 5. На ужин у нас есть рыба и зелёный салат. 6. На ужин у нас есть макароны, салат и вино.
B. 1. пью; 2. пьёшь; 3. пьёт; 4. пьют; 5. ем; 6. едите; 7. едим; 8. ешь

## How Did You Do?

Let's see how you did in this lesson. You should know how to:

☐ Name different food items and meals. (Still unsure? Go back to page 25.)

☐ Conjugate some irregular verbs related to food. (Still unsure? Go back to page 27.)

☐ Express your wants. (Still unsure? Go back to page 27.)

# ✎ Word Recall

Give Russian equivalents to the following English sentences.

1. *I have a lot of work today.*

2. *What would you (inform.) like for breakfast?*

3. *There are restaurants and cafés in the center of the city. (Watch the word order!)*

4. *Bon appétit!*

5. *Maybe I'll have pasta and wine for dinner.*

6. *He usually drinks beer.*

7. *There are sandwiches in the refrigerator.*

8. *There is a restaurant on the first floor.*

**ANSWER KEY**

1. У меня́ мно́го рабо́ты сего́дня. 2. Что ты хо́чешь на за́втрак? 3. В це́нтре го́рода есть рестора́ны и кафе́. 4. Прия́тного аппети́та! 5. Мо́жет быть, я бу́ду макаро́ны и вино́ на у́жин. 6. Он обы́чно пьёт пи́во. 7. В холоди́льнике есть бутербро́ды. 8. На пе́рвом этаже́ есть рестора́н.

# Lesson 3: Sentences

Мы ра́ды вас ви́деть! *We are glad to see you!*

In this lesson, you'll learn how to:

☐ Form commonly used sentences related to food, eating, and drinking.

☐ Conjugate eating and drinking verbs in the past tense.

☐ Say what you usually have for breakfast, lunch, or dinner.

☐ Talk about what you like.

Гото́вы? Тогда́ начнём! *Ready? Then, let's begin!*

Let's start with some useful sentences.

## Sentence Builder 1

▶ 3A Sentence Builder 1 (CD: 4, Track: 10)

| Скажи́те, пожа́луйста, где мы за́втракаем? | *Tell me, please, where are we having breakfast?* |
|---|---|
| Пойдёмте, я покажу́. | *Let's go, I'll show (you).* |
| Что там есть на за́втрак? | *What do they have for breakfast? (lit., What is there for breakfast?)* |
| Я ел(а) омле́т и бутербро́д с сы́ром. | *I ate an omelet and a sandwich with cheese.* |
| Я пил(а) во́ду и ко́фе с молоко́м. | *I drank water and coffee with milk.* |
| Я люблю́ ру́сскую ку́хню! | *I like (lit., love) Russian cuisine!* |
| Днём мы бу́дем обе́дать в ру́сском рестора́не. | *In the daytime, we'll have lunch in a Russian restaurant.* |

| Како́й э́то рестора́н? | *What kind of restaurant is it?* |
| Уви́димся в фойе́ гости́ницы. | *See you in the lobby of the hotel.* |

## Sentence Practice 1

Match the following English sentences on the left to their Russian equivalents on the right.

1. *What is there for breakfast?*

a. Она́ е́ла омле́т и бутербро́д с сы́ром.

2. *What kind of restaurant is it?*

b. Скажи́те, пожа́луйста, где мы за́втракаем?

3. *I like Russian cuisine.*

4. *She ate an omelet and a sandwich with cheese.*

c. Он пил во́ду и ко́фе с молоко́м.

d. Уви́димся в фойе́ гости́ницы.

5. *Let's go. I'll show (you).*

e. Что там есть на за́втрак?

6. *Tell me, please, where are we having breakfast?*

f. Я люблю́ ру́сскую ку́хню.

7. *See you in the lobby of the hotel.*

g. Како́й э́то рестора́н?

8. *He drank water and coffee with milk.*

h. Пойдёмте, я покажу́.

**ANSWER KEY**

1. e; 2. g; 3. f; 4. a; 5. h; 6. b; 7. d; 8. c

## Grammar Builder 1

▶ 3B Grammar Builder 1 (CD: 4, Track: 11)

### THE PAST TENSE OF ЕСТЬ (*TO EAT*) AND ПИТЬ (*TO DRINK*)

Although the present tense conjugations of the verbs есть (*to eat*) and пить (*to drink*) are irregular, the past tense is quite straightforward. Remember that Russian verbs change in the past tense according to the gender and number of the subject. The past tense does not change according to the person of the subject (e.g. the form is the same for 1st, 2nd, or 3rd person singular masculine subjects.)

| PAST TENSE OF ЕСТЬ (*TO EAT*) | |
| --- | --- |
| ел | masculine |
| éла | feminine |
| éло | neuter |
| éли | plural |

| PAST TENSE OF ПИТЬ (*TO DRINK*) | |
| --- | --- |
| пи́л | masculine |
| пила́ | feminine |
| пи́ло | neuter |
| пи́ли | plural |

Я е́л(а) омле́т и бутербро́д с сы́ром.
*I ate an omelet and a sandwich with cheese.*

Я пил(а) во́ду и ко́фе с молоко́м.
*I drank water and coffee with milk.*

As you can see, these forms don't differ from the past tense forms of the verb *to be*, был/была́/бы́ло/бы́ли. Most Russian verbs form the past tense by dropping the ending –ть of the infinitive and adding –л/–ла/–ло/–ли according to the gender/number of the noun. Notice that the stress shifts to the ending –a in the feminine past of пить (пила́) but then stays put for the other forms. This type of stress shift is common in the past tense. Notice that the verbs есть (*to eat*) and пить (*to drink*) take direct objects, which in Russian take the accusative case. The accusative of singular masculine inanimate nouns (ending in a consonant or –ь), neuter nouns (ending in –о or –е) and plural forms of inanimate nouns are the same as the nominative case.

Feminine nouns denoting direct objects drop their –а/–я endings and add –у/–ю endings in the accusative. Let's look at some examples.

| singular masc./n., plural: same as the nominative | омле́т, молоко́, фру́кты, со́ки |
|---|---|
| feminine: (у/-ю) | во́ду, о́лю |

Я е́л(а) омле́т и пи́л(а́) молоко́ и во́ду.
*I ate an omelet and drank milk and water.*

Я е́л(а) фру́кты и пи́л(а́) со́ки.
*I ate fruit(s) and drank juices.*

Remember that the Russian verbs за́втракать (*to have breakfast*), обе́дать (*to have lunch*), and у́жинать (*to have dinner*), don't take direct objects. Similar to English, if you need to specify what you had for breakfast, lunch or dinner, you should say:

Я е́л(а) омле́т на за́втрак.
*I ate an omelet for breakfast.*

# ✎ Work Out 1

A. Now let's practice. Translate the following sentences into Russian. Remember to make the past tense verbs agree with the gender and number of their subjects. Repeat the Russian sentence out loud.

1. *What did you (inform., fem.) have for breakfast?*

_____

2. *What did they eat for lunch?*

_____

3. *What did she eat for dinner?*

_____

4. *Where did you (form.) have breakfast?*

_____

5. *He had lunch at the hotel.*

_____

6. *We had dinner in a restaurant.*

_____

B. Что вы éли и пи́ли на за́втрак? *(What did you eat and drink for breakfast?)*: Answer this question using the following prompts. Remember to put the things you ate and drank into the accusative case! Я éл(а) ... и пи́л(á) ...

1. *omelet and juice*

_____

2. *fruit(s) and coffee with milk*

_____

3. *cheese sandwich and water*

_____

4. *cereal and milk*

_____

5. *omelet and water*

_____

The past tense of есть (*to eat*) and пить (*to drink*) | The future tense of быть (*to be*) and the demonstrative pronoun э́тот (*this*)

- - - - - - - - - - - - - - - - - - - - - - - - - - - - - - -

Conjugation II verbs | Conjunctions

**ANSWER KEY**

**A. 1.** Что ты е́ла на за́втрак? **2.** Что они́ е́ли на обе́д? **3.** Что она́ е́ла на у́жин? **4.** Где вы за́втракали? **5.** Он обе́дал в гости́нице. **6.** Мы у́жинали в ресторáне.

**B. 1.** Я е́л(а) омле́т и пи́л(á) сок. **2.** Я е́л(а) фру́кты и пи́л(á) ко́фе с молоко́м. **3.** Я е́л(а) бутербро́д с сы́ром и пи́л(á) во́ду. **4.** Я е́л(а) мю́сли и пи́л(á) молоко́. **5.** Я е́л(а) омле́т и пи́л(á) во́ду.

# Sentence Builder 2

▶ 3C Sentence Builder 2 (CD: 4, Track: 12)

| | |
|---|---|
| Я обы́чно за́втракаю до́ма. | *I usually have breakfast at home.* |
| Что ты хо́чешь купи́ть? | *What do you want to buy?* |
| Я хочу́ купи́ть ры́бу, помидо́ры, зелёный сала́т, лук и мя́со. | *I want to buy fish, tomatoes, lettuce, onion(s), and meat.* |
| Всё э́то есть в суперма́ркете. | *All of this is (available) in the supermarket.* |
| Я зна́ю одно́ хоро́шее и недорого́е кафе́ в це́нтре. | *I know a good and inexpensive café downtown (in the center).* |
| Извини́, сего́дня у меня́ мно́го рабо́ты. | *I'm sorry, I have a lot of work today.* |
| Дава́й пойдём туда́ за́втра ве́чером. | *Let's go there tomorrow night.* |
| Пойдём в клуб. | *Let's go to a club.* |
| Договори́лись. | *Okay. (lit., agreed)* |

## ✎ Sentence Practice 2

Let's practice the above sentences. Match the English sentences on the left to their Russian equivalents on the right. Repeat the Russian sentences out loud.

1. *What would you like to buy?*

2. *All of this is (available) in the supermarket.*

3. *Let's go there tomorrow night.*

4. *Okay (agreed).*

5. *Let's go to a club.*

6. *I'm sorry, I have a lot of work today.*

7. *I'd like to buy fish and tomatoes.*

8. *I know one inexpensive café downtown.*

a. Пойдём в клуб.

b. Я хочý купи́ть ры́бу и помидóры.

c. Извини́, сегóдня у меня́ мнóго рабóты.

d. Я знáю однó недорогóе кафé в цéнтре.

e. Всё э́то есть в супермáркете.

f. Договори́лись.

g. Что ты хóчешь купи́ть?

h. Давáй пойдём тудá зáвтра вéчером.

**ANSWER KEY**
1. g; 2. e; 3. h; 4. f; 5. a; 6. c; 7. b; 8. d

## Grammar Builder 2

▶ 3D Grammar Builder 2 (CD: 4, Track: 13)

### CONJUGATION II VERBS

Now let's review the conjugation of another type of verb, Conjugation II. Conjugation II verbs take the following endings:

| я –ю/–у | мы –им |
|---|---|
| ты –ишь | вы –ите |
| он/онá/онó –ит | они́ –ят/-ат |

Let's look at how this works with the verb люби́ть (*to like, to love*).

| ЛЮБИ́ТЬ *TO LIKE, TO LOVE* | |
| --- | --- |
| я люблю́ | мы лю́бим |
| ты лю́бишь | вы лю́бите |
| он/она́/оно́ лю́бит | они́ лю́бят |

Notice that the 1st person singular form has an –л mutation. Now remember the following rule: if there's a mutation in a Conjugation II verb, it occurs only in the 1st person singular form. The verb люби́ть takes direct objects (in the accusative case) or can be followed by an infinitive.

Я люблю́ фру́кты.
*I like fruit(s).*

Я люблю́ омле́т.
*I like omelet(s). (lit., I like an omelet.)*

Я люблю́ ру́сскую ку́хню.
*I like Russian (f. sg.) cuisine.*

The adjective ру́сская (*f. sg.*) is also in the accusative case. We will revisit the declension of adjectives later.

The verb люби́ть works with infinitives just like it does in English.

Я люблю́ за́втракать до́ма.
*I like to have breakfast at home.*

## ✎ Work Out 2

Now let's practice the important grammar and vocabulary.

A. Что вы лю́бите? (*What do you like?*) Using the prompts below, say that these people like the following things.

1. *Irina, cheese sandwich and coffee*

_____

2. *they, water*

_____

3. *I, have breakfast at home*

_____

4. *you (form.), omelet and fruit(s)*

_____

5. *you (inform.), have dinner in a restaurant*

_____

6. *we, Russian cuisine*

_____

B. Что вы хоти́те купи́ть в суперма́ркете? (*What would you like to buy in the supermarket?*) Make a shopping list of the following items using the construction я хочу́ купи́ть … (*I'd like to buy …*). Remember to put the things you want to buy in the accusative case!

1. зелёный сала́т

_____

2. чай и ко́фе

_____

3. ры́ба и мя́со

_____

4. помидо́ры и лук

_____

5. сыр и вино́

_____

**ANSWER KEY**

A. 1. Ири́на лю́бит бутербро́д с сы́ром и ко́фе. 2. Они́ лю́бят во́ду. 3. Я люблю́ за́втракать до́ма. 4. Вы лю́бите омле́т и фру́кты. 5. Ты лю́бишь у́жинать в рестора́не. 6. Мы лю́бим ру́сскую ку́хню.

B. 1. Я хочу́ купи́ть зелёный сала́т. 2. Я хочу́ купи́ть чай и ко́фе. 3. Я хочу́ купи́ть ры́бу и мя́со. 4. Я хочу́ купи́ть помидо́ры и лук. 5. Я хочу́ купи́ть сыр и вино́.

# ✎ Drive It Home

It's time for another Drive It Home section! After you've done these exercises, these aspects of Russian grammar should come to you more naturally. As always, write out each sentence completely and say the answers out loud for extra practice.

A. First, let's go over the use of the accusative case. Fill in the blanks with the correct form of each noun.

1. Я люблю́ _____ . (*tomatoes and fish*)

2. Я люблю́ _____ . (*green salad and soup*)

3. Я люблю́ _____ . (*coffee with milk*)

4. Я люблю́ _____ . (*omelet and juice*)

5. Я люблю́ пить _____ . (*water*)

B. Now let's practice conjugation of some important verbs. Fill in the blanks with the correct form of each verb.

1. Я _____ кóфе на зáвтрак. (*drink*)

2. Ты _____ кóфе на зáвтрак. (*drink*)

3. Они́ _____ кóфе на зáвтрак. (*drink*)

4. Я _____ бутербрóды на обéд. (*eat*)

5. Онá _____ бутербрóды на обéд. (*eat*)

6. Мы _____ бутербрóды на обéд. (*eat*)

7. Ты _____ бутербрóды на обéд. (*eat*)

8. Он _____ ру́сскую ку́хню. (*like*)

9. Вы _____ ру́сскую ку́хню. (*like*)

10. Я _____ ру́сскую ку́хню. (*like*)

**ANSWER KEY**
A. 1. помидóры и ры́бу; 2. зелёный салáт и суп; 3. кóфе с молокóм; 4. омлéт и сок; 5. вóду
B. 1. пью; 2. пьёшь; 3. пьют; 4. ем; 5. ест; 6. еди́м; 7. ешь; 8. лю́бит; 9. лю́бите; 10. люблю́

## How Did You Do?

Let's see how you did in this lesson. You should know how to:

☐ Form commonly used sentences related to food, eating, and drinking. (Still unsure? Go back to page 36.)

☐ Conjugate eating and drinking verbs in the past tense. (Still unsure? Go back to page 37.)

The past tense of есть (*to eat*)
and пить (*to drink*)

The future tense of быть (*to be*) and the
demonstrative pronoun э́тот (*this*)

Conjugation II verbs

Conjunctions

☐ Say what you usually have for breakfast, lunch, or dinner. (Still unsure? Go back to page 41.)

☐ Talk about what you like. (Still unsure? Go back to page 43.)

# ✎ Word Recall

Ready to practice some key vocabulary? This is a good opportunity to refresh your memory on some words and structures you learned earlier. If you're having trouble with these exercises, go back to the previous lessons and review.

A. Fill in the blanks in the following dialogue with the appropriate word from the word bank: из Аме́рики, меня́ зову́т, студе́нтка, жить, о́чень прия́тно, отку́да

1. Скажи́те, пожа́луйста, _____ вы?

2. Я _____ .

3. Я _____ и рабо́таю в Нью-Йо́рке. А вы ру́сская?

4. Да, ру́сская. Я _____ .

5. Меня́ зову́т Ната́лья. _____ .

B. Fill in the blanks according to the prompts in parentheses.

1. Мы живём _____ . (*on the second floor*)

2. Он жил в Аме́рике _____ . (*one month*)

3. Познако́мьтесь, э́то _____ . (*my wife*)

4. Она́ рабо́тает в э́той фи́рме _____ . (*four months*)

5. Вы о́чень хорошо́ _____ ! (*speak Russian*)

**ANSWER KEY**

A. 1. откýда; 2. из Амéрики; 3. живý; 4. студéнтка; 5. Óчень прия́тно

B. 1. на вторóм этажé; 2. оди́н мéсяц; 3. моя́ женá; 4. четы́ре мéсяца; 5. говори́те по-рýсски

# Lesson 4: Conversations

Мы рáды вас ви́деть снóва! *We are glad to see you again!*

In this lesson, you'll combine the words and expressions you've learned and reviewed in the first three lessons in two typical dialogues. This will enable you to:

☐ Have a basic conversation about food, eating, and drinking.

☐ Make plans for different meals.

☐ Say what you like to eat and drink for breakfast, lunch, or dinner.

☐ Find out what's available on the menu or in a supermarket.

Готóвы? Тогдá начнём! *Ready? Then, let's begin!*

Let's start with the following conversation.

## Conversation 1

▶ 4A Conversation (CD: 4, Track: 14 - Russian; Track: 15- Russian and English)

An American tourist, John, is meeting his Russian tour guide, Irina, in the lobby of his hotel in St. Petersburg in the morning. They are discussing their meal arrangements for the day.

| | |
|---|---|
| Джон: | Здрáвствуйте,Ири́на! |
| Ири́на: | Здрáвствуйте, Джон. |
| Джон: | Как у вас делá? |

| | |
|---|---|
| Ири́на: | Спаси́бо, хорошо́. А как у вас? |
| Джон: | Всё отли́чно! Скажи́те, пожа́луйста, где мы завтра́каем? |
| Ири́на: | Как, вы ещё не за́втракали? За́втрак на пе́рвом этаже́, в буфе́те. Пойдёмте, я вам покажу́. Я то́лько что отту́да. |
| Джон: | Большо́е спаси́бо. Что там есть на за́втрак? |
| Ири́на: | Я е́ла омле́т и бутербро́д с сы́ром и пила́ во́ду и ко́фе с молоко́м. |
| Джон: | Я не люблю́ мно́го есть на за́втрак. Там есть фру́кты или мю́сли? |
| Ири́на: | Да, коне́чно есть. Вы зна́ете, что днём мы бу́дем обе́дать в рестора́не в це́нтре го́рода? |
| Джон: | Како́й э́то рестора́н? |
| Ири́на: | Э́то ру́сский рестора́н на Не́вском проспе́кте. Там ру́сская ку́хня. |
| Джон: | Отли́чно! Я люблю́ ру́сскую ку́хню! Спаси́бо за по́мощь! |
| Ири́на: | Не́ за что. Вот мы и в буфе́те. Прия́тного аппети́та! |
| Джон: | Спаси́бо, Ири́на. Уви́димся в фойе́ гости́ницы. |
| Ири́на: | До встре́чи в фойе́. |

| | |
|---|---|
| *John:* | *Hello, Irina!* |
| *Irina:* | *Hello, John!* |
| *John:* | *How are you doing?* |
| *Irina:* | *Fine, thank you. And you?* |
| *John:* | *Everything is great! Tell (me) please, where are we having breakfast?* |
| *Irina:* | *Oh, you haven't had breakfast yet? Breakfast is on the first floor, in the café. Let's go, I'll show you. I've just (come) from there.* |
| *John:* | *Thank you very much. What do they have for breakfast (what is there for breakfast)?* |
| *Irina:* | *I had (ate) an omelet and a sandwich with cheese and drank water and coffee with milk.* |

John:        I don't like to eat a lot for breakfast. Do they have (lit., are there) fruit(s) and cereal?

Irina:        Yes, of course there are. Do you know that we'll have lunch in a restaurant in the center of the city?

John:        What restaurant is it?

Irina:        It's a Russian restaurant on Nevsky Prospect (Avenue). It has Russian cuisine.

John:        Great! I like Russian cuisine! Thanks for your help!

Irina:        Not at all. Here's the café (here we are in the café). Bon appétit!

John:        Thank you, Irina. See you in the lobby of the hotel.

Irina:        See you (until our meeting) in the lobby.

## ✎ Conversation Practice 1

Fill in the blanks with the appropriate phrases/sentences from the conversation above.

1. Здрáвствуйте, Ирѝна. _____ (*How are you doing?*)

2. _____, где мы зáвтракаем? (*Tell me please*)

3. Зáвтрак _____, в буфéте. (*on the first floor*)

4. На зáвтрак я éла _____. (*omelet and sandwich with cheese*)

5. На зáвтрак я пилá _____. (*coffee with milk*)

6. Днём мы бýдем обéдать в ресторáне _____. (*in the center of the city*)

7. Это рýсский ресторáн _____. (*on Nevsky Prospect*)

8. Я люблю́ _____. (*Russian cuisine*)

**ANSWER KEY**

1. Как у вас дела́? 2. Скажи́те, пожа́луйста; 3. на пе́рвом этаже́; 4. омле́т и бутербро́д с сы́ром; 5. ко́фе с молоко́м; 6. в це́нтре го́рода; 7. на Не́вском проспе́кте; 8. ру́сскую ку́хню

# Grammar Builder 1

▶ 4B Grammar Builder 1 (CD: 4, Track: 16)

## THE FUTURE TENSE OF БЫТЬ (*TO BE*) AND THE DEMONSTRATIVE PRONOUN Э́ТОТ (*THIS*)

Let's review the conjugation of the verb *to be* in the future tense.

| FUTURE TENSE OF БЫТЬ (*TO BE*) | |
| --- | --- |
| я бу́ду | мы бу́дем |
| ты бу́дешь | вы бу́дете |
| он/она́/оно́ бу́дет | они́ бу́дут |

Formally, this conjugation fully coincides with the present tense Conjugation Type I. The verb быть (*to be*) usually functions as the auxiliary verb with the infinitive that follows it. In other words, the future form of *to be* behaves like *will* in the English equivalent sentences followed by the infinitive.

Я бу́ду у́жинать до́ма.
*I will have dinner at home.*

By itself, я бу́ду can also mean *I will be.*

Я бу́ду в гости́нице.
*I will be in the hotel.*

Notice the demonstrative pronoun э́тот (*this*) in the phrase э́тот рестора́н (*this restaurant*). Like adjectives, demonstrative pronouns agree in gender, number, and case with the nouns they modify. Learn the following forms of the demonstrative pronoun э́тот (*this*) in the nominative and prepositional cases.

| NOMINATIVE CASE | |
| --- | --- |
| э́тот рестора́н (*m.*) | *this restaurant* |
| э́та гости́ница (*f.*) | *this hotel* |
| э́то кафé (*n.*) | *this café* |
| э́ти студéнты (*pl.*) | *these students* |

| PREPOSITIONAL CASE (SINGULAR) | |
| --- | --- |
| в э́том рестора́не (*m.*) | *in this restaurant* |
| в э́той гости́нице (*f.*) | *in/at this hotel* |
| в э́том кафé (*n.*) | *in this café* |

# ✎ Work Out 1

A. Say where the following people will have breakfast, lunch, or dinner using the prompts.

1. Я _____. (за́втракать, до́ма)

2. Мы _____. (обéдать, кафé)

3. Они́ _____. (у́жинать, рестора́н)

4. Никола́й _____. (за́втракать, буфéт)

5. Вы _____. (обéдать, университéт)

6. Ты _____. (у́жинать, гости́ница)

B. Translate the following sentences into Russian.

1. *I am having breakfast at this hotel.*

_____

2. *I will have breakfast at this hotel.*

_____

3. *He has lunch in this café.*

_____

4. *He will have lunch in this café.*

_____

5. *We are having dinner at this Russian restaurant.*

_____

6. *We will have dinner at this Russian restaurant.*

_____

# 🔊 Conversation 2
▶ 4C Conversation 2 (CD: 4, Track: 17- Russian; Track: 18- Russian and English)

This is a conversation between an American exchange student, Lisa, who is going food shopping, and her Russian friend, Nikolai. They are discussing their dinner plans.

Никола́й:    Ли́за, что ты хо́чешь купи́ть в суперма́ркете?

Ли́за:      Я хочу́ купи́ть ры́бу, помидо́ры, зелёный сала́т, лук, карто́шку, мя́со и макаро́ны.

Никола́й:   Что́-нибудь ещё?

Ли́за:      Да, ещё что́-нибудь на за́втрак. Мо́жет быть, я куплю́ сыр, я́йца, сок, чай, ко́фе и молоко́. Я обы́чно за́втракаю до́ма.

Никола́й:   Всё э́то есть в э́том большо́м, но́вом суперма́ркете. А где ты обе́даешь и у́жинаешь?

Ли́за:      Обы́чно я обе́даю в университе́те, в столо́вой, а у́жинаю и́ли до́ма, и́ли в рестора́не с друзья́ми.

Никола́й:   А где ты у́жинаешь сего́дня ве́чером? Я зна́ю одно́ хоро́шее и недорого́е кафе́ в це́нтре.

Ли́за:      Извини́, Ко́ля, дава́й за́втра ве́чером. Сего́дня у меня́ мно́го рабо́ты и я бу́ду у́жинать до́ма, а за́втра пя́тница.

Никола́й:   Договори́лись! За́втра ве́чером мы вме́сте бу́дем у́жинать в э́том кафе́. А пото́м пойдём в клуб.

Ли́за:      С удово́льствием!

Nikolai:   *Lisa, what would you like (lit., do you want) to buy in the supermarket?*

Lisa:      *I want to buy fish, tomatoes, lettuce, onion(s), potato(es), meat, and pasta.*

Nikolai:   *Anything else?*

Lisa:      *Yes, also something for breakfast. Maybe I'll buy cheese, eggs, juice, tea, coffee, and milk. I usually have breakfast at home.*

Nikolai:   *All of this is available in this big, new supermarket. And where do you have lunch and dinner?*

Lisa:      *Usually, I have lunch at the university, in the cafeteria, and dinner either at home or in a restaurant with my friends.*

Nikolai:   *Where are you having dinner tonight? I know one good and inexpensive café downtown.*

Lisa:      *I'm sorry, Kolya, let's (do it) tomorrow night. I have a lot of work today and I'll have dinner at home, but tomorrow's Friday.*

Nikolai:    Agreed! Tomorrow night we'll have dinner together at this café. And then we'll go to a club.

Lisa:    Great (with pleasure)!

# ✎ Conversation Practice 2

Fill in the blanks with the appropriate phrases/sentences from the conversation above. Repeat the entire line out loud.

1. Ли́за, что ты _____ в суперма́ркете? (*like to buy*)

2. Я хочу́ купи́ть _____

   _____. (*fish, tomatoes, onions, lettuce*)

3. Я ещё хочу́ купи́ть _____. (*something for*

   *breakfast*)

4. Все э́то есть _____

   _____. (*in this big, new supermarket*)

5. А где ты у́жинаешь _____? (*tonight*)

6. Извини́, Ко́ля, сего́дня _____. (*I have a lot of*

   *work*)

7. _____ туда́ за́втра ве́чером. (*Let's go*)

8. _____! А пото́м пойдём в клуб. (*Agreed*)

**ANSWER KEY**

1. хо́чешь купи́ть; 2. ры́бу, помидо́ры, лук и зелёный сала́т; 3. что́-нибудь на за́втрак; 4. в э́том большо́м, но́вом суперма́ркете; 5. сего́дня ве́чером; 6. у меня́ мно́го рабо́ты; 7. Дава́й пойдём; 8. Договори́лись

## 🌐 Culture Note

Notice how Lisa calls Никола́й "Ко́ля". She does so because they are on informal terms—they are на ты. Russian first names are rarely shortened in formal situations or when accompanied by a last name. Of course, when meeting Russians, you should call them by their full first names (Ната́лья, Влади́мир, Бори́с) and switch to nicknames only after they've suggested you do so. For your reference, here are some common Russian names and nicknames.

| FEMALE | |
|---|---|
| **FULL NAME** | **NICKNAME** |
| Алекса́ндра | Са́ша, Шу́ра |
| А́нна | А́ня |
| Еле́на | Ле́на |
| Ири́на | Ира |
| Мари́я | Ма́ша |
| Ната́лья | Ната́ша |
| О́льга | О́ля |
| Светла́на | Све́та |
| Татья́на | Та́ня |
| Ю́лия | Ю́ля |

| MALE | |
|---|---|
| **FULL NAME** | **NICKNAME** |
| Алекса́ндр | Са́ша, Шу́ра |
| Алексе́й | Алёша, Лёша |
| Бори́с | Бо́ря |
| Влади́мир | Воло́дя, Вова |
| Ива́н | Ва́ня |
| Константи́н | Ко́стя |
| Михаи́л | Ми́ша |

| MALE | |
|---|---|
| **FULL NAME** | **NICKNAME** |
| Никола́й | Ко́ля |
| Пётр | Пе́тя |
| Ю́рий | Ю́ра |

# Grammar Builder 2

▶ 4D Grammar Builder 2 (CD: 4, Track: 19)

## CONJUNCTIONS

Let's review some basic conjunctions used in this dialogue: и, а, но, и́ли, and или ... и́ли.

The conjunction и́ли means *or. Either ... or* in Russian is и́ли ... , и́ли ...

Или до́ма, и́ли в рестора́не.
*Either at home or in a restaurant.*

The Russian conjunction и means *and*, но means *but*. However, there's no direct equivalent for the Russian conjunction а. It's usually used to denote contrast rather than contradiction (for which we use но).

Я обе́даю в университе́те, а у́жинаю до́ма.
*I have lunch at the university and/but have dinner at home.*

Here we have contrast rather than contradiction. But if you say хоро́ший, но недорого́й рестора́н (*good, but inexpensive restaurant*), you present it as a contradiction: from the fact that it's good, one would expect it to be expensive but it isn't. Of course, you can simply say хоро́ший и недорого́й рестора́н (*good and inexpensive restaurant*).

и = *and* (enumeration)

Это хорóший и недорогóй рестора́н.
*This is a good and inexpensive restaurant.*

а = *and/but* (contrast)

Это дорогóй рестора́н, а э́то недорогóй.
*This is an expensive restaurant, but this one is inexpensive.*

но = *but* (contradiction)

Это хорóший, но недорогóй рестора́н.
*This is a good but inexpensive restaurant.*

# ✎ Work Out 2

A. In the following introductions, a person first states his or her full name and then suggests that you call him or her by the nickname. Fill in the blanks according to this model:
Меня́ зову́т Никола́й. Мóжно Кóля.
*My name is Nikolai. You can call me Kolya. (lit., It's possible Kolya.)*

1. Меня́ зову́т Влади́мир. Мóжно _____.

2. Меня́ зову́т Татья́на. Мóжно _____.

3. Меня́ зову́т Алекса́ндр. Мóжно _____ или _____.

4. Меня́ зову́т Светла́на. Мóжно _____.

5. Меня́ зову́т Ири́на. Мóжно _____.

6. Меня́ зову́т Ю́рий. Мо́жно _____ .

7. Меня́ зову́т Еле́на. Мо́жно _____ .

B. Fill in the blanks with the appropriate conjunctions. Repeat the entire sentence out loud.

1. Я живу́ ____ рабо́таю в Москве́.

2. Я живу́ в Москве́, ____ моя́ сестра́ живёт в Петербу́рге.

3. Я о́чень люблю́ Петербу́рг, _____ живу́ в Москве́.

4. Я хочу́ рабо́тать _____ в Москве́, _____ в Петербу́рге.

5. Я ра́ньше жил в Росси́и, ____ сейча́с я живу́ в Аме́рике.

6. Где вы хоти́те за́втракать, до́ма _____ в кафе́?

7. Это недорого́е кафе́, _____ о́чень хоро́шее.

**ANSWER KEY**
A. 1. Воло́дя; 2. Та́ня; 3. Са́ша; Шу́ра; 4. Све́та; 5. Ира; 6. Ю́ра; 7. Ле́на
B. 1. и; 2. а; 3. но; 4. или; или; 5. а; 6. или; 7. но

# ✎ Drive It Home

A. Fill in the blanks using the appropriate form of the verb люби́ть (*to like*). Repeat the entire sentence out loud.

1. На за́втрак я _____ пить ко́фе с молоко́м.

2. На у́жин мы _____ есть ры́бу и сала́т.

3. Он _____ обе́дать в э́той столо́вой.

4. Где вы _____ отдыха́ть ле́том?

5. Они́ _____ есть о́вощи и фру́кты.

6. Ты _____ рýсскую кýхню?

B. **Fill in the blanks using the appropriate form of the demonstrative pronoun** этот **(this) in the nominative or prepositional case. Repeat the entire sentence out loud.**

1. _____ студéнты—америкáнцы.

2. _____ гостúница недорогáя, но хорóшая.

3. _____ ресторáн в цéнтре гóрода.

4. Онú живýт в _____ гостúнице.

5. Онá рабóтает в _____ óфисе.

6. В _____ кафé óчень хорóший кóфе.

7. В _____ ресторáне рýсская кýхня.

8. Мой родúтели живýт в _____ гóроде.

**ANSWER KEY**
A. 1. люблю́; 2. лю́бим; 3. лю́бит; 4. лю́бите; 5. лю́бят; 6. лю́бишь
B. 1. Эти; 2. Эта; 3. Этот; 4. э́той; 5. э́том; 6. э́том; 7. э́том; 8. э́том

# How Did You Do?

Let's see how you did in this lesson. You should know how to:

☐ Have a basic conversation about food, eating, and drinking. (Still unsure? Go back to page 48.)

☐ Make plans for different meals. (Still unsure? Go back to page 48.)

☐ Say what you like to eat and drink for breakfast, lunch, or dinner. (Still unsure? Go back to page 53.)

☐ Find out what's available on the menu or in a supermarket. (Still unsure? Go back to page 53.)

The past tense of есть (*to eat*) and пить (*to drink*) | The future tense of быть (*to be*) and the demonstrative pronoun э́тот (*this*)

Conjugation II verbs | Conjunctions

# ✎ Word Recall

Match the following English expressions on the left to their Russian equivalents on the right.

| | | |
|---|---|---|
| 1. *in the morning* | | a. мо́жет быть |
| 2. *in the winter* | | b. извини́те |
| 3. *in the cafeteria* | | c. сок |
| 4. *Thank you very much!* | | d. о́сенью |
| 5. *So long!* | | e. в столо́вой |
| 6. *maybe* | | f. у́тром |
| 7. *in the afternoon* | | g. Счастли́во! |
| 8. *in the fall* | | h. Большо́е спаси́бо! |
| 9. *excuse me* | | i. зимо́й |
| 10. *juice* | | j. днём |

**ANSWER KEY**
1. f; 2. i; 3. e; 4. h; 5. g; 6. a; 7. j; 8. d; 9. b; 10. c

Don't forget to practice and reinforce what you've learned by visiting **www.livinglanguage.com/languagelab** for flashcards, games, and quizzes!

# Unit 1 Quiz

Контро́льная рабо́та №1

Now let's review. In this quiz you'll be tested on what you've learned in Unit 1. Once you've completed it, score yourself to see how well you've done. If you find that you need to go back and review, please do so before continuing on to Unit 2.

A. Где вы бы́ли? (*Where were you?*) Say where you were. Fill in the blanks following the prompts in the parentheses.

1. Я был _____ . (*at this restaurant*)

2. Мы бы́ли _____. (*on the first floor*)

3. Я была́ _____ . (*in this hotel*)

4. Мы бы́ли _____ . (*in this city*)

5. Я была́ _____ . (*at this post office*)

B. In Russian, say what these people like to eat and drink.

1. *I eat fish and potatoes for dinner.*

_____

2. *We eat meat and green salad for lunch.*

_____

3. *They eat cheese sandwiches for lunch.*

_____

4. *He drinks coffee with milk for breakfast.*

_____

5. *She drinks juice in the morning.*

_____

C. Say what these people want. Use the correct form of the verb *to want.*

1. Мы _____ купи́ть о́вощи и фру́кты.

2. Она́ _____ обе́дать. Я _____ жить в э́том го́роде.

3. Вы _____ ко́фе на за́втрак.

4. Он _____ отдыха́ть на мо́ре.

D. What did these people eat and drink for dinner? Fill in the blanks with direct objects given in parentheses.

1. Мы е́ли _____ и пи́ли _____ на у́жин. (*pasta, wine*)

2. Мы пи́ли _____ и _____ на у́жин. (*beer, tea*)

3. Мы е́ли _____ и _____ на у́жин. (*fish, potatoes*)

4. Мы пи́ли _____ и _____ на у́жин. (*water, coffee*)

5. Мы е́ли _____ и пи́ли _____ на у́жин. (*soup, juice*)

E. Say what these people like. Fill in the blanks with the correct form of the verb *to like.*

1. Они́ _____ ру́сскую ку́хню.

2. Мы _____ у́жинать в рестора́не.

3. Она́ _____ о́вощи.

4. Я _____ пить ко́фе на за́втрак.

5. Ты _____ говори́ть по-ру́сски.

F. Fill in the blanks with the correct future tense of the verb *to be*.

1. Я _____ мно́го рабо́тать сего́дня.

2. Мы _____ ку́рицу на у́жин.

3. Ты _____ говори́ть по-ру́сски.

4. Они́ _____ ко́фе и сок.

5. Он _____ пи́во.

# How Did You Do?

Give yourself a point for every correct answer, then use the following key to tell whether you're ready to move on:

**0–7 points:** It's probably a good idea to go back through the lesson again. You may be moving too quickly, or there may be too much "down time" between your contact with Russian. Remember that it's better to spend 30 minutes with Russian three or four times a week than it is to spend two or three hours just once a week. Find a pace that's comfortable for you, and spread your contact hours out as much as you can.

**8–12 points:** You would benefit from a review before moving on. Go back and spend a little more time on the specific points that gave you trouble. Re-read the Grammar Builder sections that were difficult, and do the Work Outs one more time. Don't forget about the online supplemental practice material, either. Go to **www.livinglanguage.com/languagelab** for games and quizzes that will reinforce the material from this unit.

**13–17 points:** Good job! There are just a few points that you might consider reviewing before moving on. If you haven't worked with the games and quizzes on **www.livinglanguage.com/languagelab**, please give them a try.

**18–20 points:** Great! You're ready to move on to the next unit.

points

# Unit 2:
# Family and the Home

Поздравля́ем с оконча́нием Пе́рвой главы́ и добро́ пожа́ловать во Втору́ю главу́!

*Congratulations on the completion of Unit 1 and welcome to Unit 2!*

In this unit, you'll learn how to talk about yourself and your family, for example expressing one's birthplace, profession and marital status. You'll also learn some important Russian grammar points such as the Rule of Numbers, the genitive case for possession, and negation. Let's get started!

# Lesson 5: Words

In this lesson, you'll learn how to:

☐ Talk about your family and about residences.

☐ Further use some personal and possessive pronouns.

☐ Use some irregular nouns in the prepositional case.

☐ Further use Russian numerals.

☐ Use nouns with Russian numerals that end in 2, 3, and 4.

☐ Say where you were born.

Готóвы? Тогдá начнём! *Ready? Then, let's begin!*

Let's get started with some words and phrases.

# Word Builder 1

5A Word Builder 1 (CD: 4, Track: 20)

| Дóбрый вéчер! | *Good evening!* |
|---|---|
| муж | *husband* |
| женá | *wife* |
| мнóго дел | *lots of things to do (lit., lots of things)* |
| юрúст | *lawyer* |
| консультáнт | *consultant* |
| финáнсовая компáния | *financial company* |
| мáльчик | *boy* |
| дéвочка | *girl* |
| сын | *son* |
| дочь (*f.*) (дóчка, *dim.*) | *daughter* |
| стáрший | *older (elder)* |
| млáдший | *younger* |
| брат | *brother* |
| другóй | *other (another)* |
| дéтский сад | *daycare* |
| шкóла | *school (elementary, middle, and high school)* |

# ✏ Word Practice 1

Match the following English words on the left to their Russian equivalents on the right.

| | |
|---|---|
| 1. *consultant* | a. мальчик |
| 2. *other* | b. детский сад |
| 3. *younger daughter* | c. финансовая компания |
| 4. *financial company* | d. юрист |
| 5. *good evening* | e. школа |
| 6. *lawyer* | f. добрый вечер |
| 7. *older brother* | g. младшая дочь |
| 8. *daycare* | h. другой |
| 9. *boy* | i. консультант |
| 10. *school* | j. старший брат |

**ANSWER KEY**
1. i; 2. h; 3. g; 4. c; 5. f; 6. d; 7. j; 8. b; 9. a; 10. e

# Grammar Builder

▶ 5B Grammar Builder 1 (CD: 4, Track: 21)

## SINGULAR POSSESSIVE PRONOUNS AND THE GENITIVE CASE (SINGULAR)

Review the following Russian equivalents of the 1st and 2nd person possessive pronouns *my*, *your* (*sg., inform.*), *our*, and *your* (*pl., form.*) in the nominative case. As modifiers, they have to agree with the nouns they precede.

| | MASCULINE | FEMININE | NEUTER | PLURAL |
|---|---|---|---|---|
| *my* | мой | моя | моё | мои |
| *your (sg., inform.)* | твой | твоя | твоё | твои |

Personal pronouns in the
genitive case

Reflexive verbs and the instrumental case
of pronouns and adjectives

Negation

The genitive of origin

|  | MASCULINE | FEMININE | NEUTER | PLURAL |
|---|---|---|---|---|
| *our* | наш | на́ша | на́ше | на́ши |
| *your (pl., form.)* | ваш | ва́ша | ва́ше | ва́ши |

The 3rd person possessive pronouns его́ (*his, its*), её (*her, its*), and их (*their*), agree in gender and number with the owner rather than with the object that is owned, just like their English counterparts *his*, *her*, and *their*.

мой сын

*my son*

на́ша дочь

*our daughter*

твой муж

*your husband*

Before we discuss the genitive case, let's take a look at the Russian numerals from 11 to 100.

| 11 | оди́ннадцать |
|---|---|
| 12 | двена́дцать |
| 13 | трина́дцать |
| 14 | четы́рнадцать |
| 15 | пятна́дцать |
| 16 | шестна́дцать |
| 17 | семна́дцать |
| 18 | восемна́дцать |
| 19 | девятна́дцать |
| 20 | два́дцать |

Singular possessive pronouns
and the genitive case (singular)

The instrumental case and the verbs
рабо́тать (*to work*) and жить (*to live*)

Prepositional phrases with the verb
роди́ться and rooms of the house

The dative case

| 30 | три́дцать |
|----|-----------|
| 40 | со́рок |
| 50 | пятьдеся́т |
| 60 | шестьдеся́т |
| 70 | семьдесят |
| 80 | во́семьдесят |
| 90 | девяно́сто |
| 100 | сто |

The nouns that come after Russian numerals follow a strange and counterintuitive rule known as the Rule of Numbers. Take a look at the following chart to find out which number will use which case.

| NUMBER | CASE OF THE FOLLOWING NOUN |
|--------|----------------------------|
| 1, 21, 31, etc. | nominative sg. or accusative sg. |
| 2–4, 22–24, 32–34, etc. | genitive sg. |
| 5–20, 25–30, 35–40, etc. | genitive pl. |

Before we can use this Rule of Numbers, we need to discuss another case: the genitive case. Let's start with the genitive singular.

The endings for the masculine and neuter nouns are –а/–я; the feminine endings are –ы/–и.

| GENITIVE ENDING | EXAMPLE |
|-----------------|---------|
| –а/–я (*m./n.*) | сы́на, пи́ва, словаря́ (*dictionary*) |
| –ы/–и (*f.*) | жены́, де́вочки |

The genitive case has many different functions in Russian, of which the Rule of Numbers is only one example. The quantitative word мно́го—as in the expression you learned earlier, мно́го рабо́ты (*a lot of work*)—also requires the genitive case. Let's now look at how these cases work with numbers. We'll begin with the numerals 1 through 4.

| CASE | MASCULINE | FEMININE | NEUTER |
|------|-----------|----------|--------|
| Nominative<br>1 | сын<br>оди́н сын | де́вочка, шко́ла<br>одна́ де́вочка,<br>одна́ шко́ла | пи́во<br>одно́ пи́во |
| Genitive<br>2<br>3<br>4 | сы́на<br>два сы́на<br>три сы́на<br>четы́ре сы́на | де́вочки, шко́лы<br>две де́вочки, две<br>шко́лы<br>три де́вочки,<br>три шко́лы<br>четы́ре де́вочки,<br>четы́ре шко́лы | письмо́ (letter)<br>одно́ письмо́<br>два письма́<br>три письма́<br>четы́ре письма́ |

When you count years, use the noun год (year) in the nominative for years ending in 1 (оди́н год), and its genitive singular form го́да for years ending in 2, 3, or 4 (два го́да, три го́да, четы́ре го́да). From 5 up, you need to use лет, a different form for *years*.

пять лет
*five years*

двена́дцать лет
*twelve years*

девятна́дцать лет
*nineteen years*

Singular possessive pronouns
and the genitive case (singular)

The instrumental case and the verbs
рабо́тать (*to work*) and жить (*to live*)

Prepositional phrases with the verb
роди́ться and rooms of the house

The dative case

Keep in mind that 21–24, 31–34, etc. (the numbers that end in 1–4), will use год in its appropriate form according to the final number.

два́дцать оди́н год
*twenty-one years*

со́рок четы́ре го́да
*forty-four years*

# ✎ Work Out 1

A. How do you say this in Russian? Modify the following nouns with the correct possessive pronoun and then repeat the Russian phrase out loud.

1. *my husband* _____

2. *his wife* _____

3. *our daughter* _____

4. *their son* _____

5. *your (inform.) school* _____

6. *your (form.) older brother* _____

B. How do you say this in Russian? Give Russian equivalents to the word combinations with numerals below. Remember to follow the Rule of Numbers! Also remember to make the Russian numerals *one* and *two* agree in gender with the people or things you count.

1. *one son* _____

2. *two daughters (dim.)* _____

Personal pronouns in the
genitive case

Reflexive verbs and the instrumental case
of pronouns and adjectives

Negation

The genitive of origin

3. *three mothers (dim.)* _____

4. *four letters* _____

5. *three nights* _____

6. *twenty-one companies* _____

7. *four brothers* _____

8. *three girls* _____

9. *two boys* _____

10. *twenty-three schools* _____

C. Make the noun год (*year*) agree with the numerals below.

1. 2_____

2. 5_____

3. 1_____

4. 21_____

5. 43_____

6. 74_____

7. 66_____

**ANSWER KEY**

A. 1. мой муж; 2. его жена; 3. наша дочь; 4. их сын; 5. твоя школа; 6. ваш старший брат
B. 1. один сын; 2. две дочки; 3. три мамы; 4. четыре письма; 5. три ночи; 6. двадцать одна
компания; 7. четыре брата; 8. три девочки; 9. два мальчика; 10. двадцать три школы
C. 1. года; 2. лет; 3. год; 4. год; 5. года; 6. года; 7. лет

## Word Builder 2

▶ 5C Word Builder 2 (CD: 4, Track: 22)

| | |
|---|---|
| общежи́тие | dormitory |
| роди́тели (*pl.*) | parents |
| он роди́лся | he was born |
| она́ родила́сь | she was born |
| они́ родили́сь | they were born |
| сестра́ | sister |
| программи́ст | programmer |
| библиоте́карь (*m.*) | librarian (male or female) |
| год (го́да, лет) | year |
| двухэта́жный дом | two-story house |
| за́ городом | in the suburbs, country (lit., beyond the city) |
| да́ча | dacha (Russian cottage in the country) |
| котте́дж | cottage |
| со все́ми удо́бствами | with all modern conveniences |
| кварти́ра | apartment |
| спа́льня *спальня* | bedroom |
| гости́ная *гостиная* | living room |
| столо́вая *столовая* | dining room (also cafeteria or dining hall) |
| ва́нная *ванная* | bathroom (with a tub or shower) |
| туале́т *туалет* | toilet, half-bath |

*со всеми удобствами*

# ✎ Word Practice 2

Match the following English words on the left with their Russian equivalents on the right.

1. *cottage*
2. *programmer*
3. *dormitory*
4. *country house*
5. *two-story house*
6. *in the suburbs*
7. *with all modern conveniences*
8. *bathroom*
9. *librarian*
10. *she was born*

a. общежи́тие
b. да́ча
c. ва́нная
d. она́ родила́сь
e. библиоте́карь
f. программи́ст
g. двухэта́жный дом
h. со все́ми удо́бствами
i. котте́дж
j. за́ городом

**ANSWER KEY**
1. i; 2. f; 3. a; 4. b; 5. g; 6. j; 7. h; 8. c; 9. e; 10. d

# Grammar Builder 2

▶ 5D Grammar Builder 2 (CD: 4, Track: 23)

**PREPOSITIONAL PHRASES WITH THE VERB** РОДИ́ТЬСЯ **AND ROOMS OF THE HOUSE**

The verb роди́ться (*to be born*) is a reflexive verb. We'll look at reflexive verbs in a later lesson in this unit; for now, please just remember this as an expression. Use роди́лся for men, родила́сь for women, and роди́лись for the plural. This expression will usually be followed by the prepositional case. For example,

Он роди́лся в Москве́.
*He was born in Moscow.*

Singular possessive pronouns
and the genitive case (singular)

The instrumental case and the verbs
рабóтать (*to work*) and жить (*to live*)

Prepositional phrases with the verb
родúться and rooms of the house

The dative case

Онá родилáсь в Нью-Йóрке.
*She was born in New York.*

Онú родилúсь в Россúи.
*They were born in Russia.*

Now let's look at the names of rooms in the house and the prepositional phrases with them. Notice that some of them are nouns, but some are substantivized adjectives—modifiers of the implied feminine noun кóмната (*room*). You can tell the difference by their endings.

Remember that substantivized adjectives, such as столóвая (*dining room*), should be declined as adjectives although they're used in sentences as nouns.

| | |
|---|---|
| спáльня, в спáльне | *bedroom, in the bedroom* |
| гостúная, в гостúной | *living room, in the living room* |
| столóвая, в столóвой | *dining room, in the dining room* |
| коридóр, в коридóре | *hallway, in the hallway* |
| кýхня, на кýхне | *kitchen, in the kitchen* |
| вáнная, в вáнной | *bathroom\*, in the bathroom* |
| туалéт, в туалéте | *toilet\*, in the toilet* |
| балкóн, на балкóне | *balcony, on the balcony* |
| террáса, на террáсе | *terrace/deck, on the terrace/deck* |

\*Note that in Russian speaking countries, туалéт refers to a room with only a toilet, while вáнная is a room with a bathtub or shower, and often a toilet as well.

The neuter noun общежúтие (*dorm*) belongs to a special subgroup of nouns that have the –ии ending in the prepositional case. These nouns can be masculine (кафетéрий), feminine (Россúя), or neuter (общежúтие). However, all of them have the penultimate (one before last) –и. So you should say в кафетéрии, в Россúи, в общежúтии. This rule is good to remember because the names of many countries and states in Russian end in –ия. Consequently, their

prepositional case is as follows: Фра́нция, во Фра́нции (*France, in France*); Ита́лия, в Ита́лии (*Italy, in Italy*); Япо́ния, в Япо́нии (*Japan, in Japan*); Герма́ния, в Герма́нии (*Germany, in Germany*), Калифо́рния, в Калифо́рнии (*California, in California*), etc.

Я ел(а) в кафете́рии.
*I ate in the cafeteria.*

Она́ была́ в Росси́и.
*She was in Russia.*

Он был в общежи́тии.
*He was in the dorm.*

## ⊕ Culture Note

Most Russian families live in apartments. Russians count all rooms in their apartments (rather than just bedrooms) but don't count bathrooms, kitchens, and hallways. So a standard American one-bedroom apartment is a two-room Russian apartment (двухко́мнатная кварти́ра); a two-bedroom apartment is a three-room Russian one (трёхко́мнатная кварти́ра), etc. It's fairly common to have the bathroom separate from the toilet. The first is called ва́нная, the other is туале́т. Besides an apartment in the city, most Russian families own a small country house with a small piece of land. This country house is called да́ча (*dacha*). It may or may not have all modern conveniences, such as hot and cold water, an in-house bathroom, or a heating system suitable for the Russian winter. However, many of the new *dachas* match all of the expected standards, and they are referred to as being со все́ми удо́бствами (*with all modern amenities*). Some of the more affluent residents of Russian cities can afford to buy a house in the suburbs comparable to an American single-family home, called котте́дж in Russian. This relatively new phenomenon of Russian life has lately become more popular among those who prefer, and can afford, a daily escape from the city.

Singular possessive pronouns
and the genitive case (singular)

The instrumental case and the verbs
рабо́тать (*to work*) and жить (*to live*)

Prepositional phrases with the verb
роди́ться and rooms of the house

The dative case

# ✎ Work Out 2

Где вы роди́лись? (*Where were you born?*) Answer this question using the following prompts. Remember to put the places of birth (locations) in the prepositional case and make sure the verb agrees with the subject!

1. А́нна, Калифо́рния _____

2. Никола́й, Росси́я _____

3. мы, Аме́рика _____

4. она́, Вермо́нт _____

5. вы, Москва́ _____

6. они́, Ита́лия _____

7. Ива́н, Петербу́рг _____

**ANSWER KEY**

1. А́нна родила́сь в Калифо́рнии. 2. Никола́й роди́лся в Росси́и. 3. Мы роди́лись в Аме́рике. 4. Она́ родила́сь в Вермо́нте. 5. Вы роди́лись в Москве́. 6. Они́ роди́лись в Ита́лии. 7. Ива́н роди́лся в Петербу́рге.

# ✎ Drive It Home

Say where these people were. Remember to put the words in parentheses into the prepositional case! Also, remember the special rules for the nouns with the penultimate –и– and substantivized adjectives!

1. Они́ обе́дали *в столо́вой* (dining room)

2. Он чита́л газе́ту *в гости́ной* (living room)

3. Она́ была́ *в ва́нной* (bathroom)

4. Студе́нты живу́т *в общежи́тии* (dorm)

Personal pronouns in the
genitive case

Reflexive verbs and the instrumental case
of pronouns and adjectives

Negation

The genitive of origin

5. Он роди́лся _в Ро́ссии_ . (Russia)

6. Мы пи́ли ко́фе _в столо́вой_ . (cafeteria)

7. Она́ была́ ле́том _в Ита́лии_ (Italy)

8. Мои́ роди́тели живу́т _в Калифо́рнии_ . (California)

**ANSWER KEY**

1. в столо́вой; 2. в гости́ной; 3. в ва́нной; 4. в общежи́тии; 5. в Росси́и; 6. в кафете́рии; 7. в Ита́лии; 8. в Калифо́рнии

# How Did You Do?

Let's see how you did in this lesson. You should know how to:

☐ Talk about your family and about residences. (Still unsure? Go back to page 67.)

☐ Further use some personal and possessive pronouns. (Still unsure? Go back to page 68.)

☐ Further use Russian numerals. (Still unsure? Go back to page 69.)

☐ Use nouns with Russian numerals that end in 2, 3, and 4. (Still unsure? Go back to page 70.)

☐ Say where you were born. (Still unsure? Go back to page 75.)

☐ Use some irregular nouns in the prepositional case. (Still unsure? Go back to page 76.)

# ✎ Word Recall

Now let's review some words and expressions from the earlier lessons. Read the English sentence first, then fill in the blanks in the Russian sentence, and repeat it out loud.

1. *He drinks green tea for breakfast.*

Он _пьёт_ зелёный чай на за́втрак.

Prepositional phrases with the verb
роди́ться and rooms of the house

2. *They drink red wine for dinner.*

   Они́ _пьют_ кра́сное вино́ на у́жин.

3. *You usually eat an omelet for breakfast.*

   Ты обы́чно _ешь_ омле́т на за́втрак.

4. *I often eat fish.*

   Я ча́сто _ем_ ры́бу.

5. *Would you like to buy anything?*

   Ты хо́чешь _что-нибудь_ купи́ть?

6. *He lives/stays in this hotel.*

   Он живёт _в э́той гости́нице_

7. *We will have lunch at home.*

   Мы _бу́дем обе́дать_ до́ма.

8. *In Germany, they speak German.*

   В Герма́нии говоря́т _по-неме́цки_

9. *She likes Russian cuisine.*

   Она́ лю́бит _ру́сскую ку́хню_

10. *Where are you from?*

   _Отку́да_ вы?

**ANSWER KEY**

1. пьёт; 2. пьют; 3. ешь; 4. ем; 5. что́-нибудь; 6. в э́той гости́нице; 7. бу́дем обе́дать; 8. по-неме́цки; 9. ру́сскую ку́хню; 10. Отку́да

Personal pronouns in the
genitive case

Reflexive verbs and the instrumental case
of pronouns and adjectives

Negation

The genitive of origin

# Lesson 6: Phrases

Добро́ пожа́ловать! Мы начина́ем шесто́й уро́к.
*Welcome! We're starting Lesson 6.*

In this lesson, you'll learn how to:

☐ Talk about age, marital status and occupations.

☐ Talk about residences and accommodations.

☐ Decline nouns in the instrumental and dative cases.

Гото́вы? Тогда́ начнём! *Ready? Then, let's begin!*
Let's get started with some phrases.

## Phrase Builder 1

▶ 6A Phrase Builder 1 (CD: 4, Track: 24)

| | |
|---|---|
| она́ оста́лась до́ма | she stayed at home |
| она́ рабо́тает консульта́нтом | she works as a consultant |
| е́сли я не ошиба́юсь | if I'm not mistaken |
| дво́е дете́й | two children |
| за́мужем | married (about a woman) |
| жена́т | married (about a man) |
| с на́ми живёт мла́дший сын | the younger son lives with us |
| он хо́дит в шко́лу | he goes to school (secondary school) |
| до́чери у́чатся в университе́те | daughters go to college (lit., study at university) |
| в други́х шта́тах | in other states |

Prepositional phrases with the verb родиться and rooms of the house

| они́ приезжа́ют домо́й на кани́кулы | they come home for breaks (school breaks) |
| я вас обяза́тельно познако́млю | *I'll definitely introduce you* |
| Всего́ хоро́шего! | *Take care! So long! (lit., All the best!)* |

## ✎ Phrase Practice 1

Match the following English phrases on the left with their Russian equivalents on the right.

1. *two children*
2. *married (about a woman)*
3. *married (about a man)*
4. *So long!*
5. *if I'm not mistaken*

6. *she stayed home*
7. *she works as a consultant*
8. *in other states*
9. *they come home for (school) breaks*
10. *he goes to school*

a. е́сли я не ошиба́юсь
b. она́ рабо́тает консульта́нтом
c. в други́х шта́тах
d. дво́е дете́й
e. они́ приезжа́ют домо́й на кани́кулы
f. жена́т
g. он хо́дит в шко́лу
h. она́ оста́лась до́ма
i. за́мужем
j. Всего́ хоро́шего!

**ANSWER KEY**
1. d; 2. i; 3. f; 4. j; 5. a; 6. h; 7. b; 8. c; 9. e; 10. g

## Take It Further

🔊 6B Take It Further (CD: 4, Track: 25)

The term за́мужем means *married* and refers only to women. Married men are referred to with the short adjective жена́т. Both terms follow the verb, which is omitted in the present tense.

Она́ за́мужем.
*She's married.*

Он жена́т.
*He's married.*

Она́ была́ за́мужем.
*She was married.*

Он был жена́т.
*He was married.*

## Grammar Builder 1

🔊 6C Grammar Builder 1 (CD: 4, Track: 26)

**THE INSTRUMENTAL CASE AND** РАБО́ТАТЬ (*TO WORK*) **AND** ЖИТЬ (*TO LIVE*)

Now it's time to learn one more case—the instrumental. Let's first learn the noun endings in the instrumental case.

| INSTRUMENTAL CASE | ENDING | EXAMPLES |
|---|---|---|
| *m./n.* | –ом/–ём/–ем | консульта́нтом, словарём, му́жем |

Unit 2 Lesson 6: Phrases       83

Singular possessive pronouns
and the genitive case (singular)

The instrumental case and the verbs
рабо́тать (*to work*) and жить (*to live*)

Prepositional phrases with the verb
роди́ться and rooms of the house

The dative case

*журнали́сткой*

| INSTRUMENTAL CASE | ENDING | EXAMPLES |
|---|---|---|
| *f.* | –ой/–ёй/–ей | журнали́сткой |
| *pl.* | –ами/–ями | консульта́нтами, врача́ми, журнали́стками, словаря́ми |

*врача́ми словаря́ми*

For masculine and neuter nouns, the hard ending –ом follows hard consonants and the consonants ж, ш, щ, ч, ц, if the ending is stressed. The soft stressed ending –ём follows soft consonants (–ем is the unstressed soft ending). The feminine endings are –ой or –ёй/–ей. The plural instrumental endings are –ами (*hard*) or –ями (*soft*). Also, the nominative question words кто? and что? are кем? and чем? in the instrumental case.

*кем чем*

Let's look more carefully at the conjugation of two important verbs рабо́тать (*to work*) and жить (*to live*).

| РАБО́ТАТЬ | |
|---|---|
| *TO WORK* | |
| **PRESENT** | |
| я рабо́таю | мы рабо́таем |
| ты рабо́таешь | вы рабо́таете |
| он/она́/оно́ рабо́тает | они́ рабо́тают |

Past: рабо́тал (*m.*), рабо́тала (*f.*), рабо́тало (*n.*), рабо́тали (*pl.*)

Рабо́тать is a Conjugation I verb. Its conjugation is fully predictable and standard; it has no mutations or stress shifts. In fact, this verb is so regular that you can use it as a pattern for Conjugation I verbs whose stem ends in –ай: рабо́та [й + у] = ю , > рабо́таю, and so on. You can hear the last й of the stem in every present tense form, i.e., before all vowel endings (although you can't see it since it is a part of the following "iotated" vowel—either [й + у] = ю or [й + э] = е). However, the phonetic й disappears before all consonant endings, that is, in the past tense and in the infinitive: рабо́тал, рабо́тать. We'll refer to this subtype of Conjugation I verbs as –ай verbs throughout the rest of this course.

The verb рабо́тать can take nouns in different cases depending on the specific meaning of each phrase. You've seen it used with the instrumental case. This case usually states the instrument with which or the manner in which something is done. For example, when used with occupations it takes the instrumental case.

Она́ рабо́тает консульта́нтом.
*She works as a consultant.*

Of course, there is a simpler way of expressing the same idea.

Она́ консульта́нт.
*She's a consultant.*

These options are available for other occupations as well.

Он врач. Он рабо́тает врачо́м.
*He's a doctor. He works as a doctor.*

Она́ юри́ст. Она́ рабо́тает юри́стом.
*She's a lawyer. She works as a lawyer.*

Naturally, the verb рабо́тать can also take nouns in the prepositional case to indicate location, i.e. the place where one works.

Он рабо́тает в больни́це.
*He works at the hospital.*

Она́ рабо́тает в фина́нсовой компа́нии.
*She works at a finance company.*

Singular possessive pronouns
and the genitive case (singular)

The instrumental case and the verbs
**работать** (*to work*) and **жить** (*to live*)

Prepositional phrases with the verb
роди́ться and rooms of the house

The dative case

Now let's look more closely at the conjugation of the verb жить (*to live*).

| ЖИТЬ<br>*TO LIVE* | |
|---|---|
| я живу́ | мы живём |
| ты живёшь | вы живёте |
| он/она́/оно́ живёт | они́ живу́т |

Past: жил (*m.*), жила́ (*f.*), жи́ло (*n.*), жи́ли (*pl.*)

This verb has a consonant stem жив–. All consonant stems stay intact before vowel endings, as in the present tense. However, they lose the last consonant before all consonant endings, as in the past tense or in the infinitive form. Consequently, Russians say живу́, but жил and жить. As you can guess, this verb takes the prepositional case, which denotes the location where you live.

Я живу́ в Москве́.
*I live in Moscow.*

Я живу́ в Нью-Йо́рке.
*I live in New York.*

Я живу́ в Росси́и.
*I live in Russia.*

Я живу́ в Калифо́рнии.
*I live in California.*

If this location is plural, you need to use the prepositional plural ending, either –ах (hard) or –ях (soft) for all genders since there's no gender distinction in the Russian plural. E.g., в города́х (*in cities*).

Они́ живу́т в други́х шта́тах.

*They live in other states.*

# ✎ Work Out 1

A. Now let's do some practice. Ке́м вы рабо́таете? (*What do you do? lit., As who do you work?*) Say what the following people do for a living using the verb рабо́тать. Remember to use the instrumental case!

1. Михаи́л, бизнесме́н

_____

2. она, юри́ст

_____

3. мой муж, консульта́нт

_____

4. моя́ жена́, журнали́стка

_____

5. их ста́рший сын, врач

_____

6. её роди́тели, врачи́

_____

7. на́ша дочь, библиоте́карь

_____

Singular possessive pronouns
and the genitive case (singular)

The instrumental case and the verbs
рабо́тать (*to work*) and жить (*to live*)

Prepositional phrases with the verb
роди́ться and rooms of the house

The dative case

B. Где они́ живу́т? (*Where do they live?*) Say where these people live. Use the prompts below.

1. *Bill, New York*

_____

2. *his children, other states*

_____

3. *Julia, Moscow*

_____

4. *her parents, other cities*

_____

5. *I, California*

_____

**ANSWER KEY**
A. 1. Михаил рабо́тает бизнесме́ном. 2. Она́ рабо́тает юри́стом. 3. Мой муж рабо́тает
консульта́нтом. 4. Моя́ жена́ рабо́тает журнали́сткой. 5. Их ста́рший сын рабо́тает врачо́м.
6. Её роди́тели рабо́тают врача́ми. 7. На́ша дочь рабо́тает библиоте́карем.
B. 1. Билл живёт в Нью-Йо́рке. 2. Его́ де́ти живу́т в други́х шта́тах. 3. Юлия живёт в Москве́.
4. Её роди́тели живу́т в други́х города́х. 5. Я живу́ в Калифо́рнии.

# Phrase Builder 2
▶ 6D Phrase Builder 2 (CD: 4, Track: 27)

| моя́ семья́ (*sg.*) | my family |
|---|---|
| сейча́с | now |
| я живу́ в студе́нческом общежи́тии | I live in a student dorm |
| она́ сиди́т до́ма | she stays (lit., sits) home |
| ему́ два го́да | he's two years old |
| ей два го́да | she's two years old |

| у нас дом за́ городом | we have a house in the suburbs |
| у нас да́ча под Москво́й | we have a dacha near Moscow (lit., |
| ~~у рас дача под Москвой~~ander) | |
| Ско́лько? | How much?/How many? |
| Ско́лько вам лет? (form.) | How old are you? *сколько тебе лет* |
| наприме́р | for example |
| Как интере́сно! | How interesting! |

# ✎ Phrase Practice 2

Now let's practice these phrases. Match the English phrases on the left with their Russian equivalents on the right. Repeat the Russian phrase out loud.

1. *How old are you?*
2. *How interesting!*
3. *for xample*
4. *she's two*
5. *we have a dacha near Moscow*
6. *I live in a student dorm*
7. *my family*
8. *now*

9. *she stays home*
10. *he's two*

a. у нас да́ча под Москво́й
b. моя́ семья́
c. сейча́с
d. наприме́р
e. она́ сиди́т до́ма
f. Ско́лько вам лет?
g. ему́ два го́да
h. я живу́ в студе́нческом общежи́тии
i. Как интере́сно!
j. ей два го́да

**ANSWER KEY**
1. f; 2. i; 3. d; 4. j; 5. a; 6. h; 7. b; 8. c; 9. e; 10. g

Singular possessive pronouns
and the genitive case (singular)

The instrumental case and the verbs
работать (*to work*) and жить (*to live*)

Prepositional phrases with the verb
родиться and rooms of the house

The dative case

## Grammar Builder 2

6E Grammar Builder 2 (CD: 4, Track: 28)

### THE DATIVE CASE

Now let's look at the final Russian case, the dative. This case is used to express the indirect object. It's always associated with the act of giving and denotes the recipient of the giving action, its beneficiary. When you give something to someone, this *someone* is in the dative case, whereas the *something* is in the accusative as a direct object. Let's look at how Russian nouns and pronouns change in the dative case.

|  | | SINGULAR | PLURAL |
|---|---|---|---|
| (m.) zero | | –у/–ю брáту, библиотéкарю | –ам/–ям студéнтам, гостя́м |
| (m.) –a | | –е пáпе | –ам/–ям пáпам |
| (f.) –a | | –е сестрé | –ам/–ям сёстрм |
| (f.) soft sign | | –и дóчери, мáтери | –ам/–ям дочеря́м, матеря́м |

Personal pronouns have different forms in the dative case as well.

| NOMINATIVE | DATIVE |
|---|---|
| я | мне |
| ты | тебé |
| он, оó | ем́ |
| онá | ей |

| NOMINATIVE | DATIVE |
|---|---|
| мы | нам |
| вы | вам |

Personal pronouns in the
genitive case

Reflexive verbs and the instrumental case
of pronouns and adjectives

Negation

The genitive of origin

| NOMINATIVE | DATIVE |
|---|---|
| они́ | им |

When Russians give their age (*I am X years old*), they use the dative case
construction, which literally translates as *To me (is/are) X years.*

Мне два́дцать пять лет.
*I'm 25 years old. (lit., To me, twenty-five years.)*

# ✎ Work Out 2

Ско́лько вам лет? (*How old are you?*) Say how old these people are using the
prompts below. Remember to follow the rule of numbers (see above), and use the
correct form of the noun год.

1. *my son, 21*

   _____

2. *his daughter, 5*

   _____

3. *her husband, 42*

   _____

4. *their parents, 65 and 64*

   _____

5. *I, 30*

   _____

6. *our doctor, 44*

   _____

Singular possessive pronouns
and the genitive case (singular)

The instrumental case and the verbs
рабо́тать (*to work*) and жить (*to live*)

Prepositional phrases with the verb
роди́ться and rooms of the house

The dative case

7. *my older sister, 25*

---

**ANSWER KEY**

1. Моему́ сы́ну два́дцать оди́н год. 2. Его́ до́чери пять лет. 3. Её му́жу со́рок два го́да. 4. Их роди́телям шестьдеся́т пять лет и шестьдеся́т четы́ре го́да. 5. Мне три́дцать лет. 6. На́шему врачу́ со́рок четы́ре го́да. 7. Мое́й ста́ршей сестре́ два́дцать пять лет.

# ✎ Drive It Home

Fill in the blanks with the correct dative case of the noun or pronoun in parentheses.

1. _____ два́дцать оди́н год. (я)

2. _____ два́дцать два го́да. (она́)

3. _____ два́дцать три го́да. (он)

4. _____ два́дцать четы́ре го́да. (вы)

5. _____ два́дцать пять лет. (они́)

6. _____ два́дцать шесть лет. (мы)

7. _____ два́дцать семь лет. (ты)

8. _____ два́дцать во́семь лет. (брат)

9. _____ два́дцать де́вять лет. (сестра́)

10. _____три́дцать лет. (жена́)

**ANSWER KEY**

1. Мне; 2. Ей; 3. Ему́; 4. Вам; 5. Им; 6. Нам; 7. Тебе́; 8. Бра́ту; 9. Сестре́; 10. Жене́

## How Did You Do?

Let's see how you did in this lesson. You should know how to:

☐ Talk about age, marital status, and occupations. (Still unsure? Go back to page 81.)

☐ Talk about residences and accommodations. (Still unsure? Go back to page 83.)

☐ Decline nouns in the instrumental and dative cases. (Still unsure? Go back to pages 83 and 90.)

## ✎ Word Recall

Now let's review some words and phrases from the earlier lessons. Fill in the blanks with the missing Russian word or phrase.

1. *Mr. Brown is a businessman.*

   _____Браун—бизнесме́н.

2. *He is an American.*

   Он _____.

3. *She was in Russia for two weeks.*

   Она́ была́ в Росси́и _____.

4. *I also was in Moscow.*

   Я _____ был(а) в Москве́.

5. *What else would you like?*

   Что _____ вы хоти́те?

6. *Would you like a sandwich?*

   Вы хоти́те _____?

Singular possessive pronouns
and the genitive case (singular)

The instrumental case and the verbs
рабо́тать (*to work*) and жить (*to live*)

Prepositional phrases with the verb
роди́ться and rooms of the house

**The dative case**

7. *We drank coffee in this café.*

   Мы пи́ли ко́фе _____.

8. *My wife is a lawyer.*

   Моя́ жена́—_____.

9. *They speak French well.*

   Они́ хорошо́ говоря́т _____.

10. *I don't like meat.*

    Я _____ мя́со.

**ANSWER KEY**

1. Господи́н; 2. америка́нец; 3. две неде́ли; 4. то́же; 5. ещё; 6. бутербро́д; 7. в э́том кафе́; 8. юри́ст;
9. по-францу́зски; 10. не лЮблю

# Lesson 7: Sentences

Добро́ пожа́ловать! Мы начина́ем седьмо́й уро́к.
*Welcome! We're starting Lesson 7.*

In this lesson, you'll review some words and expressions and also learn how to:

☐ Express possession.

☐ Use personal pronouns in the genitive case.

☐ Say more about residences and accommodations.

☐ Say how many children you have.

Гото́вы? Тогда́ начнём! *Ready? Then, let's begin!*
Let's get started with some phrases.

Personal pronouns in the
genitive case

Reflexive verbs and the instrumental case
of pronouns and adjectives

Negation

The genitive of origin

## Sentence Builder 1

▶ 7A Sentence Builder 1 (CD: 4, Track: 29)

| | |
|---|---|
| Вы здесь оди́н или с жено́й? | *Are you here alone or with (your) wife?* |
| У жены́ бы́ло мно́го дел. | *(My) wife had a lot of work/things (to do).* |
| У вас есть де́ти? | *Do you have children?* |
| У нас дво́е дете́й. | *We have two kids.* |
| Они́ живу́т с ва́ми? | *Do they live with you?* |
| Наш сын хо́дит в де́тский сад. | *Our son goes to daycare.* |
| На́ша дочь хо́дит в шко́лу. | *Our daughter goes to school (secondary education).* |
| Ста́ршие до́чери у́чатся в институ́те. | *The older daughters go to college.* |
| Вы, наве́рное, скуча́ете по ним. | *You probably miss them.* |
| Они́ ча́сто приезжа́ют домо́й на кани́кулы. | *They often come home for breaks.* |
| Передава́йте большо́й приве́т ва́шей жене́. | *Say hello (lit., big greeting) to your wife.* |

## ✎ Sentence Practice 1

Now let's practice these sentences. Match the following English sentences on the
left with their Russian equivalents on the right. Repeat the Russian sentence out
loud. Try repeating it again without looking.

1. *Do you have children?*

a. У нас дво́е дете́й.

2. *Our son goes to daycare.*

b. Ста́ршие до́чери хо́дят в шко́лу.

3. *Our daughter goes to school.*

c. Они́ ча́сто приезжа́ют домо́й на кани́кулы.

4. *We have two kids.*

d. У вас есть де́ти?

Singular possessive pronouns
and the genitive case (singular)

The instrumental case and the verbs
работать (*to work*) and жить (*to live*)

Prepositional phrases with the verb
родиться and rooms of the house

The dative case

5. (My) wife had a lot of things (to do).

6. The older daughters go to school.

7. They often come home for breaks.

8. You probably miss them.

9. Do they live with you?

10. Are you here alone or with your wife?

e. Вы, наве́рное, скуча́ете по ним.

f. Вы здесь оди́н или с жено́й?

g. Они́ живу́т с ва́ми?

h. На́ша дочь хо́дит в шко́лу.

i. У жены́ бы́ло мно́го дел.

j. Наш сын хо́дит в де́тский сад.

**ANSWER KEY**

1. d; 2. j; 3. h; 4. a; 5. i; 6. b; 7. c; 8. e; 9. g; 10. f

## Grammar Builder 1

▶ 7B Grammar Builder 1 (CD: 4, Track: 30)

### PERSONAL PRONOUNS IN THE GENITIVE CASE

In the last lesson you learned the forms of personal pronouns in the dative case. Now, let's look at the personal pronouns in the genitive case.

| NOMINATIVE | GENITIVE |
| --- | --- |
| я | меня́ |
| ы | тебя́ |
| н, оно́ | его́, него́ |
| она́ | её, неё |
| мы | нас |
| вы | вас |
| они́ | их, них |

Notice that the third person pronouns in the genitive will begin with н after a preposition. In Russian, personal pronouns in the genitive case are often used to express possession following the formula:

у + genitive pronoun + есть.

| Personal pronouns in the genitive case | Reflexive verbs and the instrumental case of pronouns and adjectives |
| --- | --- |

Negation                                    The genitive of origin

У вас есть де́ти?
*Do you have children?*

У нас дво́е дете́й.
*We have two kids.*

Notice that the verb есть is omitted in the answer у нас дво́е дете́й. This occurs when there is clarification on the original question, in this case дво́е.

It's idiomatic to use the collective numerals дво́е, тро́е, and че́тверо in this context in Russian, i.e., when one talks about a number of children in a family. The collective numerals from two to four are the most common in Russian. Remember that, as opposed to the standard numerals two, three, and four, which take the genitive singular (see the rule of numbers above), the collective numerals take the genitive plural: дво́е дете́й. Memorize the nominative plural noun де́ти (*children, kids*) and its genitive plural form дете́й. The singular form of де́ти is ребёнок (*child, kid*), so you should say оди́н ребёнок but дво́е дете́й.

## Take It Further

In the sentence у жены́ бы́ло мно́го дел (*my/the wife had a lot of things to do*), the verb бы́ло (*was*) is in the past tense and is in the neuter form by convention given that мно́го (*a lot of/many*) has no gender. The quantitative expression мно́го дел (*a lot of/many things*), as well as its opposite, ма́ло дел, is similar to the one in Unit 2 мно́го рабо́ты (*a lot of work [to do]*), except that the following noun is in the genitive plural form. We'll learn the genitive plural in the next unit. For now, remember this simple rule: if the noun ends in a vowel in the nominative singular (regardless of the gender), the genitive plural drops it so that the final form is truncated (has a "zero" ending) as in дел, школ, больни́ц, etc.

Singular possessive pronouns
and the genitive case (singular)

The instrumental case and the verbs
рабо́тать (*to work*) and жить (*to live*)

Prepositional phrases with the verb
роди́ться and rooms of the house

The dative case

# ✎ Work Out 1

Let's practice. Ско́лько у вас дете́й? (*How many children do you have?*) Give the Russian equivalents to the following English sentences. Don't translate the possessive pronouns in parentheses.

1. *We have three kids.*

_____

2. *They have two kids.*

_____

3. *(My) brother has three kids.*

_____

4. *Do you (form.) have one child?*

_____

5. *(My) daughter has two kids.*

_____

6. *She has four kids.*

_____

**ANSWER KEY**
1. У нас тро́е дете́й. 2. У них дво́е дете́й. 3. У бра́та тро́е дете́й. 4. У вас оди́н ребёнок? 5. У до́чери дво́е дете́й. 6. У неё че́тверо дете́й.

## Sentence Builder 2

▶ 7C Sentence Builder 2 (CD: 4, Track: 31)

| Они́ живу́т в отде́льном до́ме. | They live in a separate (single-family) home. |
| --- | --- |

Personal pronouns in the
genitive case

Reflexive verbs and the instrumental case
of pronouns and adjectives

Negation

The genitive of origin

| Они́ живу́т в кварти́ре. | *They live in an apartment.* |
|---|---|
| Это не да́ча, а котте́дж. | *This isn't a dacha; it's a cottage.* |
| Ско́лько у вас ко́мнат в до́ме? | *How many rooms do you have/are there in your house?* |
| У вас дом со все́ми удо́бствами? | *Does your house have all modern conveniences?* |
| У нас в кварти́ре есть горя́чая вода́, ва́нная и туале́т. | *We have hot water, a bathroom, and a toilet in our apartment.* |
| У нас на да́че нет горя́чей воды́. | *We don't have hot water at (our) dacha.* |
| Мы живём в двухко́мнатной/ трёхко́мнатной/четырёхко́мнатной кварти́ре в го́роде. | *We live in a two-room/three-room/ four-room apartment in the city.* |
| Это зна́чит, что у нас две спа́льни и одна́ гости́ная. | *This means that we have two bedrooms and one living room.* |
| Приезжа́йте к нам в го́сти в Вермо́нт! | *Come visit us in Vermont!* |

## ✎ Sentence Practice 2

Let's practice the following sentences. Match the following English sentences on the left with their Russian equivalents on the right. Repeat the Russian sentence out loud. Try repeating it again without looking.

1. *We live in a three-room apartment.*

2. *How many rooms do you have?*

3. *This isn't a dacha; it's a cottage.*

4. *We have hot water, a bathroom, and a toilet.*

5. *Come visit us in Vermont!*

a. У вас дом со все́ми удо́бствами?

b. У нас на да́че нет горя́чей воды́.

c. Приезжа́йте к нам в го́сти в Вермо́нт!

d. Это зна́чит, что у нас две спа́льни и одна́ гости́ная.

e. Мы живём в трёхко́мнатной кварти́ре.

Singular possessive pronouns
and the genitive case (singular)

The instrumental case and the verbs
рабо́тать (*to work*) and жить (*to live*)

Prepositional phrases with the verb
роди́ться and rooms of the house

The dative case

6. *We don't have hot water at the dacha.*

7. *Does your house have all modern conveniences?*

8. *This means that we have two bedrooms and one living room.*

f. Ско́лько у вас ко́мнат?

g. Это не да́ча, а котте́дж.

h. У нас есть горя́чая вода́, ва́нная и туале́т.

**ANSWER KEY**
1. e; 2. f; 3. g; 4. h; 5. c; 6. b; 7. a; 8. d

# Grammar Builder 2

7D Grammar Builder 2 (CD: 4, Track: 32)

## NEGATION

The phrase you just learned, не да́ча, а котте́дж (не … , а … ), is a common construction in Russian. Use it every time you contrast two things and choose one of them (*not X, but Y*). Notice that the Russian negative particle не comes immediately before the word or phrase it negates, be it a noun (with or without a preposition), a pronoun, an adjective, or a verb.

Я живу́ не в до́ме, а в кварти́ре.
*I live not in a house, but in an apartment.*

Не я живу́ в э́том до́ме, а моя́ сестра́.
*It's not I who live in this house, but my sister.*

Я не живу́ в э́том до́ме, а то́лько здесь отдыха́ю.
*I don't live in this house; I'm just on vacation here.*

When you want to express the absence of something or somebody in Russian, you need to use the genitive of negation. You do so by putting the object into the genitive case.

| Personal pronouns in the genitive case | Reflexive verbs and the instrumental case of pronouns and adjectives |
|---|---|

Negation

The genitive of origin

У нас нет горя́чей воды́.
*We don't have hot water.*

У меня́ нет дру́га.
*I don't have a friend.*

У меня́ нет да́чи.
*I don't have a dacha.*

The verb есть (*to be*) becomes нет in the negative.

# ✎ Work Out 2

A. Now, let's do some more practice. Restate the sentences below as one sentence using the construction не . . . , а . . .

1. Я не живу́ на да́че. Я живу́ в кварти́ре.

   _____

2. Он не из Кана́ды. Он из Аме́рики.

   _____

3. Моя́ дочь не у́чится в университе́те. Она́ у́чится в шко́ле.

   _____

4. Его́ жена́ не рабо́тает юри́стом. Она́ рабо́тает консульта́нтом.

   _____

5. Ва́шему бра́ту не два́дцать лет. Ему́ пятна́дцать лет.

   _____

Singular possessive pronouns
and the genitive case (singular)

The instrumental case and the verbs
рабо́тать (*to work*) and жить (*to live*)

Prepositional phrases with the verb
роди́ться and rooms of the house

The dative case

B. Restate the following sentences in the negative. Remember to use the genitive of negation.

1. У нас есть да́ча.

   _____

2. В э́том университе́те есть общежи́тие.

   _____

3. У нас есть горя́чая вода́.

   _____

4. У вас есть спа́льня.

   _____

5. В э́том до́ме есть столо́вая.

   _____

6. У них есть дочь.

   _____

**ANSWER KEY**

A. 1. Я живу́ не на да́че, а в кварти́ре. 2. Он не из Кана́ды, а из Аме́рики. 3. Моя́ дочь у́чится не в университе́те, а в шко́ле. 4. Его́ жена́ рабо́тает не юри́стом, а консульта́нтом. 5. Ва́шему бра́ту не два́дцать лет, а пятна́дцать лет.

B. 1. У нас нет да́чи. 2. В э́том университе́те нет общежи́тия. 3. У нас нет горя́чей воды. 4. У вас нет спа́льни. 5. В э́том до́ме нет столо́вой. 6. У них нет до́чери.

# ✎ Drive It Home

Now practice negation one more time. Fill in the blanks putting the nouns in parentheses into the genitive of negation.

1. У нас нет _____. (да́ча)

2. У нас нет _____ в Москве́. (кварти́ра)

3. У нас нет _____. (де́ти)

4. У нас нет _____. (молоко́)

5. У нас нет _____. (хлеб)

6. У меня́ нет _____. (сестра́)

7. У меня́ нет _____. (брат)

8. У меня́ нет _____. (маши́на)

9. У меня́ нет _____. (рабо́та)

10. У меня́ нет _____. (ку́хня)

**ANSWER KEY**

1. да́чи; 2. кварти́ры; 3. дете́й; 4. молока́; 5. хле́ба; 6. сестры́; 7. бра́та; 8. маши́ны; 9. рабо́ты; 10. ку́хни

## How Did You Do?

Let's see how you did in this lesson. You should know how to:

☐ Say how many children you have. (Still unsure? Go back to page 95.)

☐ Use personal pronouns in the genitive case. (Still unsure? Go back to page 96.)

☐ Express possession. (Still unsure? Go back to page 97.)

☐ Say more about residences and accommodations. (Still unsure? Go back to page 99.)

## ✎ Word Recall

It's time to review some older words and expressions. Read the English sentence first, then fill in the blanks and repeat the Russian sentence out loud.

1. *My name is Nikolai.*

_____ зову́т Никола́й.

Singular possessive pronouns
and the genitive case (singular)

The instrumental case and the verbs
рабо́тать (*to work*) and жить (*to live*)

Prepositional phrases with the verb
роди́ться and rooms of the house

The dative case

2. *I work as a programmer.*

   Я рабо́таю _____.

3. *We are staying in this hotel.*

   Мы живём _____.

4. *She was in Moscow for two weeks.*

   Она́ была́ в Москве́ _____.

5. *How old is he?*

   _____ ему лет?

6. *He is thirty years old.*

   Ему _____.

7. *I have one daughter and one son.*

   У меня́ _____ сын и _____ дочь.

8. *What restaurant did you go to?*

   _____ рестора́н вы ходи́ли?

9. *We went to a Russian restaurant.*

   Мы _____ в ру́сский рестора́н.

10. *I usually go to work by the metro.*

    Я обы́чно _____ на рабо́ту на метро́.

**ANSWER KEY**

1. Меня́; 2. программи́стом; 3. в э́той гости́нице; 4. две неде́ли; 5. Ско́лько; 6. три́дцать лет; 7. оди́н, одна́; 8. В како́й; 9. ходи́ли; 10. е́зжу

Personal pronouns in the
genitive case

Reflexive verbs and the instrumental case
of pronouns and adjectives

Negation

The genitive of origin

# Lesson 8: Conversations

Добро́ пожа́ловать! Мы начина́ем восьмо́й уро́к. *Welcome! We're starting Lesson 8.*

In this lesson, you'll put all of the words and expressions you've reviewed and learned in the first three lessons into two typical conversations about family and home. In this lesson, you'll learn how to:

☐ Use personal pronouns in the instrumental case.

☐ Talk more about residences and accommodations.

☐ Talk more about your family.

☐ Talk about your place of origin.

☐ Say hello to other people.

Гото́вы? Тогда́ начнём! *Ready? Then, let's begin!*

## Conversation 1

8A Conversation 1 (CD: 4, Track: 33- Russian; Track: 34- Russian and English)

At the reception after a conference, an American visitor, Bill Cooper, is talking to his Russian acquaintance and colleague, Yulia Igorevna Sidorova. They are discussing their families.

| | |
|---|---|
| Билл: | Здра́вствуйте, Ю́лия Игоревна! |
| Ю́лия: | До́брый ве́чер, господи́н Ку́пер! Вы здесь оди́н и́ли с жено́й? |
| Билл: | Оди́н. У жены́ бы́ло мно́го дел, и она́ оста́лась до́ма. |
| Ю́лия: | А кем рабо́тает ва́ша жена́? |

Singular possessive pronouns
and the genitive case (singular)

The instrumental case and the verbs
рабо́тать (*to work*) and жить (*to live*)

Prepositional phrases with the verb
роди́ться and rooms of the house

The dative case

| Билл: | Она́ юри́ст, но она́ рабо́тает консульта́нтом в фина́нсовой компа́нии. |
| Ю́лия: | А как ва́ши де́ти? Если я не ошиба́юсь, у вас дво́е дете́й? |
| Билл: | Нет, тро́е. У нас две де́вочки и оди́н ма́льчик. |
| Ю́лия: | А ско́лько им лет? |
| Билл: | Ста́ршей до́чери Джилл два́дцать оди́н год, Сюза́не девятна́дцать лет, а мла́дшему сы́ну Ге́нри четы́рнадцать. А вы за́мужем? |
| Ю́лия: | Да, за́мужем. Моего́ му́жа зову́т Никола́й Серге́евич. Он врач и рабо́тает в больни́це. |
| Билл: | А у вас есть де́ти? |
| Ю́лия: | Да, у нас оди́н сын. Ему́ четы́ре го́да. Он хо́дит в де́тский сад. Ва́ши де́ти живу́т с ва́ми? |
| Билл: | С на́ми живёт то́лько мла́дший сын Ге́нри. Он ещё хо́дит в шко́лу. А ста́ршие до́чери у́чатся в университе́тах, в други́х шта́тах. Я вас познако́млю, когда́ вы бу́дете в Аме́рике. |
| Ю́лия: | С удово́льствием познако́млюсь с ни́ми. Передава́йте ва́шей жене́ большо́й приве́т. Всего́ хоро́шего! |
| Билл: | Обяза́тельно переда́м. До свида́ния, Ю́лия Игоревна. До встре́чи. |

| Bill: | *Hello, Julia Igorevna!* |
| Julia: | *Good evening, Mr. Cooper! Are you here alone or with (your) wife?* |
| Bill: | *Alone. My wife had a lot of things to do and stayed home.* |
| Julia: | *And what does your wife do?* |
| Bill: | *She's a lawyer, but she works as a consultant in a finance company.* |
| Julia: | *And how are your children? If I'm not mistaken, you have two kids?* |
| Bill: | *No, three. We have two girls and one boy.* |
| Julia: | *How old are they?* |
| Bill: | *The older daughter, Jill, is twenty-one, Susanne is nineteen, and the younger son, Henry, is fourteen. Are you married?* |

Personal pronouns in the
genitive case

Reflexive verbs and the instrumental case
of pronouns and adjectives

Negation

The genitive of origin

| | |
|---|---|
| *Julia:* | *Yes, I am married. My husband's name is Nikolai Sergeevich. He's a doctor and (he) works in a hospital.* |
| *Bill:* | *Do you have children?* |
| *Julia:* | *Yes, we have one son. He's four. He goes to daycare. Do your children live with you?* |
| *Bill:* | *Only our younger son, Henry, lives with us. He still goes to (high) school. But the older daughters go to colleges in other states. I'll introduce you when you come to America (lit., are in America).* |
| *Julia:* | *I'll be glad to meet them. Say hello to your wife. Take care!* |
| *Bill:* | *I definitely will. Good bye, Julia Igorevna. See you!* |

# ✎ Conversation Practice 1

Now let's practice some of the phrases and sentences from the conversation above. Read the English sentence first, then fill in the blanks, and finally repeat the Russian sentence out loud.

1. *Are you here alone or with your wife?*

   Вы здесь оди́н _____ ?

2. *My wife had a lot of things (to do) and stayed home.*

   У мое́й жены́ бы́ло мно́го дел, и она́ _____ .

3. *She's a lawyer, but she works as a consultant.*

   Она́ юри́ст, но она́ _____ .

4. *If I'm not mistaken, you have two kids?*

   _____ , у вас дво́е дете́й.

5. *Julia Igorevna, are you married?*

   Ю́лия Иго́ревна, вы _____ ?

Singular possessive pronouns
and the genitive case (singular)

The instrumental case and the verbs
рабо́тать (*to work*) and жить (*to live*)

Prepositional phrases with the verb
роди́ться and rooms of the house

The dative case

6. *My husband's name is Nikolai Sergeevich.*

_____ Никола́й Сергеевич.

7. *He's a doctor.*

Он _____.

8. *Our son is four.*

_____ четы́ре го́да.

9. *Do your children live with you?*

Ва́ши де́ти живу́т _____?

10. *Say hello to your wife.*

_____ ва́шей жене́.

**ANSWER KEY**

1. или с жено́й; 2. оста́лась до́ма; 3. рабо́тает консульта́нтом; 4. Если я не ошиба́юсь; 5. за́мужем; 6. Моего́ му́жа зову́т; 7. врач; 8. На́шему сы́ну; 9. с ва́ми; 10. Передава́йте приве́т

## ● Culture Note

In addition to a first name (и́мя) and a last name (фами́лия), all complete Russian personal names also have another formal part, called a patronymic (о́тчество). The patronymic always consists of the person's father's first name with a particular suffix: –ович (–евич) for males, and –овна (–евна) for females. For example, if Никола́й's father's first name was, say, Ива́н, his patronymic would be Ива́нович. If Ната́лья Петро́ва's father's first name is Бори́с, her patronymic would be Бори́совна, and her complete фами́лия, и́мя, о́тчество (last name, first name, patronymic) would be Петро́ва Ната́лья Бори́совна. Notice also that in formal situations and all legal documents, Russian names are given in this order: 1. фами́лия (*last or family name*), 2. и́мя (*first name*), 3. о́тчество (*patronymic*). The common acronym for all three is Ф. И. О. The и́мя and о́тчество can be initialized, so instead of Пу́шкин Алекса́ндр Серге́евич, you will often see А. С. Пу́шкин. As opposed to English, these initials are never pronounced as individual letters in Russian but are either left out altogether from pronunciation or deciphered as the full name and patronymic.

## Take It Further 1

Note that Bill Cooper is calling Ms. Sidorova by her first name and patronymic. They are on formal terms; however, calling her госпожа́ Си́дорова, would have been too official and impersonal. Because English doesn't have a social equivalent to this type of address (formal yet not impersonal), Ms. Sidorova has no choice but to call Bill Cooper господи́н Ку́пер (Mr. Cooper). Addressing him as Bill, while he addresses her as Юлия Игоревна, would be awkward.

The adverb ещё in the sentence он ещё хо́дит в шко́лу translates as *still*: It is common for Russians to put "old" (i.e., already stated in the discourse) information first in a sentence. Since Ms. Sidorova discussed the living arrangements in her previous statement, Ва́ши де́ти живу́т с ва́ми? (*Do your children live with you?*), Bill Cooper begins his reply where she's left off, С на́ми живёт то́лько мла́дший сын. (*lit., With us lives our younger son only.*) In English, this kind of changed word order is less common and restricted to special contexts, such as when one wants to emphasize or contrast one part of the sentence with respect to the rest, e.g. *I can't stand the Yankees, but the Mets, I love*; however, word order is more flexible in Russian and these do not carry such special meaning, but rather depend on the previous context outside of the sentence in question.

Singular possessive pronouns
and the genitive case (singular)

The instrumental case and the verbs
рабо́тать (*to work*) and жить (*to live*)

Prepositional phrases with the verb
роди́ться and rooms of the house

The dative case

## Grammar Builder 1

▶ 8B Grammar Builder 1 (CD: 4, Track: 35)

### REFLEXIVE VERBS AND THE INSTRUMENTAL CASE OF PRONOUNS AND ADJECTIVES

Éсли я не ошиба́юсь is an idiomatic expression equivalent to the English *if I'm not mistaken.*

Ошиба́ться is a Conjugation Type I verb, and it's also a reflexive verb. In Russian, reflexive verbs are conjugated using the same pattern as non-reflexive verbs with the particle –ся/–сь added to the end. The ending –ся follows consonants, and –сь is added after vowels. Now, take a look at the following paradigm:

| ОШИБА́ТЬСЯ TO BE MISTAKEN | |
|---|---|
| я ошиба́юсь | мы ошиба́емся |
| ты ошиба́ешься | вы ошиба́етесь |
| он/она́/оно́ ошиба́ется | они́ ошиба́ются |

Past: ошиба́лся, ошиба́лась, ошиба́лось, ошиба́лись.

The stress is stable.

The verb роди́ться (*to be born*) is also reflexive.

| РОДИ́ТЬСЯ TO BE BORN | |
|---|---|
| я рожу́сь | мы роди́мся |
| ты роди́шься | вы роди́тесь |
| он/она́/оно́ роди́тся | они́ родя́тся |

Past: роди́лся, родила́сь, родило́сь, родили́сь.

Notice the end stress shift in the past.

Personal pronouns in the
genitive case

Reflexive verbs and the instrumental case
of pronouns and adjectives

Negation

The genitive of origin

You should say роди́лся for males, родила́сь for females, and родили́сь for plurals. Predictably, this verb takes the prepositional case, because the place where you were born is a location.

Он роди́лся в Росси́и.
*He was born in Russia.*

Она́ родила́сь во Фра́нции.
*She was born in France.*

Мы родили́сь в Калифо́рнии.
*We were born in California.*

Let's look at the instrumental case of personal pronouns. The instrumental case of pronouns is used especially to express *with someone* or *with something*. Remember that you need the preposition с in the instrumental case only in the sense of accompaniment, as in ко́фе с молоко́м (*coffee with milk*) or с жено́й (*with [my] wife*), and never in the purely instrumental sense, as in *I'm writing with a pen* (we'll discuss the instrumental of means later). Therefore, it will be helpful if you think of the instrumental case as the case without a preposition in the "default setting," and with the preposition с only in the sense of accompaniment.

| NOMINATIVE | INSTRUMENTAL |
| --- | --- |
| я | со мно́й |
| ты | с тобо́й |
| он, оно́ | с им |
| она́ | с ней |
| мы | с на́ми |
| вы | с ва́ми |
| они́ | с ни́ми |

Singular possessive pronouns
and the genitive case (singular)

The instrumental case and the verbs
рабо́тать (*to work*) and жить (*to live*)

Prepositional phrases with the verb
роди́ться and rooms of the house

The dative case

Let's also look at the adjectival endings in the instrumental case. They are –ым / –им for masculine and neuter adjectives, –ой /–ей for feminine adjectives, and –ыми /–ими for plurals.

с мое́й мла́дшей сестро́й
*with my younger sister*

с мои́м мла́дшим бра́том
*with my younger brother*

с мои́ми ру́сскими друзья́ми
*with my Russian friends*

Let's review the adjectival endings in the nominative, prepositional, and instrumental cases. Learn them through the familiar examples in the chart below.

| | MASCULINE | FEMININE | NEUTER | PLURAL |
|---|---|---|---|---|
| Nom. | мла́дший брат | мла́дшая сестра́ | до́брое у́тро | ру́сские друзья́ |
| Prep. | в большо́м до́ме | в ва́нной ко́мнате | в студе́нческом общежи́тии | в други́х шта́тах |
| Inst. | с ру́сским дру́гом | с мла́дшей сестро́й | с кра́сным вино́м | с ру́сскими друзья́ми |

# ✎ Work Out 1

A. Now let's practice. Translate the following sentences into Russian. Repeat the Russian sentence out loud.

1. *You're mistaken (form.), she's twenty-one.*

Personal pronouns in the
genitive case

Reflexive verbs and the instrumental case
of pronouns and adjectives

Negation

The genitive of origin

2.  *If I'm not mistaken, your children live with you (form.).*

_____

3.  *You're mistaken (inform.), he works as a doctor.*

_____

4.  *He was born in Russia.*

_____

5.  *They were born in Cleveland.*

_____

B. Rewrite the following sentences replacing the nouns in the instrumental case with the appropriate pronouns. Repeat the final sentence out loud.

1. Мы живём с детьми́ в отде́льном до́ме.

_____

2. Я живу́ с бра́том в гости́нице.

_____

3. Я жил с роди́телями.

_____

4. Они́ рабо́тают с Ю́ристом.

_____

5. Вы здесь с жено́й?

_____

Singular possessive pronouns
and the genitive case (singular)

The instrumental case and the verbs
рабо́тать (*to work*) and жить (*to live*)

Prepositional phrases with the verb
роди́ться and rooms of the house

The dative case

C. Fill in the blanks by putting the phrases in the parentheses in the instrumental case.

1. Я живу́ со _____. (ста́рший брат)

2. Вы рабо́таете с _____. (хоро́ший юри́ст)

3. Я живу́ с _____. (америка́нский студе́нт)

4. Она́ сидит до́ма с _____. (мла́дшая сестра́)

5. Мы рабо́таем с _____. (ру́сские врачи́)

**ANSWER KEY**

A. 1. Вы ошиба́етесь, ей два́дцать оди́н год. 2. Если я не ошиба́юсь, ва́ши де́ти живу́т с ва́ми. 3. Ты ошиба́ешься, он рабо́тает врачо́м. 4. Он роди́лся в Росси́и. 5. Они́ родили́сь в Кли́вленде.

B. 1. Мы живём с ни́ми в отде́льном до́ме. 2. Я живу́ с ним в гости́нице. 3. Я жил с ни́ми. 4. Они́ рабо́тают с ним. 5. Вы здесь с ней?

C. 1. ста́ршим бра́том; 2. хоро́шим юри́стом; 3. америка́нским студе́нтом; 4. мла́дшей сестро́й; 5. ру́сскими врача́ми

# Conversation 2

▶ 8C Conversation 2 (CD: 5, Track: 1- Russian; Track: 2- Russian and English)

Christy Doyle, an American exchange student, is talking to her Russian host, Aleksei Gregorovich, in her apartment in Moscow. They are having tea and discussing their respective families.

Алексе́й:   Кри́сти, где вы живёте в Аме́рике?

Кри́сти:   Я из Вермо́нта. Я там родила́сь, и моя́ семья́ живёт в Вермо́нте. Но сейча́с я студе́нтка в университе́те в Калифо́рнии. Я там живу́ в студе́нческом общежи́тии.

Алексе́й:   А кто ва́ши роди́тели? Кем они́ рабо́тают?

Кри́сти: Моего́ отца́ зову́т Па́трик. Он программи́ст. Моя́ ма́ма библиоте́карь, но она́ сейча́с не рабо́тает. Она́ сиди́т до́ма с мое́й мла́дшей сестро́й Дже́ннифер. Она́ ещё ма́ленькая. Ей то́лько два го́да.

Алексе́й: А они́ живу́т в до́ме или в кварти́ре?

Кри́сти: У нас дом за́ городом.

Алексе́й: А ско́лько в нём ко́мнат?

Кри́сти: У нас четы́ре спа́льни, гости́ная, столо́вая, две ва́нных ко́мнаты.

Алексе́й: Вы живёте на да́че?

Кри́сти: Нет, э́то не да́ча, а котте́дж – большо́й двухэта́жный дом со все́ми удо́бствами.

Алексей: Зна́чит, у вас шесть ко́мнат?

Кри́сти: Да, но в Аме́рике мы счита́ем то́лько спа́льни. Наприме́р, у вас в Москве́ четырёхко́мнатная кварти́ра—э́то зна́чит, что у вас три спа́льни и одна́ гости́ная.

Алексе́й: Как интере́сно!

Кри́сти: Приезжа́йте к нам в го́сти в Вермо́нт!

Aleksei: *Christy, where do you live in America?*

Christy: *I'm from Vermont. I was born there and my family lives in Vermont. But now, I'm a student at a university in California. I live in a student dorm there.*

Aleksei: *And who are your parents? What do they do?*

Christy: *My father's name is Patrick. He's a programmer. My mother is a librarian, but she's not working now. She's staying home with my younger sister, Jennifer. She's still small. She's only two (years old).*

Aleksei: *Do they live in a house or in an apartment?*

Christy: *We have a house in the country (suburbs).*

Aleksei: *How many rooms are there (in it)?*

Christy: *We have four bedrooms, a living room, a dining room, and two bathrooms.*

Singular possessive pronouns
and the genitive case (singular)

The instrumental case and the verbs
работать (*to work*) and жить (*to live*)

Prepositional phrases with the verb
родиться and rooms of the house

The dative case

| Aleksei: | Do you live at a dacha? |
|---|---|
| Christy: | No, it isn't a dacha; it is a cottage—a big, two-story house with all the conveniences. |
| Aleksei: | Then (this means) you have six rooms? |
| Christy: | Yes, but in America, we count only bedrooms. For example, you have a four-room apartment in Moscow—this means that you have three bedrooms and one living room. |
| Aleksei: | How interesting! |
| Christy: | Come visit us in Vermont! |

## ✎ Conversation Practice 2

Let's practice now. Match the following English phrases and sentences on the left with their Russian equivalents on the right. Repeat the Russian sentence out loud.

1. *I live in a student dorm.*

2. *What do your parents do?*

3. *My mother stays home with my younger sister.*

4. *We have a house in the suburbs.*

5. *How many rooms are there in your house?*

6. *We have four bedrooms.*

7. *You have a four-room apartment in Moscow.*

8. *How interesting!*

a. У нас четы́ре спа́льни.

b. Ско́лько ко́мнат в ва́шем до́ме?

c. У вас четырёхко́мнатная кварти́ра в Москве́.

d. Как интере́сно!

e. Кем рабо́тают ва́ши роди́тели?

f. Я живу́ в студе́нческом общежи́тии.

g. Моя́ ма́ма сиди́т до́ма с мое́й мла́дшей сестро́й.

h. У нас дом за́ городом.

**ANSWER KEY**

1. f; 2. e; 3. g; 4. h; 5. b; 6. a; 7. c; 8. d

Personal pronouns in the
genitive case

Reflexive verbs and the instrumental case
of pronouns and adjectives

Negation

The genitive of origin

# Grammar Builder 2

▶ 8D Grammar Builder 2 (CD: 5, Track: 3)

## THE GENITIVE OF ORIGIN

Notice the genitive case in Christy's statement Я из Вермо́нта (*I'm from Vermont*). This is the genitive of origin. You already learned the expressions Я из Аме́рики (*I'm from America*) and Я из Нью-Йо́рка (*I'm from New York*). Now you know that all places of origin take the genitive case in Russian and are usually preceded by the preposition из (*from*). The nouns that take the preposition на in the prepositional case have the preposition с in the genitive of origin. For example, на рабо́те (*at work*) becomes с рабо́ты (*from work*).

Remember to differentiate among different declensions. Masculine nouns (zero endings or –ь) take –а (or soft –я) in the genitive case (из Вермо́нта); feminine nouns (–а /–я endings and some irregular masculine –а nouns) take –ы (or soft –и) (из Аме́рики). Also remember that the irregular feminine nouns that end in –ия (Росси́я and other countries ending in –ия, etc.) change their endings to –ии in the genitive singular (из Росси́и, из Фра́нции, из Герма́нии, etc.), just as they do in the prepositional case (в Росси́и, во Фра́нции, etc.).

Я из Вермо́нта.
*I'm from Vermont.*

Я из Аме́рики.
*I'm from America.*

Я из Нью-Йо́рка.
*I'm from New York.*

Он из Росси́и.
*He's from Russia.*

Singular possessive pronouns
and the genitive case (singular)

The instrumental case and the verbs
рабо́тать (*to work*) and жить (*to live*)

Prepositional phrases with the verb
роди́ться and rooms of the house

The dative case

Она́ из Фра́нции.

*She's from France.*


# ✎ Work Out 2

Отку́да вы? (*Where are you from?*) Restate the answers below using the genitive
of origin. Repeat the final Russian sentence out loud.


1. Он роди́лся в Москве́.

_____

2. Она́ родила́сь в Вермо́нте.

_____

3. Они́ родили́сь в Росси́и.

_____

4. Я родила́сь в Аме́рике.

_____

5. Ты роди́лся в Петербу́рге.

_____

6. Вы родили́сь в Герма́нии.

_____

**ANSWER KEY**

**1.** Он из Москвы́. **2.** Она́ из Вермо́нта. **3.** Они́ из Росси́и. **4.** Я из Аме́рики. **5.** Ты из
Петербу́рга. **6.** Вы из Герма́нии.

# Take It Further 2

▶ 8E Take It Further 2 (CD: 5, Track: 4)

How do you use foreign geographical names in Russian? Well, if the foreign geographical name (American, English, French, etc.) fits into any Russian declension, meaning, if it ends in a consonant (1st declension) or the vowel –a (2nd declension), you decline it as a Russian noun of the same class: Вермо́нт (*Vermont*) becomes в Вермо́нте/из Вермо́нта, and Аризо́на (*Arizona*) becomes в Аризо́не/из Аризо́ны. If the foreign name has any other ending, so that it doesn't fit the above patterns, it will stay indeclinable in Russian: Ога́йо (*Ohio*) becomes в Ога́йо/из Ога́йо, and Миссиси́пи (*Mississippi*) becomes в Миссиси́пи/из Миссиси́пи, etc.

There is also a way to avoid declining the foreign geographical name if you're not sure how to go about it: introduce the foreign name with a generic noun, such as го́род (*city*) or штат (*state*). The generic noun assumes the case, relieving the following noun from the need to change.

Я живу́ в Мичига́не.
*I live in Michigan.*

Я живу́ в шта́те Мичига́н.
*I live in the state of Michigan.*

Я роди́лся в Фи́никсе.
*I was born in Phoenix.*

Я роди́лся в го́роде Фи́никс.
*I was born in the city of Phoenix.*

Singular possessive pronouns
and the genitive case (singular)

The instrumental case and the verbs
работать (*to work*) and жить (*to live*)

Prepositional phrases with the verb
родиться and rooms of the house

The dative case

# ✎ Drive It Home

Now it's time to commit the new structures to your memory. These fairly easy exercises will help make these Russian constructions seem natural to you. Don't forget to write out and repeat each sentence out loud.

Fill in the blanks with the words and phrases in parentheses using the instrumental case. Remember not to use the preposition с in the instrumental of means (the purely instrumental sense) and use it only in the sense of accompaniment!

1. Он рабо́тает _____. (врач)

2. Он рабо́тает _____. (программи́ст)

3. Она́ рабо́тает _____. (юри́ст)

4. Он был в Росси́и _____. (жена́)

5. Я лЮблЮ ко́фе _____. (молоко́)

6. Я была́ в ресторáне _____. (ру́сский друг)

7. Я живу́ в общежи́тии _____.

   (америка́нский студе́нт)

8. На обе́д мы е́ли суп _____. (сала́т)

9. Я жил _____ в одно́й кварти́ре. (он)

10. Я рабо́тал _____ в одно́й компа́нии. (она́)

**ANSWER KEY**

1. врачо́м; 2. программи́стом; 3. юри́стом; 4. с жено́й; 5. с молоко́м; 6. с ру́сским дру́гом; 7. с америка́нским студе́нтом; 8. с сала́том; 9. с ним; 10. с ней

Personal pronouns in the
genitive case

Reflexive verbs and the instrumental case
of pronouns and adjectives

Negation

The genitive of origin

## How Did You Do?

Let's see how you did in this lesson. You should know how to:

☐ Say hello to other people. (Still unsure? Go back to page 107.)

☐ Use personal pronouns in the instrumental case. (Still unsure? Go back to page 110.)

☐ Talk more about residences and accommodations. (Still unsure? Go back to page 115.)

☐ Talk more about your family. (Still unsure? Go back to page 115.)

☐ Talk about your place of origin. (Still unsure? Go back to page 117.)

## ✎ Word Recall

Now it's time to review some of the expressions and structures you've learned earlier. Read the English sentence first and fill in the blanks in the corresponding Russian sentence. Repeat the Russian sentence out loud.

1. *We have two kids.*

   У нас _____.

2. *My daughter is five.*

   _____ пять лет.

3. *My son is fourteen.*

   Моему́ сы́ну _____ лет.

4. *My husband is forty two.*

   _____ со́рок два го́да.

Singular possessive pronouns
and the genitive case (singular)

The instrumental case and the verbs
работать (*to work*) and жить (*to live*)

Prepositional phrases with the verb
роди́ться and rooms of the house

The dative case

5. *They are from America.*

   Они́ _____.

6. *What do they have for breakfast?*

   Что _____ на за́втрак?

7. *In the summer, I vacation by the sea.*

   _____ я отдыха́ю на мо́ре.

8. *What will you do on Saturday night?*

   Что ты _____ в суббо́ту ве́чером?

9. *These are my Russian friends.*

   _____ мои́ ру́сские друзья́.

10. *This is an inexpensive, but good restaurant.*

    Это _____ хоро́ший рестора́н.

**ANSWER KEY**

1. дво́е дете́й; 2. Мое́й до́чери; 3. четы́рнадцать лет; 4. Моему́ му́жу; 5. из Аме́рики; 6. у них
есть; 7. Ле́том; 8. бу́дешь де́лать; 9. Это; 10. недорого́й, но

Don't forget to practice and reinforce what you've
learned by visiting **www.livinglanguage.com/
languagelab** for flashcards, games, and quizzes!

# Quiz 2

## Контро́льная рабо́та №2

Now let's review. In this section you'll be tested on what you've learned in Unit 2. Once you've completed it, score yourself to see how well you've done. If you find that you need to go back and review, please do so before continuing on to Unit 3.

**Let's get started!**

A. Ско́лько вам лет? (*How old are you?*) Say how old these people are. Fill in the blanks following the prompts in the parentheses

1. _____ со́рок лет. (*my husband*)

2. _____ восемна́дцать лет. (*my sister*)

3. _____ два́дцать де́вять лет. (*her friend*)

4. _____ восемна́дцать лет. (*she*)

5. _____ три́дцать три го́да. (*he*)

B. Say what these people don't have. Fill in the blanks following the prompts in the parentheses.

1. У нас нет _____ . (*children*)

2. У нас нет _____ . (*dacha*)

3. У них нет _____ . (*hot water*)

4. У них нет _____ . (*dorm*)

5. У вас в кварти́ре нет _____ . (*balcony*)

C. Say where these people are from. Fill in the blanks using the nouns in parentheses with correct prepositions and in the correct case.

1. Моя́ жена́ _____. (America)

2. Мой муж _____. (Russia)

3. Её роди́тели _____. (California)

4. Эта де́вушка _____. (Vermont)

5. Они́ неда́вно _____. (work)

D. What do these people do for a living? Fill in the blanks with their occupation given in the parentheses.

1. Мой муж рабо́тает _____. (programmer)

2. Моя́ жена́ рабо́тает _____. (lawyer)

3. Наш сын рабо́тает _____. (doctor)

4. _____ рабо́тает ваш оте́ц? (what/who)

5. Эта студе́нтка рабо́тает _____. (waitress)

E. Say where these people were born. Fill in the blanks with the correct form of the verb to be born.

1. Они́ _____ в Москве́.

2. Она́ _____ в Вермо́нте.

3. Мой сын _____ в Нью-Йо́рке.

4. Я _____ в Аме́рике. (use your own gender)

5. Мои́ роди́тели _____ в Петербу́рге.

F. Say how many children these people have. Fill in the blanks according to the prompts in parentheses.

1. У неё _____ . (*two kids*)

2. У нас _____ . (*four kids*)

3. У них _____ . (*one daughter*)

4. У вас _____ . (*one son*)

5. У мое́й сестры́ _____ . (*three kids*)

**ANSWER KEY**
A. 1. Моему́ му́жу; 2. Мое́й сестре́; 3. Её дру́гу; 4. Ей; 5. Ему́
B. 1. дете́й; 2. да́чи; 3. горя́чей воды́; 4. общежи́тия; 5. балко́на
C. 1. из Аме́рики; 2. из Росси́и; 3. из Калифо́рнии; 4. из Вермо́нта; 5. с рабо́ты
D. 1. программи́стом; 2. юри́стом; 3. врачо́м; 4. Кем; 5. официа́нткой
E. 1. родили́сь; 2. родила́сь; 3. роди́лся; 4. роди́лся/родила́сь; 5. родили́сь
F. 1. дво́е дете́й; 2. че́тверо дете́й; 3. одна́ дочь; 4. оди́н сын; 5. тро́е дете́й

# How Did You Do?

Give yourself a point for every correct answer, then use the following key to tell whether you're ready to move on:

**0–7 points:** It's probably a good idea to go back through the lesson again. You may be moving too quickly, or there may be too much "down time" between your contact with Russian. Remember that it's better to spend 30 minutes with Russian three or four times a week than it is to spend two or three hours just once a week. Find a pace that's comfortable for you, and spread your contact hours out as much as you can.

**8–12 points:** You would benefit from a review before moving on. Go back and spend a little more time on the specific points that gave you trouble. Re-read the Grammar Builder sections that were difficult, and do the Work Outs one more time. Don't forget about the online supplemental practice material, either. Go to **www.livinglanguage.com/languagelab** for games and quizzes that will reinforce the material from this unit.

**13-17 points:** Good job! There are just a few points that you might consider reviewing before moving on. If you haven't worked with the games and quizzes on **www.livinglanguage.com/languagelab**, please give them a try.

**18–20 points:** Great! You're ready to move on to the next unit.

|  |  |
|--|--|

points

# Unit 3:
# Everyday Life

Поздравля́ем с оконча́нием второ́й главы́, и добро́ пожа́ловать в тре́тью гла́ву! *Congratulations on the completion of Unit 2 and welcome to Unit 3!*

In this unit, you'll learn some important aspects of Russian grammar such as imperfective and perfective verbs, more verbs of motion and more about cases such as the accusative of duration. You'll also learn important vocabulary related to talking about dates and activities such as shopping and playing music and sports. Let's get started!

# Lesson 9: Words

In this lesson, you'll review some of the old words and expressions and also learn how to:

☐ Use more words and phrases related to everyday activities.

☐ Differentiate and use perfective and imperfective verbs.

☐ Talk about renting a place.

☐ Talk about seasons and months.

Гото́вы? Тогда́ начнём! *Ready? Then, let's begin!*
Let's get started with some words and phrases.

# Word Builder 1

▶ 9A Word Builder 1 (CD: 5, Track: 5)

| | |
|---|---|
| снима́ть/снять | *to rent (an apartment)* |
| ста́нция метро́ | *metro station* |
| остано́вка | *stop (bus, trolley, streetcar)* |
| на метро́ | *by metro, by subway* |
| пешко́м | *on foot* |
| ка́ждый день | *every day* |
| иногда́ | *sometimes* |
| теа́тр | *theater* |
| музе́й | *museum* |
| удо́бно | *convenient, comfortable* |
| спорти́вный зал (спортза́л) | *gym (lit., sports hall)* |
| спорти́вный клуб (спортклу́б) | *gym (lit., sports club)* |

## Take It Further 1

The Russian verb снима́ть has several meanings: *to rent* (*to hire*, not *to rent out*) as in снима́ть кварти́ру; *to take photographs*; and *to take off (an article of clothing)*. This is possible because the verb literally means *to take off*, so in the first case, you *take an apartment off someone*; in the second, you *take an image (photograph) (off) of* someone; in the third, you *take off* your shoes, etc. This verb belongs to Conjugation I.

The genitive plural case
and telling time

Expressing likes and dislikes

The accusative of duration, numbers
100—1,000, and ordinal numbers

The verbs занима́ться (to
study) and игра́ть (to play)

# ✎ Word Practice 1

Let's practice what you just learned. Match the following English words and
phrases on the left with their Russian equivalents on the right. Repeat the Russian
words and phrases out loud.

1. *by metro*                          a. остано́вка

2. *on foot*                           b. удо́бно

3. *sometimes*                         c. музе́й

4. *every day*                         d. снима́ть кварти́ру

5. *museum*                            e. иногда́

6. *convenient or comfortable*         f. пешко́м

7. *gym*                               g. ста́нция метро́

8. *top (bus)*                         h. на метро́

9. *metro station*                     i. спорти́вный зал/клуб

10. *rent an apartment*                j. ка́ждый день

**ANSWER KEY**
1. h; 2. f; 3. e; 4. j; 5. c; 6. b; 7. i; 8. a; 9. g; 10. d

## Grammar Builder 1

▶ 9B Grammar Builder 1 (CD: 5, Track: 6)

### IMPERFECTIVE AND PERFECTIVE VERBS

Now, let's learn some important information regarding Russian verbs. All Russian
verbs can be either imperfective or perfective. This grammatical distinction is
called "aspect," and it doesn't correspond perfectly to anything in English (or
French, or Spanish, or German) grammar. Imperfective verbs often describe
continuous or repeated actions. For example, when you want to emphasize the
fact that you stayed in a rented apartment for several months (duration), or when
you say that you rented the same apartment several times (repetition), you have
to use the imperfective verb снима́ть (я снима́л кварти́ру). Such adverbs as

ча́сто (*often*), обы́чно (*usually*), всегда́ (*always*), иногда́ (*sometimes*), and even никогда́ (*never*) are good signs of the imperfective aspect because they clearly indicate repetition. Follow them and you'll never be wrong!

Perfective verbs, on the other hand, denote one-time, completed actions that form a link in a causal chain. So, for example, when you present the act of renting an apartment in such a way that this act either is a consequence of something stated earlier (e.g., you told me to rent it and I did) or leads to something that your interlocutor is aware of (e.g., I rented this apartment and now we have a place to stay), you need to use the perfective aspect. In other words, perfective actions denote completed actions usually lined up in a sequence – explicitly or implied. Consider another example:

Я прочита́л э́тот рома́н.
*I read this novel.*

This statement can occur in different contexts but it always presupposes an expectation (I was supposed to read it, it was on the syllabus, and my interlocutor knows about it) or a consequence (now I can write an essay about it). Without any of these contextual references obvious to your interlocutor, the perfective aspect wouldn't be appropriate. The fact that you read the novel once and through to the end isn't enough to justify the perfective.

Moreover, if you use the imperfective aspect, it doesn't mean that you read it many times or that you never finished it:

Я чита́л э́тот рома́н.
*I read this novel.*

This statement means that you happened to have read this novel at some point in the past without any immediate relevance to the current context. This type of statement becomes "a mere statement of fact." This statement may also mean, *I*

The genitive plural case
and telling time

Expressing likes and dislikes

The accusative of duration, numbers
100—1,000, and ordinal numbers

The verbs занима́ться (*to
study*) and игра́ть (*to play*)

*was reading this novel*, but then it would require the context to justify it, such as "I was reading this novel when you called."

You should note that when the imperfective and perfective forms of a verb are presented as a pair, for example in a dictionary, the first one is imperfective. So, when you see two hyphenated or slashed verbs in a dictionary, e.g., снима́ть— снять (*to rent*), you can assume that the first one is imperfective. Usually, but not always, imperfective verbs don't have prefixes and perfectives do: чита́ть— прочита́ть (*to read*); де́лать—сде́лать (*to do*); sometimes, it is the suffix that marks the difference, а is imperfective, и is perfective: реша́ть—реши́ть (*to decide, to solve*); покупа́ть—купи́ть (*to buy*).

One very important thing to remember is that perfective verbs don't occur in the present tense; they denote future when you conjugate them with the present tense endings. Let's take a look at the conjugation of the perfective verb снять (*to rent*), which has the present tense endings but signifies the future tense.

| СНЯТЬ *TO RENT* | |
| --- | --- |
| я сниму́ | мы сни́мем |
| ты сни́мешь | вы сни́мите |
| он/она́/оно́ сни́мет | они́ сни́мут |

Past: снял, сняла́, сня́ло, сня́ли
Both the perfective and imperfective forms of this verb take a noun in the accusative case.

# ✎ Work Out 1

Fill in the blanks using the correct perfective or imperfective form of the verb снима́ть—снять in the following sentences and indicate the reason for your choice: present tense, repetition, duration for imperfective; one-time completed action/sequence/result for perfective.

1. Когда́ я в Москве́, я всегда́ _____ э́ту кварти́ру.

2. Сейча́с я живу́ в це́нтре, я _____ о́чень хоро́шую двухко́мнатную кварти́ру.

3. Моему́ дру́гу понра́вилась (*my friend liked*) э́та кварти́ра, и он _____ её.

4. Ты обы́чно _____ кварти́ру о́коло метро́.

5. Мы _____ э́ту кварти́ру всё ле́то (*during the whole summer*).

6. Я _____ э́ту кварти́ру, когда́ у меня́ бу́дет мно́го де́нег (*when I have a lot of money*).

7. Вы _____ э́ту да́чу ка́ждое ле́то.

**ANSWER KEY**

1. снима́ю (repetition); 2. снима́ю (present tense); 3. снял (sequence); 4. снима́ешь (repetition); 5. снима́ли (duration); 6. сниму́ (sequence); 7. снима́ете (repetition)

# Word Builder 2

▶ 9C Word Builder 2 (CD: 5, Track: 7)

Let's learn more useful vocabulary.

| ме́сяц | *month* |
|---|---|
| проду́кты | *groceries* |
| покупа́ть (*conj. I; –ай*) —купи́ть (*conj. II; –и*) | *to buy* |
| гото́вить/пригото́вить | *to cook* |
| стира́льная маши́на | *washing machine* |
| стира́ть (*conj. I*) —постира́ть | *to wash, to do laundry* |
| суши́лка | *dryer* |
| химчи́стка | *dry cleaner* |

The genitive plural case
and telling time

Expressing likes and dislikes

The accusative of duration, numbers
100—1,000, and ordinal numbers

The verbs заниматься (to
study) and играть (to play)

| вещь (*f.*), ве́щи (*pl.*) | *thing, things* |
|---|---|
| зима́ | *winter* |
| весна́ | *spring* |
| ле́то | *summer* |
| о́сень | *fall* |

# ✎ Word Practice 2

Now, let's practice these words and phrases. Match the following English words and phrases on the left with their Russian equivalents on the right. Repeat the Russian words and phrases out loud.

1. *to buy* (*imperf.*)       a. суши́лка

2. *to buy* (*perf.*)       b. проду́кты

3. *washing machine*       c. ве́щи

4. *dry cleaner*       d. стира́ть

5. *dryer*       e. гото́вить

6. *things*       f. стира́льная маши́на

7. *to cook* (*imperf.*)       g. покупа́ть

8. *to have cooked* (*perf.*)       h. купи́ть

9. *to wash* (*imperf.*)       i. химчи́стка

10. *groceries*       j. пригото́вить

**ANSWER KEY**
1. g; 2. h; 3. f; 4. i; 5. a; 6. c; 7. e; 8. j; 9. d; 10. b

# Grammar Builder 2

▶ 9D Grammar Builder 2 (CD: 5, Track: 8)

## THE VERBS ПОКУПА́ТЬ—КУПИ́ТЬ (*TO BUY*)

*To buy* is покупа́ть or купи́ть in Russian. This is another aspectual pair where
покупа́ть is imperfective and купи́ть is perfective. Покупа́ть is a Conjugation
I verb, just like the verbs рабо́тать (*to work*), снима́ть (*to rent*), etc. Купи́ть is
a Conjugation II verb. Notice in the chart below that it adds the letter –л in the
first person singular (л–mutation) and has a present tense stress shift. Look at the
following future tense conjugation of the verb купи́ть and note how it is identical
to the verb люби́ть, which you already know well.

| КУПИ́ТЬ<br>*TO BUY* | |
|---|---|
| я куплю́ | мы ку́пим |
| ты ку́пишь | вы ку́пите |
| он/она́/оно́ ку́пит | они́ ку́пят |

Past: купи́л, купи́ла, купи́ло, купи́ли

Remember that the same endings as in the imperfective present tense denote the
future tense with the perfective verbs. The imperfective future is formed with the
conjugated auxiliary verb *to be* and an imperfective infinitive.

Compare the following sentences:

Я иногда́ покупа́ю проду́кты в э́том магази́не.
*I sometimes buy groceries at this store.* (present tense, imperfective, repetition)

Я за́втра куплю́ проду́кты в э́том магази́не.
*Tomorrow I will buy groceries at this store.* (future, perfective, one-time action)

Я всегда́ бу́ду покупа́ть проду́кты в э́том магази́не.

*I will always buy groceries at this store.* (future, imperfective, repetition)

## Take It Further 2

▶ 9E Take It Further 2 (CD: 5, Track: 9)

Let's review the four seasons in Russian. They are зима́ (*winter*), весна́ (*spring*), ле́то (*summer*), о́сень (*fall*). Notice that зима́ and весна́ are feminine nouns, о́сень is also a feminine noun ending in –ь, and ле́то is neuter. In order to say *in the winter, in the spring*, etc., you need to put these nouns into the instrumental case without prepositions.

| зимо́й | *in the winter* |
|---|---|
| весно́й | *in the spring* |
| ле́том | *in the summer* |
| о́сенью | *in the fall* |

Now let's learn the names of the months in Russian. In order to say in January, in February, etc., use the preposition в and the month in the prepositional case.

| янва́рь | *January* | в январе́ | *in January* |
|---|---|---|---|
| февра́ль | *February* | в феврале́ | *in February* |
| март | *March* | в ма́рте | *in March* |
| апре́ль | *April* | в апре́ле | *in April* |
| май | *May* | в ма́е | *in May* |
| ию́нь | *June* | в ию́не | *in June* |
| ию́ль | *July* | в ию́ле | *in July* |
| а́вгуст | *August* | в а́вгусте | *in August* |
| сентя́брь | *September* | в сентябре́ | *in September* |
| октя́брь | *October* | в октябре́ | *in October* |
| ноя́брь | *November* | в ноябре́ | *in November* |

**The verbs покупа́ть – купи́ть** (*to buy*)

| дека́брь | *December* | в декабре́ | *in December* |
|----------|------------|-----------|---------------|

All Russian months are masculine and are never capitalized (unless in
the beginning of the sentence). Notice the following stress pattern in the
prepositional case: all "cold" (fall and winter) months from September to
February have end stress; all "warm" (spring and summer) months from March to
August have stem stress.

# ✎ Work Out 2

A. Translate the following sentences into Russian. Pay attention to your choice of
aspect and tense! Indicate the reason for your choice of aspect from the following
list: present tense, repetition, duration—for imperfective; one-time action/result
for perfective.

1. *We buy groceries at this store.*

   _____

2. *Tomorrow, he will buy groceries at this store.*

   _____

3. *She sometimes would buy groceries at this store.*

   _____

4. *They will do laundry tomorrow all day long* (весь день).

   _____

5. *He has washed all of his clothes* (все его́ ве́щи).

   _____

The genitive plural case
and telling time

Expressing likes and dislikes

The accusative of duration, numbers
100—1,000, and ordinal numbers

The verbs занима́ться (*to
study*) and игра́ть (*to play*)

6. *You (infml.) always do laundry at home.*

_____

B. Когда́ они́ жи́ли и рабо́тали в Росси́и? (*When did they live and work in
   Russia?*) Restate the sentences below replacing the seasons with the three
   appropriate months so that *in the winter* indicates *in December, in January, and
   in February; in the spring* indicates *in March, in April,* and *in May,* etc.

1. Грэг жил в Росси́и весно́й.

   Грэг жил в Росси́и _____.

2. Мэри рабо́тала в Москве́ зимо́й.

   Мэри рабо́тала в Москве́ _____

   _____.

3. Дженнифер жила́ в Петербу́рге о́сенью.

   Дженнифер жила́ в Петербу́рге _____

   _____.

4. Билл рабо́тал в Росто́ве ле́том.

   Билл рабо́тал в Росто́ве _____.

**ANSWER KEY**
A. 1. Мы покупа́ем проду́кты в э́том магази́не. (**present tense**) 2. За́втра он ку́пит проду́кты
в э́том магази́не. (**one-time action**) 3. Она́ иногда́ покупа́ла проду́кты в э́том магази́не.
(**repetition**) 4. Они́ бу́дут стира́ть завтра́ весь день. (**duration**) 5. Он постира́л все его́ ве́щи.
(**one-time action/result**) 6. Ты всегда́ стира́ешь до́ма. (**repetition**)
B. 1. в ма́рте, в апре́ле и в ма́е; 2. в декабре́, в январе́ и в феврале́; 3. в сентябре́, в октябре́ и
в ноябре́; 4. в ию́не, в ию́ле и в а́вгусте

## 🌐 Culture Note

It's customary in Russia to consider the first day of the appropriate month to be the beginning of a new season, not the equinox or solstice. So winter officially starts on the 1st of December, spring, on the 1st of March, summer, on the 1st of June, and fall, on the 1st of September. In addition, September 1st is traditionally the first day of the new academic year for all schools and universities (unless, of course, it falls on a weekend), and the official День зна́ний (*The Day of Knowledge*). Before 1918, Russia followed the Julian calendar (ста́рый стиль, "the old style"), which is approximately two weeks behind the Gregorian calendar (но́вый стиль, "the new style") now commonly accepted everywhere in the world, including Russia. However, the Russian Orthodox Church still keeps the Julian calendar. Consequently, Christmas (Рождество́) in Russia falls on January 7. Many government and private institutions are closed for the entire week between New Year's Day (Но́вый год) and Christmas. So, don't plan to do any serious business in Russia at this time!

## ✎ Drive It Home

Now, let's review the basic distinctions between imperfective and perfective verbs. Fill in the blanks with the correct form of the aspectual pair given in parentheses. The English translations of the Russian sentences will guide you through the process of choosing the right aspect.

1. *I stayed home for the entire day yesterday and did my laundry.*

   Я вчера́ сиде́л весь день до́ма и_____ оде́жду. (стира́ть—постира́ть)

2. *I did all of my laundry and then went to the movies.*

   Я _____ всю оде́жду и пото́м пошёл в кино́. (стира́ть—постира́ть)

The genitive plural case
and telling time          Expressing likes and dislikes

- - - - - - - - - - - - - | - - - - - | - - - - - - - - - - - - | - - - - - - - - - - | - - - - - - -

The accusative of duration, numbers          The verbs занима́ться (to
100—1,000, and ordinal numbers          study) and игра́ть (to play)

3. *Every day, I read this newspaper.*

   Ка́ждый день я _____ э́ту газе́ту. (чита́ть—прочита́ть)

4. *I read the entire newspaper and gave it to my friend.*

   Я _____ всю газе́ту и дал её моему́ дру́гу. (чита́ть—
   прочита́ть)

5. *This is a very good apartment! I will definitely rent it!*

   Это о́чень хоро́шая кварти́ра! Я её обяза́тельно _____! (снима́ть—
   снять)

6. *We always rent a dacha in the summer.*

   Мы всегда́ _____ да́чу ле́том. (снима́ть—снять)

7. *They bought vegetables at the market and made a salad for lunch.*

   Они́ _____ о́вощи на ры́нке и _____ сала́т на
   обе́д. (покупа́ть—купи́ть; гото́вить—пригото́вить)

8. *Where did you buy such good groceries?*

   Где ты _____ таки́е хоро́шие проду́кты? (покупа́ть—купи́ть)

9. *When we lived in Moscow, we often made omelet(s) for breakfast.*

   Когда́ мы жи́ли в Москве́, мы ча́сто _____ омле́т на за́втрак.
   (гото́вить—пригото́вить)

10. *Where did you vacation last (lit., this) summer?*

    Где вы _____ э́тим ле́том? (отдыха́ть—отдохну́ть)

**ANSWER KEY**
1. стира́л; 2. постира́л; 3. чита́ю; 4. прочита́л; 5. сниму́; 6. снима́ем; 7. купи́ли, пригото́вили; 8. купи́л; 9. гото́вили; 10. отдыха́ли

## How Did You Do?

Let's see how you did in this lesson. You should know how to:

☐ Use more words and phrases related to everyday activities. (Still unsure? Go back to page 128.)

☐ Differentiate and use perfective and imperfective verbs. (Still unsure? Go back to page 129.)

☐ Talk about renting a place. (Still unsure? Go back to page 131.)

☐ Talk about seasons and months. (Still unsure? Go back to page 135.)

## ✎ Word Recall

Now, it's time to review some words and expressions from the earlier lessons. Listen to the English sentence first, then fill in the blanks with the correct word or phrase, and then repeat the Russian sentence out loud.

1. *My wife had a lot of things (to do).*

   У мое́й жены́ бы́ло _____.

2. *She lives in America now, but she was born in Russia.*

   Она́ сейча́с живёт в Аме́рике, но она́ _____ в Росси́и.

3. *I worked with him in one financial company in New York.*

   Я рабо́тал _____ в одно́й фина́нсовой компа́нии в Нью-Йо́рке.

4. *They had lunch with a Russian friend.*

   Они́ обе́дали _____.

The genitive plural case
and telling time

Expressing likes and dislikes

The accusative of duration, numbers
100—1,000, and ordinal numbers

The verbs занима́ться (*to
study*) and игра́ть (*to play*)

5. *Bon appétit!*

   _____ аппети́та!

6. *My older daughter works as a lawyer.*

   Моя́ ста́ршая дочь рабо́тает _____.

7. *This restaurant is on Nevsky Prospect.*

   Э́тот рестора́н _____.

8. *I always drink coffee with milk.*

   Я всегда́ пью ко́фе _____.

9. *This hotel is in the center of the city.*

   Э́та гости́ница _____.

10. *Thank you very much!*

    _____ спаси́бо!

**ANSWER KEY**
1. мно́го дел; 2. родила́сь; 3. с ним; 4. с ру́сским дру́гом; 5. Прия́тного; 6. юри́стом; 7. на
Не́вском проспе́кте; 8. с молоко́м; 9. в це́нтре го́рода; 10. Большо́е

# Lesson 10: Phrases
Как всегда́, мы ра́ды вас ви́деть! *As always, we're glad to see you!*

In this lesson, you'll learn how to:

☐ Further use perfective and imperfective verbs.

☐ Say *to begin* and *to finish*.

The verbs покупа́ть – купи́ть (*to buy*)

☐ Use days of the week.

☐ Further use some motion verbs.

☐ Talk about going to work and on trips.

☐ Talk about playing sports.

Гото́вы? Тогда́ начнём! *Ready? Then, let's begin!*

Let's get started with some words and phrases.

## Phrase Builder 1

▶ 10A Phrase Builder 1 (CD: 5, Track: 10)

| Как жизнь? (*infml.*) | *How's life?* |
|---|---|
| Рад(а) тебя́/вас ви́деть! | *Glad to see you!* |
| начина́ть (*conj. I; –ай*)—нача́ть | *to begin, to start* |
| конча́ть (*conj. I; –ай*) (зака́нчивать)—ко́нчить | *to end, to finish* |
| гуля́ть по го́роду | *walk around town* |
| отдыха́ть | *to rest, to vacation* |
| чита́ть (*conj. type I; –ай*) кни́гу | *to read a book* |
| смотре́ть—посмотре́ть телеви́зор | *to watch TV* |
| де́лать—сде́лать | *to do* |
| по́сле рабо́ты | *after work* |
| выходны́е (дни) | *weekend (lit., days off)* |
| дни неде́ли | *days of the week* |
| по вечера́м | *in the evenings* |

The genitive plural case
and telling time

Expressing likes and dislikes

The accusative of duration, numbers
100—1,000, and ordinal numbers

The verbs занима́ться (*to study*) and игра́ть (*to play*)

# Take It Further 1

The verbs начина́ть—нача́ть (*to begin*) and конча́ть—ко́нчить (*to finish*) take either a noun in the accusative case (e.g., нача́ть рабо́ту, *to begin work*) or an imperfective infinitive (e.g., нача́ть рабо́тать, *to begin to work*). The infinitive must be imperfective because whatever action you begin or finish, presupposes a duration.

# Phrase Practice 1

Let's practice the new expressions. Match the English phrases on the left with their Russian equivalents on the right. Repeat the Russian phrases out loud.

1. *I'm glad (masc.) to see you (fml.)!*
2. *How's life?*
3. *after work*
4. *weekend*
5. *days of the week*
6. *to watch TV*
7. *in the evenings*
8. *to walk around town*
9. *to begin (perf.)*
10. *to finish (perf.)*

a. выходны́е
b. дни неде́ли
c. смотре́ть телеви́зор
d. Я рад вас ви́деть!
e. Как жизнь?
f. по́сле рабо́ты
g. нача́ть
h. ко́нчить
i. по вечера́м
j. гуля́ть по го́роду

**ANSWER KEY**
1. d; 2. e; 3. f; 4. a; 5. b; 6. c; 7. i; 8. j; 9. g; 10. h

## Grammar Builder 1

▶ 10B Grammar Builder 1 (CD: 5, Track: 11)

### MORE IMPERFECTIVE-PERFECTIVE VERB PAIRS AND THE DAYS OF THE WEEK

The imperfective-perfective verbs начина́ть —нача́ть (*to begin, to start*) and зака́нчивать —зако́нчить (*to end, to finish*) can take either a complement in the accusative case:

Он на́чал рабо́ту.
*He started work.*

or an imperfective infinitive:

Он на́чал рабо́тать.
*He started to work.*

Notice that the infinitive must be imperfective. This is so because it is presupposed that the action is ongoing when one speaks of a beginning of something. The conjugated verbs themselves, however, can be either perfective or imperfective depending on the context. Sometimes the synonymous imperfective verb конча́ть (*to end, to finish*) is used instead of зака́нчивать.

All three imperfective verbs начина́ть, зака́нчивать, конча́ть belong to Conjugation I.

The perfective verb нача́ть has the same endings as the present tense Conjugation I, but it is formed from the perfective infinitive with the stem начн–.

| НАЧА́ТЬ *TO BEGIN* | |
|---|---|
| я начну́ | мы начнём |

The genitive plural case
and telling time

Expressing likes and dislikes

The accusative of duration, numbers
100—1,000, and ordinal numbers

The verbs занима́ться (*to study*) and игра́ть (*to play*)

| НАЧА́ТЬ | |
|---|---|
| *TO BEGIN* | |
| ты начнёшь | вы начнёте |
| он/она́/оно́ начнёт | они́ начну́т |

The past tense на́чал, начала́, на́чало, на́чали has feminine stress shift: the stress shifts back to the –а in the feminine form but then stays put for the other forms.

The perfective verb зако́нчить (ко́нчить) belongs to Conjugation Type II.

| ЗАКО́НЧИТЬ | |
|---|---|
| *TO END* | |
| я зако́нчу | мы зако́нчим |
| ты зако́нчишь | вы зако́нчите |
| он/она́/оно́ зако́нчит | они́ зако́нчат |

The past tense зако́нчил, зако́нчила, зако́нчило, зако́нчили has a stable stem stress.

Now, let's learn дни неде́ли (*the days of the week*) in Russian:

| дни неде́ли | *days of the week* | Когда́? | *When?* |
|---|---|---|---|
| понеде́льник | *Monday* | в понеде́льник | *on Monday* |
| вто́рник | *Tuesday* | во вто́рник | *on Tuesday* |
| среда́ | *Wednesday* | в сре́ду | *on Wednesday* |
| четве́рг | *Thursday* | в четве́рг | *on Thursday* |
| пя́тница | *Friday* | в пя́тницу | *on Friday* |
| суббо́та | *Saturday* | в суббо́ту | *on Saturday* |
| воскресе́нье | *Sunday* | в воскресе́нье | *on Sunday* |

Notice that the days of the week are not capitalized in Russian, just like the names of the months. Also, in order to say on Monday, on Tuesday, etc., you need to use the preposition в /во with the accusative case (not prepositional).

Выходны́е (дни) is the traditional Russian word for weekend. The term уик-энд is stylistically marked as new, trendy, and potentially ironic.

Выходны́е—э́то суббо́та и воскресе́нье.
*(The) weekend is Saturday and Sunday.*

## ✎ Work Out 1

A. Translate the following sentences into Russian.

1. *I'm starting a new job.*

   _____

2. *They started watching TV.*

   _____

3. *He finished working and started reading.*

   _____

4. *She will finish this job.*

   _____

5. *We start every day after work.*

   _____

B. Что вы де́лали в выходны́е? (*What did you do on the weekend?*) Fill in the blanks using the phrases provided in the parentheses. Be sure to use the past tense of the verb.

1. В пя́тницу ве́чером мы _____. (смотре́ть телеви́зор)

The genitive plural case
and telling time

Expressing likes and dislikes

The accusative of duration, numbers
100—1,000, and ordinal numbers

The verbs занима́ться (*to study*) and игра́ть (*to play*)

2. В суббо́ту у́тром я (*fem.*)_____. (чита́ть кни́гу)

3. В суббо́ту ве́чером я (*masc.*) _____. (отдыха́ть)

4. В воскресе́нье днём мы _____. (гуля́ть по

го́роду)

### ANSWER KEY

**A.** 1. Я начина́ю но́вую рабо́ту. 2. Они́ на́чали смотре́ть телеви́зор. 3. Он зако́нчил рабо́тать и на́чал чита́ть. 4. Она́ зако́нчит э́ту рабо́ту. 5. Мы начина́ем ка́ждый день по́сле рабо́ты.
**B.** 1. смотре́ли телеви́зор; 2. чита́ла кни́гу; 3. отдыха́л; 4. гуля́ли по го́роду

# Phrase Builder 2

▶ 10C Phrase Builder 2 (CD: 5, Track: 12)

| ходи́ть в го́сти | to visit someone, to drop in on someone |
|---|---|
| ходи́ть в магази́н | to go to the store |
| е́здить на экску́рсии | to go on excursions/tours |
| встреча́ться с друзья́ми | to meet with friends |
| занима́ться (*conj. I;*–ай) спо́ртом | to do/play sports |
| ката́ться (*conj. I;*–ай) на лы́жах | to ski |
| ката́ться (*conj. type I;*–ай) на велосипе́де | to ride a bicycle |
| игра́ть (*conj. type I;*–ай) в те́ннис | to play tennis |
| сдава́ть—сдать ве́щи в химчи́стку | to take things to the dry cleaner |
| не́которые ве́щи | some things |
| поэ́тому | therefore, so, thus |

# ✎ Phrase Practice 2

Now, let's practice. Match the English phrases on the left with their Russian equivalents on the right. Repeat the Russian phrases out loud.

| | |
|---|---|
| 1. *to ride a bike* | a. поэ́тому |
| 2. *to ski* | b. ходи́ть в го́сти |
| 3. *to play sports* | c. не́которые ве́щи |
| 4. *to play tennis* | d. встреча́ться с друзья́ми |
| 5. *to go to the store* | e. игра́ть в те́ннис |
| 6. *to meet with friends* | f. ходи́ть в магази́н |
| 7. *therefore* | g. ката́ться на велосипе́де |
| 8. *to visit* | h. ката́ться на лы́жах |
| 9. *some things* | i. занима́ться спо́ртом |

**ANSWER KEY**
1. g; 2. h; 3. i; 4. e; 5. f; 6. d; 7. a; 8. b; 9. c

# Grammar Builder 2

▶ 10D Grammar Builder 2 (CD: 5, Track: 13)

## MORE ON VERBS OF MOTION

As you already know, the Russian verb of motion ходи́ть (e.g., ходи́ть в шко́лу) literally means *to walk*. All motion verbs in Russian are distinguished by two general criteria:

1. the method of motion—walking, riding a vehicle, sailing, flying, etc.;
2. direction—multidirectional (including round-trips) or unidirectional (one way).

The verb ходи́ть is a walking verb, whereas the verb е́здить is a vehicular one. Remember that you'll almost always use a vehicular motion verb when a

The genitive plural case
and telling time

Expressing likes and dislikes

The accusative of duration, numbers
100—1,000, and ordinal numbers

The verbs занима́ться (*to
study*) and игра́ть (*to play*)

geographical name is mentioned, because this always implies traveling by vehicle
rather than walking.

Both ходи́ть and е́здить are multidirectional verbs. This means that they denote
one of the following:

A. recurrent action

Ка́ждый день я хожу́ на рабо́ту.
*Every day I go to work.*

Ка́ждое ле́то я е́зжу в Росси́ю.
*I go to Russia every summer.*

B. round-trip action in the past

Вчера́ я ходи́л(а) в кино́.
*I went to the movies yesterday (and I'm back now).*

Ле́том я е́здил(а) в Росси́ю.
*I went to Russia in the summer (and I'm back now).*

C. general physical action

Я люблю́ ходи́ть пешко́м.
*I like to walk.*

Я люблю́ е́здить на маши́не.
*I like to drive.*

Unidirectional verbs, on the other hand, denote an action that is happening at a
given point in time, be it in the present, past, or future.

The two unidirectional verbs you need to learn for now are идти́ (*to go on foot, to walk*) and éхать (*to go by vehicle, to ride, to drive*).

Let's look at how the verb идти́ is conjugated in the present tense.

| ИДТИ́ TO GO ON FOOT, TO WALK | |
|---|---|
| я иду́ | мы идём |
| ты идёшь | вы идёте |
| он/онá/онó идёт | они́ иду́т |

As you can see, it is a Conjugation I verb. Its past tense, however, is irregular: он шёл, онá шлá, онó шло, они́ шли. Notice that the root vowel –ё "flees" in the past tense forms that have a vowel ending.

The verb éхать is also a Conjugation I verb.

| ÉХАТЬ TO GO BY VEHICLE, TO RIDE, TO DRIVE | |
|---|---|
| я éду | мы éдем |
| ты éдешь | вы éдете |
| он/онá/онó éдет | они́ éдут |

The past tense is он éхал, онá éхала, онó éхало, они́ éхали. No stress shifts either in the present or past.

Normally, the unidirectional motion verbs идти́ and éхать are used for background actions in the past or for current, ongoing actions in the present. (Background actions in the future are rare.) For instance,

Когдá я шёл/шла на рабóту, я купи́л(а) газéту.
*As I was walking to work, I bought a newspaper.*

The genitive plural case
and telling time

Expressing likes and dislikes

The accusative of duration, numbers
100—1,000, and ordinal numbers

The verbs занима́ться (to
study) and игра́ть (to play)

The first action in the above example когда́ я шла на рабо́ту (*when I was walking to work*) serves as a background for the main action я купи́л(а) газе́ту (*I bought a newspaper*). Also use unidirectional verbs in the present tense when you catch an action as it unfolds in front of you as you would in taking a snapshot. For example,

Смотри́, Ва́ня идёт!
*Look, Vanya is coming/going!*

Сейча́с я иду́ на рабо́ту.
*I am walking to work now.*

In addition, remember that the walking verbs ходи́ть—идти́ often refer to a local activity (within the city bounds), regardless of the exact mode of transportation. So it's normal to say я вчера́ ходи́л(а) в теа́тр (*I went to the theater yesterday*), even if you took the metro, because going to the theater is a local activity.

Both multidirectional and unidirectional motion verbs are imperfective. Naturally, all of them take a noun in the accusative case of direction: you go to a place in contrast to being at one.

Я был(а) в теа́тре.
*I was at the theater. (prepositional, location)*

Я ходи́л(а) в теа́тр.
*I went to the theater. (accusative, direction)*

# Grammar Practice 2

Restate the following sentences replacing the past forms of the verb быть with the appropriate motion verbs. Remember to change the case of the destination noun from the prepositional to the accusative!

1. Вчера́ мы бы́ли в теа́тре.

_____

2. Ле́том они́ бы́ли в Росси́и.

_____

3. Я сего́дня была́ на рабо́те.

_____

4. Вы бы́ли в гостя́х в суббо́ту?

_____

5. Ты был на экску́рсии в Но́вгороде?

_____

6. Я был в магази́не у́тром.

_____

**ANSWER KEY**
1. Вчера́ мы ходи́ли в теа́тр. 2. Ле́том они́ е́здили в Росси́ю. 3. Я сего́дня ходи́ла на рабо́ту. 4. Вы ходи́ли в го́сти в суббо́ту? 5. Ты е́здил на экску́рсию в Но́вгород? 6. Я ходи́л в магази́н у́тром.

# Drive It Home

Now, let's do more practice with motion verbs. Listen to the English sentence first, then fill in the blanks with the appropriate motion verb, and finally, repeat the entire Russian sentence out loud.

The genitive plural case
and telling time

Expressing likes and dislikes

The accusative of duration, numbers
100—1,000, and ordinal numbers

The verbs занима́ться (*to study*) and игра́ть (*to play*)

1. *Yesterday, we went on a tour of Novgorod.*

   Вчера́ мы _____ на экску́рсию в Но́вгород.

2. *She went to work on Saturday.*

   Она́ _____ на рабо́ту в суббо́ту.

3. *When I (masc.) was walking to work, I saw my sister.*

   Когда́ я _____ на рабо́ту, я ви́дел мою́ сестру́.

4. *I often go to the movies.*

   Я ча́сто _____ в кино́.

5. *I like to walk around the city.*

   Я люблю́ _____ по го́роду.

6. *We went to Russia in the summer.*

   Мы _____ в Росси́ю ле́том.

7. *We always go to the sea in the summer.*

   Мы всегда́_____ на мо́ре ле́том.

8. *We talked about our children when we were going/traveling in/by the car.*

   Мы говори́ли о на́ших де́тях, когда́ мы _____ на маши́не.

9. *He likes to go to work on foot.*

   Он лю́бит _____ на рабо́ту пешко́м.

10. *We went to the dacha by car.*

    Мы _____ на да́чу на маши́не.

    **ANSWER KEY**
    1. е́здили; 2. ходи́ла; 3. шёл; 4. хожу́; 5. ходи́ть; 6. е́здили; 7. е́здим; 8. е́хали; 9. ходи́ть; 10. е́здили

## How Did You Do?

Let's see how you did in this lesson. You should know how to:

☐ Further use perfective and imperfective verbs. (Still unsure? Go back to page 143.)

☐ Say *to begin* and *to finish*. (Still unsure? Go back to page 144.)

☐ Use days of the week. (Still unsure? Go back to page 145.)

☐ Talk about playing sports. (Still unsure? Go back to page 147.)

☐ Further use some motion verbs. (Still unsure? Go back to page 148.)

☐ Talk about going to work and on trips. (Still unsure? Go back to page 148.)

## ✎ Word Recall

Now it's time to review some words, phrases, and constructions from the earlier lessons. Read the English sentence first, then fill in the blanks, and finally, repeat the Russian sentence out loud.

1. *I'm renting a comfortable apartment in the center of the city.*

   Я _____ удо́бную кварти́ру в це́нтре го́рода.

2. *We don't have a gym.*

   У нас нет _____.

3. *They have a three-room apartment.*

   У них _____ кварти́ра.

4. *This is not a dacha, but a cottage.*

   Это не да́ча, _____.

5. *Come visit us in Vermont!*

   _____ к нам в го́сти в Вермо́нт!

The genitive plural case
and telling time

Expressing likes and dislikes

The accusative of duration, numbers
100—1,000, and ordinal numbers

The verbs занима́ться (to
study) and игра́ть (to play)

6. *My older daughter attends school (secondary education).*

   Моя́ ста́ршая дочь _____ в шко́ле.

7. *Say hello to your wife.*

   _____ ва́шей жене́!

8. *He lives in a student dorm.*

   Он живёт _____.

9. *Take care! (lit., All the best!)*

   Всего́ _____!

10. *If I'm not mistaken.*

    Если я _____.

    **ANSWER KEY**
    1. снима́ю; 2. спорти́вного зала; 3. трёхко́мнатная; 4. а котте́дж; 5. Приезжа́йте; 6. у́чится;
    7. Передава́йте приве́т; 8. в студе́нческом общежи́тии; 9. хоро́шего; 10. не ошиба́юсь

# Lesson 11: Sentences

Добро́ пожа́ловать, ещё раз! *Welcome once again!*

In this lesson, you'll review some old words and expressions and also learn how
to:

☐ Tell basic time.

☐ Use nouns and adjectives in the genitive plural case.

☐ Say a.m. and p.m.

☐ Say on what date, in what month or year something happened.

☐ Use numerals from 100 to 1000.

Гото́вы? Тогда́ начнём! *Ready? Then, let's begin!*
Let's get started with some words and phrases.

## Sentence Builder 1

▶ 11A Sentence Builder 1 (CD: 5, Track: 14)

| | |
|---|---|
| Я снима́ю кварти́ру в са́мом це́нтре, о́коло ста́нции метро́ «Пу́шкинская». | *I'm renting an apartment in the center, near Pushkinskaya metro station.* |
| Я живу́ недалеко́ от рабо́ты. | *I live not far from work.* |
| Это далеко́? | *Is it far?* |
| Нет, одна́ остано́вка на метро́. | *No, one stop on the metro.* |
| Ско́лько сейча́с вре́мени? | *What time is it now?* |
| Сейча́с де́вять часо́в утра́. | *Now it's nine o'clock in the morning.* |
| Во ско́лько ты начина́ешь рабо́тать? | *What time do you start work?* |
| Я начина́ю рабо́тать в де́вять часо́в утра́. | *I start work at nine a.m.* |
| Я зака́нчиваю в пять часо́в три́дцать мину́т. | *I finish at five-thirty.* |
| В це́нтре мно́го теа́тров, музе́ев, магази́нов, кафе́, краси́вых у́лиц и площаде́й. | *In downtown, there are a lot of theaters, museums, stores, cafés, beautiful streets and squares.* |
| Везде́ мо́жно ходи́ть пешко́м. | *You can go everywhere on foot.* |
| В э́ту суббо́ту я иду́ на бале́т в Большо́й теа́тр. | *This Saturday I'm going to a ballet at the Bolshoi Theater.* |

The genitive plural case
and telling time

Expressing likes and dislikes

The accusative of duration, numbers
100—1,000, and ordinal numbers

The verbs занима́ться (*to study*) and игра́ть (*to play*)

# ✎ Sentence Practice 1

Let's practice. Match the English sentences on the left to their Russian equivalents on the right. Repeat the Russian sentences out loud.

1. *In downtown, there are many stores, beautiful streets and squares.*

2. *You can go everywhere on foot.*

3. *Is it far?*

4. *No, one stop on the metro.*

5. *What time is it now?*

6. *It's nine a.m.*

7. *I'm renting an apartment near a metro station.*

8. *I start work at nine a.m.*

9. *I finish work at five-thirty p.m.*

10. *I live not far from work.*

a. Я снима́ю кварти́ру о́коло ста́нции ме́тро.

b. Это далеко́?

c. Нет, одна́ остано́вка на метро́.

d. Везде́ мо́жно ходи́ть пешко́м.

e. Я живу́ недалеко́ от рабо́ты.

f. Я начина́ю рабо́тать в де́вять часо́в утра́.

g. В це́нтре мно́го магази́нов, краси́вых у́лиц и площаде́й.

h. Сейча́с де́вять часо́в утра́.

i. Ско́лько сейча́с вре́мени?

j. Я зака́нчиваю рабо́тать в пять три́дцать ве́чера.

**ANSWER KEY**
1. g; 2. d; 3. b; 4. c; 5. i; 6. h; 7. a; 8. f; 9. j; 10. e

# Grammar Builder 1

▶ 11B Grammar Builder 1 (CD: 5, Track: 15)

## THE GENITIVE PLURAL CASE AND TELLING TIME

You've already learned the genitive singular for nouns: стола́ (*table*), словаря́ (*dictionary*), ма́мы (*mom*), кни́ги (*book*), окна́ (*window*), мо́ря (*sea*). Now let's learn the genitive plural. You've seen that the genitive plural is used after the quantitative word мно́го (*a lot of/many*). The genitive is also used to mark the possessor (e.g., ма́мы (*of mom or mom's*); or the origin (e.g., из Нью-Йо́рка [*from New York*] or из Москвы́ [*from Moscow*]), as well as after many specific prepositions. There are three basic endings in the genitive plural –ов, –ей, or a null or zero ending. The choice of the ending generally depends on the nature of the last letter of the noun.

| NOMINATIVE SINGULAR | GENITIVE PLURAL ENDING |
|---|---|
| *ending in a hard consonant: add* –ов | |
| магази́н | магази́нов |
| час | часо́в |
| *ending in* й *and* ц: *add* –ев | |
| трамва́й | трамва́ев |
| ме́сяц | ме́сяцев |
| *ending in* ь, ж, ш, щ, *and* ч,: *add* –ей (*notice that if there's is a soft sign it is replaced with a soft vowel*) | |
| пло́щадь | площаде́й |
| рубль | рубле́й |
| врач | враче́й |
| нож | ноже́й |
| *ending in a vowel: zero ending (sometimes you need to insert either an* о *or* е *between the two last consonants before the zero ending*) | |
| мину́та | мину́т |
| у́лица | у́лиц |
| я́блоко | я́блок |
| окно́ | о́ко |
| письмо́ | пи́см |

Adjectives in the genitive plural have the hard ending –ых or the soft ending –их (also following the spelling rule): мно́го краси́вых у́лиц (*many beautiful streets*), мно́го больши́х музе́ев (*many big museums*).

The non-count noun вре́мя (*time*) is irregular. Although it looks like a feminine noun, it's actually neuter, as all nouns ending in –мя. Consequently, many Russian

The genitive plural case
and telling time                    Expressing likes and dislikes

The accusative of duration, numbers          The verbs занима́ться (to
100—1,000, and ordinal numbers               study) and игра́ть (to play)

native speakers mispronounce it in the genitive plural as ско́лько "вре́мя" (*What time is it?*), instead of its proper form ско́лько вре́мени (мно́го вре́мени, etc.).

There are several ways to tell time in Russian. The easiest one is to say the number of hours first and then the number of minutes. Remember to apply the rule of numbers:

1 use the nominative/accusative singular after one;
2–4 use the genitive singular after two, three, and four;
5+ use the genitive plural after five and higher.

Ско́лько сейча́с вре́мени?
*What time is it now?*

Сейча́с (оди́н) час два́дцать одна́ мину́та.
*It's 1:21. (lit., Now (it is one) hour, twenty-one minutes.)*

Сейча́с два часа́ три мину́ты.
*It's 2:03. (lit., Now (it is) two hours, three minutes.)*

Сейча́с пять часо́в де́сять мину́т.
*It's 5:10. (lit., Now (it is) five hours, ten minutes.)*

Note that it is customary to leave out оди́н before час.

Сейча́с час.
*It's 1:00. (lit., Now (it is one) hour.).*

To indicate a.m. and p.m., use утра́, дня, ве́чера, or но́чи. For the hours between 4 and 11 a.m., you should say утра́ (*lit., of the morning*). For the hours between 12 and 4 p.m., you should say дня (*lit., of the afternoon*). For the hours between 5 and 11 p.m., you should say ве́чера (*lit., of the evening*). And for the hours between

12 and 3 a.m., you should say но́чи (*lit., of the night*). Pay special attention to the stress! Also, keep in mind that it's customary to use the Russian equivalents of the English a.m. and p.m. only on the hour (e.g. 5:00 p.m.).

Я начина́ю рабо́ту в де́вять часо́в утра́.
*I start work at nine a.m.*

# ✎ Work Out 1

A. Fill in the blanks by putting the nouns in parentheses into the genitive singular or plural. Note that the choice depends on whether the noun is count or non-count as the latter cannot be plural.

1. У Ива́на мно́го _____. (рабо́та)

2. В Москве́ мно́го _____. (хоро́шие магази́ны)

3. В це́нтре мно́го _____. (интере́сные музе́и)

4. В Петербу́рге мно́го _____. (краси́вые у́лицы)

5. У меня́ мно́го _____. (вре́мя)

6. На столе́ мно́го _____. (письмо́)

7. В одно́м ча́се шестьдеся́т_____. (мину́та)

B. Ско́ько сейча́с вре́мени? (*What time is it now?*) Write out full answers in the blanks and repeat the entire sentence out loud.

1. *2:30*

   Сейча́с _____.

The genitive plural case
and telling time

Expressing likes and dislikes

The accusative of duration, numbers
100—1,000, and ordinal numbers

The verbs занима́ться (*to
study*) and игра́ть (*to play*)

2. *6:15*

   Сейча́с _____ .

3. *3:25*

   Сейча́с _____ .

4. *1:42*

   Сейча́с _____ .

5. *10:00 a.m.*

   Сейча́с _____ .

6. *2:00 p.m.*

   Сейча́с _____ .

7. *8:00 p.m.*

   Сейча́с _____ .

8. *12:00 a.m.*

   Сейча́с _____ .

**ANSWER KEY**

A. 1. рабо́ты; 2. хоро́ших магази́нов; 3. интере́сных музе́ев; 4. краси́вых у́лиц; 5. вре́мени;
6. пи́сем; 7. мину́т

B. 1. два часа́ три́дцать мину́т; 2. шесть часо́в пятна́дцать мину́т; 3. три часа́ два́дцать пять
мину́т; 4. час со́рок две мину́ты; 5. де́сять часо́в утра́; 6. два часа́ дня; 7. во́семь часо́в ве́чера;
8. двена́дцать часо́в но́чи

# Sentence Builder 2

▶ 11C Sentence Builder 2 (CD: 5, Track: 16)

| Ско́лько вре́мени ты жила́ в Аме́рике? | *How long (lit., how much time) did you live in America?* |
|---|---|

| | |
|---|---|
| Я жил(а) в Аме́рике де́вять ме́сяцев. | *I lived in America for nine months.* |
| Я прие́хал(а) в Аме́рику пе́рвого сентября́. | *I arrived in America on the first of September.* |
| Я верну́лся/верну́лась в Росси́ю деся́того ма́я. | *I came back to Russia on the tenth of May.* |
| Она́ е́здила в Росси́ю в две ты́сячи деся́том году́. | *She went to Russia in 2010.* |
| Он роди́лся в ты́сяча девятьсо́т во́семьдесят седьмо́м году́. | *He was born in 1987.* |
| Она́ жила́ одна́. | *She lived alone.* |
| Она́ сама́ покупа́ла проду́кты, гото́вила и стира́ла. | *She bought groceries, cooked, and did the laundry herself.* |
| У неё в до́ме была́ стира́льная маши́на и суши́лка. | *She had a washer and dryer in her house.* |
| Иногда́ она́ ходи́ла в кафе́ и в рестора́н. | *Sometimes she went to a café and to a restaurant.* |

## ✎ Sentence Practice 2

Let's practice. Match the English sentences on the left with their Russian equivalents on the right. Repeat the Russian sentences out loud.

1. *She went to Russia in 2010.*

2. *He was born in 1987.*

a. Она́ жила́ одна́.

b. Я прие́хал(а) в Аме́рику пе́рвого сентября́.

The genitive plural case
and telling time

Expressing likes and dislikes

The accusative of duration, numbers
100—1,000, and ordinal numbers

The verbs занима́ться (to
study) and игра́ть (to play)

3. *I lived in America for nine months.*

c. Я верну́лась/верну́лся в Росси́ю деся́того ма́я.

4. *She lived alone.*

d. Он роди́лся в ты́сяча девятьсо́т во́семьдесят седьмо́м году́.

5. *I arrived in America on the first of September.*

e. У неё в до́ме была́ стира́льная маши́на и суши́лка.

6. *I came back to Russia on the tenth of May.*

f. Она́ сама́ стира́ла.

7. *She had a washer and dryer in the house.*

g. Я жил(а́) в Аме́рике де́вять ме́сяцев.

8. *She did laundry herself.*

h. Она́ е́здила в Росси́ю в две ты́сячи деся́том году́.

**ANSWER KEY**
1. h; 2. d; 3. g; 4. a; 5. b; 6. c; 7. e; 8. f

# Grammar Builder 2

⊙ 11D Grammar Builder 2 (CD: 5, Track: 17)

## THE ACCUSATIVE OF DURATION, NUMBERS 100–1,000 AND ORDINAL NUMBERS

When an action continues for a certain time, you should use the accusative case to indicate this time. This is called the accusative of duration.

Я жила́ в Аме́рике оди́н год/одну́ неде́лю/де́вять ме́сяцев.
*I lived in America for one year/one week/nine months.*

As you see, оди́н год and одну́ неде́лю are in the accusative case. The phrase де́вять ме́сяцев is also in the accusative case except that the "rule of numbers" took over and replaced the "original" accusative with the genitive plural (ме́сяцев) after the numeral nine (because it is more than five).

If you need to ask about duration, you can use the expression ско́лько вре́мени (*how much time*).

Ско́лько вре́мени ты жил в Москве́?
*How long did you live in Moscow?*

Remember to use the rule of numbers for time periods with the numerals other than 1: я жила́ в Аме́рике два го́да/пять лет.

Before we learn how to say dates and years in Russian, let's look at the numerals from 100 to 1,000.

| | |
|---|---|
| сто | *100* |
| две́сти | *200* |
| три́ста | *300* |
| четы́реста | *400* |
| пятьсо́т | *500* |
| шестьсо́т | *600* |
| семьсо́т | *700* |
| восемьсо́т | *800* |
| девятьсо́т | *900* |
| ты́сяа | *1,000* |

In order to say a year in Russian—for example, 1979—you need to say ты́сяча девятьсо́т се́мьдесят девя́тый год, literally, *(one) thousand nine hundred seventy-ninth year*. The numeral *one* in *one thousand* is usually left out in spoken Russian. The last digit of the year (if it's not a zero) becomes an ordinal numeral. If it's a zero, e.g., 1960, then the last digit before the zero forms one ordinal numeral: ты́сяча девятьсо́т шестидеся́тый год (*[one] thousand nine hundred sixtieth year*). Ordinal numerals have adjectival endings and function just like adjectives.

The genitive plural case
and telling time

Expressing likes and dislikes

The accusative of duration, numbers
100—1,000, and ordinal numbers

The verbs занима́ться (*to
study*) and игра́ть (*to play*)

Let's look at the ordinal numbers in Russian.

| пе́рвый | *first* |
|---|---|
| второ́й | *second* |
| тре́тий | *third* |
| четвёртый | *fourth* |
| пя́тый | *fifth* |
| шесто́й | *sixth* |
| седьмо́й | *seventh* |
| восьмо́й | *eighth* |
| девя́тый | *ninth* |
| деся́тый | *tenth* |
| двадца́тый | *twentieth* |
| тридца́тый | *thirtieth* |
| сороково́й | *fortieth* |
| пятидеся́тый | *fiftieth* |
| шестидеся́тый | *sixtieth* |
| семидеся́тый | *seventieth* |
| восьмидеся́тый | *eightieth* |
| девяно́стый | *ninetieth* |
| со́тый | *hundredth* |

In order to answer the question когда́? (*when?*), you might answer with any combination of the date + month + year. The cases that you will use depend on what information is expressed. These rules are shown in the table below.

| КОГДА́? | | |
|---|---|---|
| ЧИСЛО́ | Ме́яЦ | ГОД |
| | | в + prepositional<br>в ты́сяча девятьсо́т се́мьдесят девя́том году́ |
| | в + prepositional<br>в сентябре́ | genitive<br>ты́сяча девятьсо́т се́мьдесят девя́того го́да |
| genitive<br>семна́дцатого | genitive<br>сентября́ | genitive<br>ты́сяча девятьсо́т се́мьдесят девя́того го́да |

Here is an example with all three expressed.

Я роди́лся/Я родила́сь семна́дцатого сентября́ ты́сяча девятьсо́т се́мьдесят девя́того го́да.
*I was born on September 17, 1979.*

Notice that the date comes first: *on the 17th of September, 1979.* If there's a date, you should use no preposition and put the date in the genitive case of the ordinal numeral (since what happened is an event *of* the seventeenth). The month and the year follow in the genitive case (because it was the date *of* a given month, *of* a given year). If you don't have the date, but just the month and the year or just the year, follow the examples in the chart above.

And finally, the year 2000 is двухты́сячный год, в двухты́сячном году́ (*in 2000*); the year 2001 is две ты́сячи пе́рвый год, в две ты́сячи пе́рвом году́ (*in 2001*), etc.

# ✎ Work Out 2

A. Когда́ вы роди́лись? (*When were you born?*) Say when the following people were born using the information in parentheses. Fill out the blanks writing out the numerals in full words as well as choosing the correct gender of the verb роди́ться (*to be born*) in the past tense.

1. Ната́лья _____

   _____ . (1 сентября́ 1975)

2. Её дочь _____

   _____ . (май 2002)

3. Мой муж _____

   _____ . (8 декабря́ 1965)

4. Моя́ мать _____

   _____ . (1950)

5. Мой друг _____

   _____ . (октя́брь 1975)

6. Мой сын _____ . (апре́ль 20)

B. Answer the following questions by filling the blanks below. Use the information in parentheses for your answers. Write out the dates in full and repeat the entire answer out loud.

1. Когда́ Ле́на прие́хала в Аме́рику? (сентя́брь 2005 го́да)

   Ле́на прие́хала в Аме́рику _____

   _____.

2. Когда́ она́ верну́лась в Росси́ю? (10 ма́я)

   Она́ верну́лась в Росси́ю _____.

3. Когда́ вы е́здили в Петербу́рг? (1999)

   Мы е́здили в Петербу́рг _____

   _____.

4. Когда́ вы на́чали рабо́тать в э́той компа́нии? (21 ию́ня 2000)

   Я начала́ рабо́тать в э́той компа́нии _____

   _____.

5. Когда́ мы бу́дем ката́ться на лы́жах? (февра́ль)

   Мы бу́дем ката́ться на лы́жах _____.

**ANSWER KEY**

A. 1. родила́сь пе́рвого сентября́ ты́сяча девятьсо́т се́мьдесят пя́того го́да; 2. родила́сь в мае́ две ты́сячи второ́го го́да; 3. роди́лся восьмо́го декабря́ ты́сяча девятьсо́т шестьдеся́т пя́того го́да; 4. родила́сь в ты́сяча девятьсо́т пятидеся́том году́; 5. роди́лся в октябре́ ты́сяча девятьсо́т се́мьдесят пя́того го́да; 6. роди́лся двадца́того апре́ля

B. 1. в сентябре́ две ты́сячи пя́того го́да; 2. деся́того ма́я; 3. в ты́сяча девятьсо́т девяно́сто девя́том году́; 4. два́дцать пе́рвого ию́ня двухты́сячного го́да; 5. в феврале́

# ✎ Drive It Home

Let's do additional practice on the genitive case, both singular and plural. Fill in the blanks by choosing the correct form of the genitive case (singular or plural), then repeat the Russian sentence out loud.

The genitive plural case
and telling time

Expressing likes and dislikes

The accusative of duration, numbers
100—1,000, and ordinal numbers

The verbs занима́ться (*to study*) and игра́ть (*to play*)

1. У неё мно́го _____. (де́ло)

2. У нас ма́ло _____. (вре́мя)

3. В го́роде мно́го _____. (рестора́н)

4. В Петербу́рге мно́го _____.

   (больша́я и краси́вая пло́щадь)

5. Сейча́с де́сять _____. (час)

6. Ско́лько _____ в одно́м году́? (ме́сяц)

7. У меня́ есть сто _____. (рубль)

8. У меня́ есть три _____. (рубль)

**ANSWER KEY**

1. дел; 2. вре́мени; 3. рестора́нов; 4. бо́льших и краси́вых площаде́й; 5. часо́в; 6. ме́сяцев; 7. рубле́й; 8. рубля́

# How Did You Do?

Let's see how you did in this lesson. You should know how to:

☐ Tell basic time. (Still unsure? Go back to page 156.)

☐ Use nouns and adjectives in the genitive plural case. (Still unsure? Go back to page 157.)

☐ Say a.m. and p.m. (Still unsure? Go back to page 159.)

☐ Say on what date, in what month or year something happened. (Still unsure? Go back to page 163.)

☐ Use numerals from 100 to 1000. (Still unsure? Go back to page 163.)

# ✎ Word Recall

Now it's time to review some words, phrases, and constructions from the earlier lessons. Read the English sentence first, then fill in the blanks, and finally, repeat the Russian sentence out loud.

1. *On Wednesday(s), I always go to the gym.*

   _____ я всегда́ хожу́ в спорти́вный зал.

2. *We always go to the store in the morning.*

   Мы всегда́ хо́дим в магази́н _____.

3. *When will you finish working?*

   Когда́ ты _____ рабо́тать?

4. *We will be either at the hotel or in the restaurant.*

   Мы бу́дем _____ в гости́нице, _____ в рестора́не.

5. *His office is on the third floor.*

   Его́ о́фис _____.

6. *Our younger son lives with us.*

   Наш мла́дший сын живёт _____.

7. *She is not married.*

   Она́ не _____.

8. *How interesting!*

   _____ интере́сно!

9. *He is from Florida.*

   Он _____.

The genitive plural case
and telling time

Expressing likes and dislikes

The accusative of duration, numbers
100—1,000, and ordinal numbers

The verbs занима́ться (*to study*) and игра́ть (*to play*)

10. *We like to have dinner at home.*

Мы лю́бим _____ до́ма.

**ANSWER KEY**

1. В сре́ду; 2. у́тром; 3. зако́нчишь; 4. или или; 5. на третье́м этаже́; 6. с на́ми; 7. за́мужем; 8. Как; 9. из Флори́ды; 10. у́жинать

# Lesson 12: Conversations

Добро́ пожа́ловать, ещё раз! *Welcome once again!*

In this lesson, you'll review some words and expressions and also learn how to:

☐ Express likes and dislikes.

☐ Comment on one's impression of something.

☐ Ask a newcomer if he or she is settled.

☐ Use more "studying verbs".

☐ Differentiate playing sports from playing musical instruments.

Гото́вы? Тогда́ начнём! *Ready? Then, let's begin!*

Now, let's put it all together in a typical conversation!

## Conversation 1

▶ 12A Conversation 1 (CD: 5, Track: 18- Russian; Track 19- Russian and English)

Greg Campbell, an American who has recently relocated to Moscow for a year, is telling his Russian friend, Inna Gribova, about his new life and daily routine there.

Инна: Приве́т, Грэг! Как жизнь в Москве́? Как ты устро́ился?

| Грэг: | Приве́т, Инна! Рад тебя́ ви́деть! У меня́ всё отли́чно. Я прекра́сно устро́ился. Я снима́ю прекра́сную двухко́мнатную кварти́ру в це́нтре, о́коло ста́нции метро́ «Пу́шкинская». |
|---|---|
| Инна: | Здо́рово! Это недале́ко от твое́й рабо́ты? |
| Грэг: | Всего́ одна́ остано́вка на метро́. Иногда́ я да́же хожу́ пешко́м. |
| Инна: | Ты рабо́таешь ка́ждый день? |
| Грэг: | Да, коне́чно, ка́ждый день кро́ме суббо́ты и воскресе́нья. Начина́ю в де́вять часо́в утра́ и зака́нчиваю в пять часо́в три́дцать мину́т, а иногда́ в шесть ве́чера. |
| Инна: | Тебе́ нра́вится жить в це́нтре? |
| Грэг: | О́чень! Здесь мно́го интере́сных теа́тров и музе́ев, хоро́ших магази́нов, рестора́нов, кафе́, краси́вых у́лиц и площаде́й, и везде́ мо́жно ходи́ть пешко́м. Это о́чень удо́бно. Я люблю́ ходи́ть пешко́м. |
| Инна: | А что ты де́лаешь по́сле рабо́ты по вечера́м и в выходны́е? |
| Грэг: | В понеде́льник, сре́ду и пя́тницу я хожу́ в спорти́вный зал, а пото́м или в магази́н за поку́пками, или с друзья́ми в кино́. А иногда́ я про́сто гуля́ю по го́роду или отдыха́ю до́ма—чита́ю и смотрю́ телеви́зор. А в э́ту суббо́ту я иду́ на бале́т в Большо́й теа́тр. |
| Инна: | Я уве́рена, что тебе́ о́чень понра́вится. |

| Inna: | *Hi, Greg! How's life in Moscow? Are you settled?* |
|---|---|
| Greg: | *Hi, Inna! (I'm) glad to see you! Everything's great. I'm well settled. I'm renting a wonderful two-room apartment in the city center, near the metro station Pushkinskaya.* |
| Inna: | *Great! Is it close to (lit., not far from) your job?* |
| Greg: | *Just one stop on the metro. Sometimes I even walk (lit., go on foot).* |
| Inna: | *Do you work every day?* |

The genitive plural case
and telling time

Expressing likes and dislikes

The accusative of duration, numbers
100—1,000, and ordinal numbers

The verbs занима́ться (to
study) and игра́ть (to play)

| Greg: | Yes, of course, every day except Saturday(s) and Sunday(s). (I) start at nine in the morning and finish at five-thirty, sometimes at six in the evening. |
| Inna: | Do you like living in the (city) center? |
| Greg: | Very much! There are many interesting theaters and museums, good stores, restaurants, cafés, beautiful streets and squares here, and you can walk everywhere. It's very convenient. I like walking. |
| Inna: | And what do you do after work in the evenings and on weekends? |
| Greg: | On Monday, Wednesday, and Friday, I go to the gym, and then either shopping (lit., to the store for goods) or to the movies with friends. Sometimes I just walk around the city or rest at home—read and watch TV. And this Saturday, I'm going to a ballet at the Bolshoi Theater. |
| Inna: | I'm sure (fem.) you'll like it very much. |

# ✎ Conversation Practice 1

Now let's practice some of the phrases and sentences from the conversation above. Read the English sentence first, then fill in the blanks, and finally repeat the Russian sentence out loud.

1. *I'm well settled.*

   Я _____.

2. *Everything's great!*

   Всё _____.

3. *I work every day except Saturday(s) and Sunday(s).*

   Я рабо́таю _____ суббо́ты и воскресе́нья.

4. *Sometimes, I finish (working) at six p.m.*

   Иногда́ я зака́нчиваю _____.

5. *Do you like living in the (city) center?*

   _____ жить в це́нтре?

6. *It's very convenient.*

   Это о́чень _____.

7. *I like walking.*

   Я люблю́ _____.

8. *What do you do after work in the evenings?*

   Что ты де́лаешь _____?

9. *I often go shopping (lit., to the store for goods).*

   Я ча́сто _____.

10. *I'm sure (fem.) you'll like the ballet very much.*

    Я уве́рена, что бале́т _____.

**ANSWER KEY**

1. прекра́сно устро́ился; 2. отли́чно; 3. ка́ждый день, кро́ме; 4. в шесть ве́чера; 5. Тебе́ нра́вится; 6. удо́бно; 7. ходи́ть пешко́м; 8. по́сле рабо́ты по вечера́м; 9. хожу́ в магази́н за поку́пками; 10. тебе́ о́чень понра́вится

## Grammar Builder 1

▶ 12B Grammar Builder 1 (CD: 5, Track: 20)

### EXPRESSING LIKES AND DISLIKES

You already know the verb люби́ть (*to like*). It is most commonly used with infinitives when you like doing something: я люблю́ гуля́ть; я люблю́ ходи́ть пешко́м (*I like to go for a walk; I like to go on foot*). It is also used with food and drinks, as in я люблю́ ко́фе (*I like coffee*) and with aesthetic preferences, as in я люблю́ бале́т (*I like ballet*). However, when used to refer to people, this verb actually means *to love*: он лю́бит её (*he loves her*).

The genitive plural case
and telling time

Expressing likes and dislikes

The accusative of duration, numbers
100—1,000, and ordinal numbers

The verbs занима́ться (*to
study*) and игра́ть (*to play*)

There's another way of expressing likes and dislikes in Russian. For this, you can
use the Conjugation II reflexive verb нра́виться (*to like*). Because this verb is
reflexive, what is liked is either a noun in the nominative case or verb infinitive
while the "liker", or literally the person who is being pleased with something, is a
pronoun or noun in the dative case.

Мне нра́вится жить в це́нтре.
*I like living in the city center. (lit., Living in the center pleases me.)*

Мне нра́вится моя́ но́вая жизнь в Москве́.
*I like my new life in Moscow. (lit., My new life in Moscow pleases me.)*

The verb нра́виться is less common than the verb люби́ть. You should primarily
use it in the present tense when you are in the middle of a new experience and
you like it. For example, if you recently moved to Moscow and you're enjoying
it, then you should say: Мне нра́вится жить в Москве́. Conversely, if you've
always liked walking (it's not a new experience for you), then you should say: Я
люблю́ ходи́ть пешко́м.

When you put the verb нра́виться in the perfective form понра́виться, then it
refers to your impression of any recent experience—tasting some food, seeing a
show, meeting a friend. For example:

Мне понра́вился бале́т.
*I liked the ballet (the one I just saw).*

Мне понра́вилась твоя́ сестра́.
*I liked your sister (after I met her).*

Мне понра́вилось вино́.
*I liked the wine (the one I just tried).*

Мне понра́вились музе́и в Москве́.
*I liked the museums in Moscow (the ones I visited).*

Notice how the gender of the thing you liked affects the gender of the past
perfective verb понра́виться. If the thing you liked is expressed by an infinitive,
the verb понра́виться should be in neuter form. For example:

Мне понра́вилось гуля́ть по го́роду.
*I liked walking/strolling around the city (after I tried it).*

This verb is used mostly in the past tense. However, if you conjugate the
perfective verb понра́виться, it denotes the future tense and means *will like
something.* For instance:

Тебе́ понра́вится бале́т.
*You will like the ballet.*

## Take It Further

▶ 12C Take It Further (CD: 5, Track: 21)

Устро́иться is a reflexive perfective verb that doesn't have a direct equivalent
in English. It can be translated as to *get settled, to set up one's accommodations.*
When a person moves, it takes time before he or she is comfortable and
settled. When this happens, you'd say that он устро́ился or она́ устро́илась,
они́ устро́ились. Как вы устро́ились? is a common courtesy question to a
newcomer. This is why Inna asked her friend Greg, who recently arrived in
Moscow, Как ты устро́ился? And Greg responded, Я прекра́сно устро́ился (*I
got settled nicely*).

Notice the difference between the adverb прекра́сно (я прекра́сно устро́ился)
and the adjective прекра́сный (я снима́ю прекра́сную кварти́ру). Adjectives

The genitive plural case
and telling time

Expressing likes and dislikes

The accusative of duration, numbers
100—1,000, and ordinal numbers

The verbs заниматься (*to
study*) and играть (*to play*)

and adverbs are strictly differentiated in Russian. Russian adverbs usually end in −o /e; they only change in the comparative degree. Adverbs modify actions, they tell you how you do something: хорошо (*well*), плохо (*bad/badly*), быстро (*quickly, fast*), отлично (*great*), прекрасно (*nicely/wonderfully*), etc. Russian adjectives, on the other hand, modify nouns and change in accordance with the gender, number, and case of the nouns they modify: прекрасная квартира, я снял прекрасную квартиру, я живу в прекрасной квартире, etc.

The Russian adverb удобно means both *convenient* and *comfortable*. It's often used with the logical subject in the dative case мне удобно (*lit., [it is] convenient/ comfortable for me,* where мне is the logical subject). In the past tense, you simply insert the past tense of the verb *to be* in the neuter form (because the subject *it* is implied): мне /ей /ему было удобно; or in the future, third person singular: мне / ей /ему будет удобно. Notice that in the dialogue above, удобно is used as an adjective: Это очень удобно. (*It is very convenient.*)

---

# ✎ Work Out 1

A. Say what the following people like doing. Use the conjugated verb любить with the prompts below.

1. Мы _____ смотреть телевизор вечером.

2. Я _____ гулять по городу.

3. Володя _____ театр.

4. Моя дочь _____ читать книги.

5. Вы _____ ходить пешком.

B. Traslate the following sentences into Russian using the word in parentheses.

1. *I like ballet.* (люби́ть)

2. *I liked the ballet.* (понра́виться)

3. *My wife likes Russian cuisine.* (люби́ть)

4. *I love my wife.* (люби́ть)

5. *I like (I'm enjoying) my new job.* (нра́виться)

6. *Do you like walking? (infml.* люби́ть)

7. *Yesterday I went to the museum and I liked it.* (понра́виться)

8. *I like Russians.* (люби́ть)

9. *You'll be comfortable in this apartment. (infml.)* (удобно)

**ANSWER KEY**
A. 1. лю́бим; 2. люблю́; 3. лю́бит; 4. лю́бит; 5. лю́бите
B. 1. Я люблю́ бале́т. 2. Мне понра́вился бале́т. 3. Моя́ жена́ лю́бит ру́сскую ку́хню. 4. Я люблю́

The genitive plural case
and telling time

Expressing likes and dislikes

The accusative of duration, numbers
100—1,000, and ordinal numbers

The verbs занима́ться (to
study) and игра́ть (to play)

мою́ жену́. **5.** Мне нра́вится моя́ но́вая рабо́та. **6.** Ты лю́бишь ходи́ть пешко́м? **7.** Вчера́ я ходи́л(а) в музе́й, и он мне понра́вился. **8.** Я люблю́ ру́сских. **9.** Тебе́ бу́дет удо́бно в э́той кварти́ре.

# Conversation 2

12D Conversation 2 (CD: 5, Track: 22- Russian; Track 23- Russian and English)

**A Russian graduate student, Igor Zubov, spent a year in the U.S. as an exchange student. He's talking to his friend Tanya Petrova about his daily life in America.**

| | |
|---|---|
| Та́ня: | Ско́лько вре́мени ты жил в Аме́рике в про́шлом году́? |
| Игорь: | Я прие́хал в Аме́рику пе́рвого сентября́ и верну́лся в Росси́ю в ма́е – всего́ де́вять ме́сяцев. |
| Та́ня: | Ты жил оди́н или в общежи́тии? |
| Игорь: | Я снима́л ко́мнату в отде́льном до́ме. |
| Та́ня: | Зна́чит, ты сам ходи́л в магази́н, покупа́л проду́кты и гото́вил? |
| Игорь: | Да, но иногда́ я ходи́л в столо́вую, кафе́ или рестора́н. |
| Та́ня: | А у тебя́ в до́ме была́ стира́льная маши́на? |
| Игорь: | Да, коне́чно! И стира́льная маши́на, и да́же суши́лка. Поэ́тому я обы́чно стира́л до́ма, а не́которые ве́щи сдава́л в химчи́стку. |
| Та́ня: | А что ты де́лал ве́чером, и в суббо́ту и в воскресе́нье? |
| Игорь: | Я мно́го занима́лся, но ещё я ходи́л в го́сти, встреча́лся с друзья́ми и е́здил на экску́рсии в други́е города́. |
| Та́ня: | А ты занима́лся спо́ртом в Аме́рике? |
| Игорь: | Да, все америка́нцы мно́го занима́ются спо́ртом. И я то́же зимо́й ката́лся на лы́жах, а весно́й и о́сенью игра́л в те́ннис и ката́лся на велосипе́де. |
| Та́ня: | Я ра́да, что тебе́ понра́вилось в Аме́рике! |

*Tanya:*      *How long did you live in America last year?*

| | |
|---|---|
| Igor: | *I went to America on the first of September and came back to Russia in May—nine months total.* |
| Tanya: | *Did you live alone or in a dorm?* |
| Igor: | *I rented a room in a separate house.* |
| Tanya: | *This means you went to the store by yourself, bought groceries, and cooked?* |
| Igor: | *Yes, but sometimes, I went to the dining hall, a café, or a restaurant.* |
| Tanya: | *Did you have a washer in your house?* |
| Igor: | *Yes, of course! Both a washer and (even) a dryer. This is why I usually did laundry (lit., washed) at home, but I took some things to the dry cleaner.* |
| Tanya: | *What did you do in the evenings and on Saturday(s) and Sunday(s)?* |
| Igor: | *I studied a lot, but I also went to parties, met with friends, and went on tours to other cities.* |
| Tanya: | *Did you do sports (exercise) in America?* |
| Igor: | *Yes, all Americans exercise a lot. I also skied in the winter, and played tennis and rode a bicycle in the spring and fall.* |
| Tanya: | *I'm glad (fem.) you liked (it) in America!* |

## ✎ Conversation Practice 2

Now let's practice some of the phrases and sentences from the conversation above. Read the English sentence first, then fill in the blanks, and finally repeat the Russian sentence out loud.

1. *How long did you live in America last year?*

   Ско́лько вре́мени ты жил в Аме́рике _____.

2. *I arrived in America on the first of September.*

   Я прие́хал в Аме́рику _____.

The genitive plural case
and telling time

Expressing likes and dislikes

The accusative of duration, numbers
100—1,000, and ordinal numbers

The verbs занима́ться (*to study*) and игра́ть (*to play*)

3.  *I came back to Russia in May.*

    Я _____ в Росси́ю _____.

4.  *This means you went to the store by yourself, bought groceries, and cooked?*

    _____, ты _____, _____

    _____ и гото́вил?

5.  *I studied a lot.*

    Я мно́го _____.

6.  *I also went to parties.*

    Я ещё _____.

7.  *I went on tours to other cities.*

    Я е́здил на экску́рсии _____.

8.  *Did you do sports (exercise)?*

    Ты _____?

9.  *I skied in the winter, played tennis and rode a bike in the spring and fall.*

    Я _____ зимо́й, _____ и

    _____ весно́й и о́сенью.

10. *I'm glad (fem.) you liked (it) in America.*

    Я _____, что _____ в Аме́рике!

**ANSWER KEY**

1. в про́шлом году́; 2. пе́рвого сентября́; 3. верну́лся, в мае́; 4. Зна́чит, сам ходи́л в магази́н, покупа́л проду́кты; 5. занима́лась; 6. ходи́л в го́сти; 7. в други́е города́; 8. занима́лся спо́ртом; 9. ката́лся на лы́жах, игра́л в те́ннис, ката́лся на велосипе́де; 10. ра́да, тебе́ понра́вилось

# Grammar Builder 2

▶ 12E Grammar Builder 2 (CD: 5, Track: 24)

### THE VERBS ЗАНИМА́ТЬСЯ (*TO STUDY*) AND ИГРА́ТЬ (*TO PLAY*)

The verb занима́ться refers to the actual process of studying (different from other "study verbs" which you will study in Unit 4 of *Advanced Russian*.) It's a Conjugation I verb. Being a reflexive verb, it doesn't take a direct object. It literally means "occupy oneself." Занима́ться is usually modified by a location (где?, *where?*) or by an adverb (как?, *how?*): занима́ться в кафе́, до́ма, etc., or мно́го, ма́ло, хорошо́ занима́ться. You can also use it by itself.

You should avoid specifying what exactly you studied. So for example, if you want to state what you studied, you'll have to start a new sentence stating specifically what you did: Я учил но́вые слова́. *I studied/memorized the new words.*

Что ты де́лал вчера́ ве́чером?
*What did you do last night?*

Я занима́лся.
*I studied.*

It's important to differentiate the above verb from another "studying verb," учи́ться (*to be formally a student in a school, to go to school*). You will learn more about this verb later.

The genitive plural case
and telling time                          Expressing likes and dislikes

The accusative of duration, numbers
100—1,000, and ordinal numbers

The verbs занима́ться (*to
study*) and игра́ть (*to play*)

The verb занима́ться is also used in another expression, занима́ться спо́ртом, which refers to any kind of sport and means *to do sports* or *to play sports*. Notice that the noun спорт is in the instrumental case. The verb игра́ть (*to play*) is used strictly with games and is followed by the preposition в and the name of the sport in the accusative: игра́ть в те́ннис (*to play tennis*), игра́ть в футбо́л (*to play soccer*), игра́ть в баскетбо́л (*to play basketball*), etc.

You can also use the verb игра́ть with musical instruments. In this case, игра́ть will be followed by the preposition на and the musical instrument in the prepositional case: игра́ть на пиани́но (*to play the piano*).

## Take It Further 2

▶ 12F Take It Further 2 (CD: 5, Track: 25)

The pronoun сам means *by oneself, by myself, by yourself,* etc. It agrees with the gender of the person it refers to. In the question Ты сам ходи́л в магази́н? (*Did you go to the store yourself?*), сам is masculine, because the question is addressed to Igor. Had it been addressed to a woman, it would've been, Ты (*sg. infml.*) сама́ ходи́ла в магази́н? or Вы (*pl. or sg. fml.*) са́ми ходи́ли в магази́н?

Similarly, оди́н, одна́, and одни́, when used to mean *alone,* reflect the gender and number of the person(s) they refer to. You should say он жил оди́н (*he lived alone*) about a male person, она́ жила́ одна́ (*she lived alone*) about a female person, and они́ жи́ли одни́ (*they lived alone*) about two or more people.

When the conjunction и is repeated twice и . . . и, it usually means *both.*

Там была́ и стира́льная маши́на, и да́же суши́лка.
*There were both a washer and even a dryer.*

Igor is making a point that there was a dryer, because dryers are relatively uncommon in Russia: people usually wash clothes in a washer and then hang them out to dry.

The verb ката́ться denotes the general *riding for fun*. Consequently, it's used to describe such activities as ката́ться на велосипе́де (*riding a bicycle*), ката́ться на лы́жах (*skiing, lit., riding on skis*), and ката́ться на конька́х (*skating, lit., riding on skates*).

## ✎Work Out 2

A. Fill in the blanks using the correct studying verb: занима́ться or учи́ться.

1. Вчера́ ве́чером мы _____ в кафе́.

2. Она́ студе́нтка, она́ _____ в университе́те.

3. Вы отли́чные (*excellent*) студе́нты, вы мно́го _____.

4. Обы́чно я _____ оди́н до́ма.

5. Сего́дня у меня́ мно́го дел, я бу́ду _____ весь ве́чер.

B. Чемони́ занима́ются? (*What do they busy themselves with?*) Say what the following people do as their hobby. Use the prompts below, and conjugate the appropriate verbs in the present tense.

1. моя́ сестра́, велосипе́д

   _____

2. мои́ роди́тели, лы́жи

   _____

3. мы, те́ннис

   _____

The genitive plural case
and telling time

Expressing likes and dislikes

The accusative of duration, numbers
100—1,000, and ordinal numbers

The verbs занима́ться (*to study*) and игра́ть (*to play*)

4. америка́нцы, спорт

_____

5. мой брат, гита́ра

_____

6. мои́ де́ти, пиани́но

_____

**ANSWER KEY**

A. 1. занима́лись; 2. у́чится; 3. занима́етесь; 4. занима́юсь; 5. занима́ться

B. 1. Моя́ сестра́ ката́ется на велосипе́де. 2. Мои́ роди́тели ката́ются на лы́жах. 3. Мы игра́ем в те́ннис. 4. Америка́нцы занима́ются спо́ртом. 5. Мой брат игра́ет на гита́ре. 6. Мои́ де́ти игра́ют на пиани́но.

# ✎ Drive It Home

Now, let's practice how to say that one liked a person, a thing, or an activity. Fill in the blanks using the perfective verb понра́виться in the past tense. Repeat the entire sentence out loud.

1. Мне _____ жить в Москве́.

2. Твои друзья́ нам о́чень _____.

3. Мне _____ э́тот фильм.

4. Мне _____ ката́ться на лы́жах.

5. Она́ мне о́чень _____.

6. Он мне о́чень _____.

7. Вы мне о́чень _____.

8. Ей _____ ката́ться на велосипе́де.

9. Ему́ _____ учи́ться в Аме́рике.

10. Нам _____ занима́ться в э́том кафе́.

**ANSWER KEY**

1. понра́вилось; 2. понра́вились; 3. понра́вился; 4. понра́вилось; 5. понра́вилась; 6.
понра́вился; 7. понра́вились; 8. понра́вилось; 9. понра́вилось; 10. понра́вилось

# How Did You Do?

Let's see how you did in this lesson. You should know how to:

☐ Express likes and dislikes. (Still unsure? Go back to page 174.)

☐ Comment on one's impression of something. (Still unsure? Go back to page 175.)

☐ Ask a newcomer if he or she is settled. (Still unsure? Go back to page 176.)

☐ Use more "studying verbs". (Still unsure? Go back to page 182.)

☐ Differentiate playing sports from playing musical instruments. (Still unsure? Go
back to page 182.)

# ✎ Word Recall

Now it's time to review some words, phrases, and constructions from the earlier
lessons. Read the English sentence first, then fill in the blanks, and finally, repeat
the Russian sentence out loud.

1. *He lived in America for one year.*

   Он жил в Аме́рике _____.

2. *I have four hundred rubles.*

   У меня́ есть _____.

3. *When I was walking to work, I bought a newspaper.*

   Когда́ я _____ на рабо́ту, я _____ газе́ту.

The genitive plural case
and telling time

Expressing likes and dislikes

The accusative of duration, numbers
100—1,000, and ordinal numbers

The verbs занима́ться (*to study*) and игра́ть (*to play*)

4. *Every day, as I walk to work, I buy a newspaper.*

   Ка́ждый день, когда́ я _____ на рабо́ту, я _____ газе́ту.

5. *What time do you finish working?*

   _____ ты _____ рабо́тать?

6. *He is glad to see us.*

   Он _____ нас ви́деть.

7. *On weekend(s), we buy groceries at this supermarket.*

   _____ мы покупа́ем _____ в э́том

   суперма́ркете.

8. *I'll rent this apartment in September.*

   Я _____ э́ту кварти́ру _____.

9. *She studied at this university.*

   Она́ _____ в э́том университе́те.

10. *The children were at home alone.*

    Де́ти бы́ли до́ма _____.

**ANSWER KEY**

1. оди́н год; 2. четы́реста рубле́й; 3. шёл, купи́л; 4. иду́, покупа́ю; 5. Во ско́лько, зака́нчиваешь; 6. рад; 7. В выходны́е, проду́кты; 8. сниму́, в сентябре́; 9. учи́лась; 10. одни́

Don't forget to practice and reinforce what you've learned by visiting **www.livinglanguage.com/languagelab** for flashcards, games, and quizzes!

# Unit 3 Quiz

Контро́льная рабо́та №3

Now let's review. In this quiz you'll be tested on what you've learned in Unit 3. Once you've completed it, score yourself to see how well you've done. If you find that you need to go back and review, please do so before continuing on to Unit 4.

Let's get started!

A. Fill in the blanks using the correct aspect of the verb in parentheses. Remember also to make the verb agree with its subject in person, number, tense, and gender.

1. Я всегда́ _____ проду́кты в э́том суперма́ркете. (покупа́ть—купи́ть)

2. Мы вчера́ весь ве́чер_____ телеви́зор. (смотре́ть—посмотре́ть)

3. Он _____ ку́рицу, помидо́ры, сала́т и хлеб на у́жин. (покупа́ть—купи́ть)

4. Она́ обы́чно _____ рабо́тать в де́вять часо́в, но сего́дня она́ _____ в семь. (начина́ть—нача́ть)

5. Ка́ждое ле́то мы _____ да́чу. (снима́ть—снять)

B. Когда́ вы роди́лись? Say when these people were born. Use the information in parentheses.

1. Мой оте́ц роди́лся _____. (September 1)

2. Моя́ жена́ родила́сь _____. (October)

3. Моя́ сестра́ родила́сь _____

   _____. (1978)

4. Мой сын роди́лся _____

   _____. (April 20, 2007)

5. Моя́ дочь родила́сь _____. (in the fall)

C. Fill in the blanks using the correct motion verb—ходи́ть, идти́, е́здить, or е́хать.

1. Я обы́чно _____ на рабо́ту пешко́м.

2. Вчера́ мы _____ в кино́.

3. Вчера́, когда́ мы _____ домо́й, мы ви́дели мою́ сестру́.

4. Она́ _____ в Росси́ю в про́шлом году́.

5. Мы всегда́ _____ отдыха́ть на мо́ре ле́том.

D. Ско́лько сейча́с вре́мени? Say what time it is now using the prompts in parentheses.

1. Сейча́с _____. (4 p.m.)

2. Сейча́с _____. (8:15)

3. Сейча́с _____. (7 a.m.)

4. Сейча́с _____. (1 a.m.)

5. Сейча́с _____. (3:22)

E. Fill in the blanks using the correct "liking" verb—люби́ть, нра́виться, or понра́виться.

1. Я _____ ру́сскую ку́хню.

2. Мы бы́ли вчера́ в одно́м рестора́не, он нам о́чень _____. Я сейча́с живу́ в Москве́.

3. Мне о́чень _____ Москва́.

4. Толсто́й _____ ката́ться на велосипе́де.

5. Когда́ она́ прочита́ла кни́гу, она́ ей о́чень _____.

F. Fill in the blanks using the correct "studying verb"—учи́ться or занима́ться.

1. Моя́ мла́дшая дочь _____ в шко́ле.

2. Когда́ я был студе́нтом, я _____ в Моско́вском университе́те.

3. Я люблю́ _____ в э́той библиоте́ке.

4. Ве́чером она́ обы́чно _____ у себя́ в ко́мнате.

5. Все америка́нцы лю́бят _____ спо́ртом.

**ANSWER KEY**

A. 1. покупа́ю; 2. смотре́ли; 3. купи́л; 4. начина́ет, начала́; 5. снима́ем

B. 1. пе́рвого сентября́; 2. в октябре́; 3. в ты́сяча девятьсо́т се́мьдесят восьмо́м году́; 4. двадца́того апре́ля две ты́сячи седьмо́го го́да; 5. о́сенью

C. 1. хожу́; 2. ходи́ли; 3. шли; 4. е́здила; 5. е́здим

D. 1. четы́ре часа́ дня; 2. во́семь часо́в пятна́дцать мину́т; 3. семь часо́в утра́; 4. час но́чи; 5. три часа́ два́дцать две мину́ты

E. 1. люблю́; 2. понра́вился; 3. нра́вится; 4. люби́л; 5. понра́вилась

F. 1. у́чится; 2. учи́лся; 3. занима́ться; 4. занима́ется; 5. занима́ться

# How Did You Do?

Give yourself a point for every correct answer, then use the following key to tell whether you need to review Unit 3:

**0–7 points:** It's probably a good idea to go back through the lesson again. You may be moving too quickly, or there may be too much "down time" between your contact with Russian. Remember that it's better to spend 30 minutes with Russian three or four times a week than it is to spend two or three hours just once a week. Find a pace that's comfortable for you, and spread your contact hours out as much as you can.

**8–12 points:** You would benefit from a review before moving on. Go back and spend a little more time on the specific points that gave you trouble. Re-read the Grammar Builder sections that were difficult, and do the Work Outs one more time. Don't forget about the online supplemental practice material, either. Go to **www.livinglanguage.com/languagelab** for games and quizzes that will reinforce the material from this unit.

**13–17 points:** Good job! There are just a few points that could consider reviewing. If you haven't worked with the games and quizzes on **www.livinglanguage.com/languagelab**, please give them a try.

**18–20 points:** Great! Congratulations! You're ready for Unit 4!

points

# Unit 4:
# Health and the Human Body

Поздравля́ем с оконча́нием тре́тьей главы́ и нача́лом четвёртой!
*Congratulations on the completion of Unit 3 and the beginning of Unit 4!*

In this unit, you'll learn important vocabulary for discussing ailments and health issues. You'll also continue to learn about important points of Russian grammar such as the genitive case and aspect and learn more important grammar such as indefinite and definite prounouns and imperatives in Russian. Finally, you'll put it all together in a couple of typical conversations about health.

# Lesson 13: Words

In this lesson, you'll learn how to:

☐ Refer to different parts of the human body.

☐ Talk about sickness and health.

☐ Use more adverbs, adjectives, and comparatives.

☐ Further use perfective and imperfective verbs.

☐ Further use plurals.

Гото́вы? Тогда́ начнём! *Ready? Then, let's begin!*
Let's get started with some words and phrases.

# Word Builder 1

▶ 13A Word Builder 1 (CD: 5, Track: 26)

| всё норма́льно | *everything is okay (lit., normal)* |
|---|---|
| температу́ра | *temperature* |
| боле́ть (*imperf.*) | *to be sick* |
| заболе́ть (*perf.*) | *to fall ill* |
| голова́ | *head* |
| го́рло | *throat* |
| нос | *nose* |
| рот | *mouth* |
| живо́т | *abdomen, stomach, belly* |
| зуб | *tooth* |
| рука́ | *hand, arm* |
| нога́ | *foot, leg* |
| спина́ | *back* |
| лицо́ | *face* |
| у́хо | *ear* |
| гла́з | *eye* |
| тепле́е | *warmer* |
| лу́чше | *better* |
| бо́льше | *more* |
| побо́льше | *a little more (colloquial)* |
| ме́ньше | *less* |
| поме́ньше | *a little less (colloquial)* |
| апте́ка | *drug store, pharmacy* |
| е́сли | *if* |
| Молоде́ц! | *Good job!* |

Body parts and the plural of neuter
nouns and the verb боле́ть (*to be sick*)

The imperfective verbs каза́ться and
чу́вствовать and the modal verb мочь

The verb боле́ть (*to hurt*)
and expressing ailments

Irregular genitive plurals

# ✎ Word Practice 1

Let's practice these words. Match the English words on the left with their Russian equivalents on the right. Repeat the Russian words out loud.

| | |
|---|---|
| 1. *nose* | a. рука́ |
| 2. *throat* | b. голова́ |
| 3. *ear* | c. рот |
| 4. *foot, leg* | d. го́рло |
| 5. *hand, arm* | e. лицо́ |
| 6 *abdomen* | f. глаз |
| 7. *head* | g. апте́ка |
| 8. *face* | h. нос |
| 9. *mouth* | i. заболе́ть |
| 10. *eye* | j. у́хо |
| 11. *pharmacy* | k. живо́т |
| 12. *to fall ill* | l. нога́ |

**ANSWER KEY**
1. h; 2. d; 3. j; 4. l; 5. a; 6. k; 7. b; 8. e; 9. c; 10. f; 11. g; 12. i

# Grammar Builder 1

▶ 13B Grammar Builder 1 (CD: 5, Track: 26)

## BODY PARTS AND THE PLURAL OF NEUTER NOUNS AND THE VERB БОЛЕ́ТЬ (*TO BE SICK*)

First, let's learn the following basic body parts in the nominative plural.

| SINGULAR | PLURAL | TRANSLATION |
|---|---|---|
| нос | носы́ | *nose, noses* |
| рот | рты | *mouth, mouths* |
| живо́т | животы́ | *stomach, stomachs* |

*nething* and *anything* and negative
pronouns and adverbs

Perfective aspect in
negative sentences

The accusative of personal
pronouns

Imperatives and aspect

| SINGULAR | PLURAL | TRANSLATION |
|----------|--------|-------------|
| зуб | зу́бы | *tooth, teeth* |
| рука́ | ру́ки | *hand/arm, hands/arms* |
| нога́ | но́ги | *foot/leg, feet/legs* |
| спина́ | спи́ны | *back, backs* |
| лицо́ | ли́ца | *face, faces* |
| у́хо | у́ши | *ear, ears* |
| глаз | глаза́ | *eye, eyes* |

Notice the irregular plurals for у́хо—у́ши (х/ш mutation) and глаз—глаза́
(–а plural); some other –а/я plurals are дом—дома́, учи́тель—учителя́. Most
neuter nouns end in –а in the plural form (often with a stress shift): лицо́—ли́ца,
письмо́—пи́сьма, окно́—о́кна. The noun рот—рты has a fleeting о in the root.
All other plurals in the above chart are regular: they end in –ы (for hard endings)
or –и (for soft endings and the spelling rule).

The imperfective verb боле́ть means to be sick. It belongs to Conjugation I.

| БОЛЕ́ТЬ *TO BE SICK* | |
|----------------------|--|
| я боле́ю | мы боле́ем |
| ты боле́ешь | вы боле́ете |
| он/она́/оно́ боле́ет | они́ боле́ют |

The past tense is боле́л, боле́ла, боле́ло, боле́ли. The verb has no mutations or
stress shifts.

Its perfective counterpart заболе́ть means *to fall ill* and denotes the beginning of
the action rather than its duration. Он заболе́л means that he fell ill in the past
and he's still sick (он ещё боле́ет).

The verb боле́ть (*to be sick*) can be followed by the name of the illness in the
instrumental case: я боле́ю гри́ппом (*I'm sick/came down with the flu*), он боле́л

Body parts and the plural of neuter
nouns and the verb болеть (*to be sick*)

The imperfective verbs каза́ться and
чу́вствовать and the modal verb мочь

The verb боле́ть (*to hurt*)
and expressing ailments

Irregular genitive plurals

воспале́нием лёгких (*he was sick with/he had pneumonia*), etc. When you ask
what a person is sick with, you need to put the interrogative что (*what*) into the
instrumental case as well: Чем вы боле́ете/заболе́ли/боле́ли? (*lit., What are you
sick/have you been sick/were you sick with?*)

## Take It Further 1

▶ 13C Take It Further 1 (CD: 5, Track: 28)

The adverb норма́льно often refers to the *normal* state of affairs. Всё
норма́льно means *everything is okay* in the most general sense. The adjective
норма́льный is a modifier in such set phrases as норма́льная температу́ра
(*normal temperature*), норма́льное давле́ние (*normal [blood] pressure*),
норма́льный пульс (*normal pulse*), норма́льные результа́ты ана́лиза
(*normal test results*), etc. Notice the change in the ending of the adjective, as it
agrees in number and gender with the noun it modifies. All of the examples above
are in the nominative case. If the noun appears in any other case, the modifying
adjective will change accordingly.

Лу́чше and тепле́е are comparatives. Most Russian comparatives end in –ее.
However, some have just one –е following one of these "hushers": ж, ш, щ, or ч,
as in the comparative лу́чше.

Молоде́ц is a term of approval of a person. It can roughly be translated as *you
do/did a great/good job*. Although it's a masculine noun, it equally refers to males
and females. The plural form is молодцы́ (notice the "fleeting" –е, which will be
discussed in Take It Further 2).

# ✎Work Out 1

A. What are the nominative plural forms of the nouns below? Fill in the blanks with the correct form. Remember to follow the spelling rule.

1. у́хо— _____

2. дом— _____

3. голова́— _____

4. лицо́— _____

5. нога́— _____

6. молоде́ц— _____

7. рука́— _____

8. зуб— _____

B. Translate the following sentences into Russian.

1. *I'm often sick in the winter.*

_____

2. *She has normal temperature.*

_____

3. *He fell sick yesterday.*

_____

4. *It's warmer today.*

_____

5. *We were sick for the whole winter.*

_____

**ANSWER KEY**

A. 1. у́ши; 2. дома́; 3. го́ловы; 4. ли́ца; 5. но́ги; 6. молодцы́; 7. ру́ки; 8. зу́бы

B. 1. Я ча́сто боле́ю зимо́й. 2. У неё норма́льная температу́ра. 3. Он заболе́л вчера́. 4. Сего́дня тепле́е. 5. Мы боле́ли всю зи́му.

# Word Builder 2

▶ 13D Word Builder 2 (CD: 5, Track: 29)

| Что у вас боли́т? | *What's hurting you?* |
|---|---|
| бо́льно | *painful(ly)* |
| больни́ца | *hospital* |
| на́сморк | *cold, runny nose* |
| ка́шель (*m.*) | *cough* |
| ка́шлять (*imperf., conj. I, –ай*) | *to cough* |
| воспале́ние лёгких | *pneumonia* |
| грипп | *the flu* |
| просту́да | *common cold* |
| простуди́ться (*perf., conj. II, –и*) | *to catch a cold* |
| вы́здороветь (*perf., conj. I, –ей*) | *to get well, to get healthy* |
| лека́рство от | *medication for (lit., from)* |
| мно́гие | *many (people)* |

# Word Practice 2

Let's practice these words. Match the English words and expressions on the left with their Russian equivalents on the right. Repeat the Russian words out loud.

1. *the flu*

2. *common cold*

3. *runny nose*

4. *cough*

a. воспале́ние лёгких

b. лека́рство от

c. больни́ца

d. Что у вас боли́т?

*mething* and *anything* and negative
pronouns and adverbs

The accusative of personal
pronouns

Perfective aspect in
negative sentences

Imperatives and aspect

5. *pneumonia*      e. вы́здороветь

6. *painful(ly)*      f. просту́да

7. *medication for*      g. ка́шель

8. *to get well*      h. бо́льно

9. *What's hurting you?*      i. грипп

10. *hospital*      j. на́сморк

**ANSWER KEY**
1. i; 2. f; 3. j; 4. g; 5. a; 6. h; 7. b; 8. e; 9. d; 10. c

# Take It Further 2
⊙ 13E Take It Further 2 (CD: 5, Track: 30)

The genitive form of ка́шель (*cough*) is ка́шля. This noun has a so-called
fleeting vowel: the vowel e vanishes when another vowel is added to the stem.
This phenomenon has historical reasons and is common in many words such as
америка́нец—америка́нцы (*American—Americans*), он шёл—она́ шла (*he
walked—she walked*), etc.

The noun лека́рство (*medication*) takes the preposition от + *genitive,* when it
denotes *medication for something.* So you would say лека́рство от гри́ппа (*flu
medication*), which literally means *medication from the flu.* You might remember
that medication helps one "get away from" an illness.

# Grammar Builder 2
⊙ 13F Grammar Builder 2 (CD: 5, Track: 31)

### THE VERB БОЛЕ́ТЬ (*TO HURT*) AND EXPRESSING AILMENTS

Что у вас боли́т? (*lit., What do you have hurting?*) is the question you hear most
often in a doctor's office. Notice that боли́т (*hurts*) is different from боле́ет (*is*

Body parts and the plural of neuter
nouns and the verb боле́ть (*to be sick*)

The imperfective verbs каза́ться and
чу́вствовать and the modal verb мочь

The verb боле́ть (*to hurt*)
and expressing ailments

Irregular genitive plurals

*sick*), which is the 3rd person singular of боле́ть you learned before. Even though both infinitives look the same—боле́ть (*to be sick*) and боле́ть (*to hurt*)—the first боле́ть (*to be sick*) is a Conjugation I verb with the stem ending in –ей, while the second боле́ть (*to hurt*) belongs to Conjugation II with the stem ending in –е. This –е disappears before vowel endings (in the present tense) but stays before consonant endings (in the past and in the infinitive). The verb боле́ть (*to hurt*) has only two forms in the present tense—the third person singular and plural (боли́т, боля́т).

Голова́ боли́т.
*I have a headache. (lit., [My] head hurts.)*

Зу́бы боля́т.
*I have a toothache. (lit., [My] teeth hurt.)*

The past tense forms are just like those for *to be sick:* боле́л, боле́ла, боле́ло, боле́ли.

Russian has one uniform expression for all aches and pains. You say: У + the suffering person in genitive case + a form of боле́ть + the ailing body part. For example,

У меня́ боли́т голова́.
*My head hurts.*

У неё боля́т зу́бы.
*Her teeth hurt.*

У него́ боле́ла спина́.
*His back hurt.*

У вас боле́ли но́ги.
*Your legs hurt.*

Бо́льно is an adverb meaning *painful*, as in the impersonal expression мне
бо́льно (*it hurts; lit., it's painful to me*). Compare this expression with the one you
learned earlier: мне удо́бно (*it's convenient to me*).

The nouns на́сморк, ка́шель, воспале́ние лёгких, грипп, and просту́да are
the names of common ailments. In order to say that you have any of them, you
need to use the expression у меня́ (*I have*). For example,

У меня́ ка́шель.
*I have a cough.*

У меня́ грипп.
*I have the flu.*

У меня́ просту́да.
*I have a cold.*

The adjectives си́льный (*strong, severe*) and небольшо́й (*light, minor*) can
be used to modify the nouns: си́льный на́сморк, небольшо́й ка́шель.
There are also verbs corresponding to the nouns ка́шель and просту́да:
ка́шлять (ка́шляю, ка́шляешь, ка́шляют, *to cough*) and простуди́ться (он
простуди́лся, она́ простуди́лась, *to catch a cold*). Си́льно and немно́го are the
commonly used adverbs in these situations.

Я си́льно ка́шляю.
*I'm coughing heavily.*

У меня́ немно́го боли́т голова́.
*I have a minor headache.*

The verb болéть (*to hurt*)
and expressing ailments

# ✎ Work Out 2

A. Что у вас болúт? (*What hurts?/Where does it hurt?*) Answer this question in the present tense using the prompts below. Remember to put personal pronouns into the genitive case after the preposition у.

1. я, головá

_____

2. он, зýбы

_____

3. вы, спинá

_____

4. онá, ногá

_____

5. ты, живóт

_____

B. Translate the following sentences into Russian.

1. *I've gotten sick. I have the flu.*

_____

2. *He's caught a cold. He has a runny nose and he has a cough.*

_____

3. *I was sick, but I've recovered.*

_____

4. *They bought the flu medication in the pharmacy.*

_____

…mething and *anything* and negative
pronouns and adverbs

Perfective aspect in
negative sentences

The accusative of personal
pronouns

Imperatives and aspect

5. *What do you have for (lit., from) a cough?*

_____

6. *This is a cold medication.*

_____

**ANSWER KEY**
A. 1. У меня́ боли́т голова́. 2. У него́ боля́т зу́бы. 3. У вас боли́т спина́. 4. У неё боли́т нога́. 5. У тебя́ боли́т живо́т.
B. 1. Я заболе́л. У меня́ грипп. 2. Он простуди́лся. У него́ на́сморк и ка́шель. 3. Я боле́л(а), но я вы́здоровел(а). 4. Они́ купи́ли лека́рство от гри́ппа в апте́ке. 5. Что у вас есть от ка́шля? 6. Это лека́рство от просту́ды.

## Culture Note

In the nineteenth century, pharmacies in Russia also offered first aid. In a way, this tradition has been carried over into the modern day pharmacy, where, in addition to medication, customers often receive medical advice. It's common to approach the pharmacist with a detailed description of symptoms and expect that he or she will suggest the suitable remedy. So customers often say: что у вас есть от гри́ппа, у меня́ боли́т живо́т, etc. In more serious cases, the pharmacist will recommend that the customer see a doctor. As a mnemonic device, compare the English word apothecary to the Russian апте́ка.

## Drive It Home

Now let's drive home the different expressions of sickness. Fill out the blanks using one of the following verbs in the correct form—боле́ть (–ей), боле́ть (–е), заболе́ть. Repeat the Russian sentence out loud.

1. Я ча́сто _____ гри́ппом.

2. Он вдруг (*suddenly*) простуди́лся и _____.

3. У него́ си́льно _____ голова́.

The verb боле́ть (*to hurt*)
and expressing ailments

4. У моего́ сы́на _____ зу́бы.

5. Вчера́ моя́ дочь _____: у неё температу́ра и ка́шель.

6. У меня́ _____ нога́: мне бо́льно ходи́ть.

7. Что у вас _____?

8. У меня́ _____ у́ши.

9. Де́ти ча́сто _____ зимо́й.

10. В про́шлом году́ она́ _____ всю зи́му.

**ANSWER KEY**
1. боле́ю; 2. заболе́л; 3. боли́т; 4. боля́т; 5. заболе́ла; 6. боли́т; 7. боли́т; 8. боля́т; 9. боле́ют; 10. боле́ла

## How Did You Do?

Let's see how you did in this lesson. You should know how to:

☐ Refer to different parts of the human body. (Still unsure? Go back to page 193.)

☐ Talk about sickness and health. (Still unsure? Go back to page 194.)

☐ Further use perfective and imperfective verbs. (Still unsure? Go back to page 194.)

☐ Further use plurals. (Still unsure? Go back to page 194.)

☐ Use more adverbs, adjectives, and comparatives. (Still unsure? Go back to page 196.)

## ✎ Word Recall

Now it's time to review some words, phrases, and constructions from the earlier lessons. Fill in the blanks with the word(s) based on the translation, and finally, repeat the Russian sentence out loud.

1. *She was born in nineteen eighty-five.*

Она́ родила́сь _____

_____.

*mething* and *anything* and negative
pronouns and adverbs

Perfective aspect in
negative sentences

The accusative of personal
pronouns

Imperatives and aspect

2. *In the winter, we ski.*

Зимóй мы _____.

3. *Every week, I ride my bicycle.*

Кáждую недéлю я _____.

4. *He cooked and did laundry by himself in America.*

Он готóвил и _____ в Амéрике.

5. *I usually take my things to the dry cleaner.*

Я обы́чно _____.

6. *I don't work on Saturday(s).*

Я не рабóтаю _____.

7. *I like to watch TV in the evenings.*

Я люблю́ смотрéть телеви́зор _____.

8. *I'll be in Moscow in September.*

Я бýду в Москвé _____.

9. *I rent an apartment by the metro station.*

Я снимáю кварти́ру_____ _____.

10. *Every day, I go to work by the metro.*

Кáждый день я éзжу на рабóту _____.

**ANSWER KEY**

1. в ты́сяча девятьсот вóсемьдесят пя́том годý; 2. катáемся на лы́жах; 3. катáюсь на велосипéде; 4. стирáл сам; 5. сдаю́ мои́ вéщи в химчи́стку; 6. в суббóту; 7. по вечерáм; 8. в сентябрé; 9. óколо стáнции метрó; 10. на метрó

# Lsson 14: Phrases

Добро́ пожа́ловать ещё раз! *Welcome once again!*

In this lesson, you'll review some of the old words and expressions and also learn how to:

☐ Express uncertainty and ability.

☐ Say that one is right or wrong.

☐ Talk more about sickness and health.

☐ Use more reflexive verbs.

☐ Use some irregular genitive plurals.

Гото́вы? Тогда́ начнём! *Ready? Then, let's begin!*

Let's get started with some words and phrases.

## Phrase Builder 1

▶ 14A Phrase Builder 1 (CD: 5, Track: 32)

| мне ка́жется | *it seems to me* |
| я себя́ пло́хо чу́вствую | *I feel bad (sick)* |
| (из)ме́рить температу́ру | *take (lit., measure) (one's) temperature* |
| на вся́кий слу́чай | *just in case* |
| мочь | *be able to, can or may* |
| пить чай с мёдом | *to drink tea with honey (as a traditional remedy)* |
| он прав | *he's right* |

| онá правá | she's right |
|---|---|
| онú прáвы | they're right |
| Мне лýчше пойтú домóй. | I'd better go home. |
| одевáться (*imperf., conj. I, –ай*) | to get dressed |
| (с)дéлать зарáдку | to exercise in the mornings |
| брать примéр с дрýга | to follow (your) friend's example |

## Take It Further

The Russian expression дéлать зарáдку doesn't have a good English equivalent. Nevertheless, it's quite common in Russian. It means to exercise for 5–20 minutes in the morning in order to get "charged" for the day. Зарáдка literally means *charge* (as in *phone battery charge*—зарáдка для телефóна). This is a Russian cultural phenomenon that should be taken for what it is: it's generally believed in Russia that, in order to have good physical and mental health, one needs to start the day with a set of morning exercises. The Soviet government even used to broadcast a short exercise program on the national radio every day, early in the morning, in order to keep the entire country motivated and fit.

## Phrase Practice 1

Let's practice the new expressions. Match the English phrases on the left with their Russian equivalents on the right. Repeat the Russian phrases out loud.

1. *She is right.*
2. *I'd better go home.*
3. *to exercise in the morning*
4. *just in case*
5. *it seems to me*
6. *to take (one's) temperature*

a. на вся́кий слу́чай
b. изме́рить температу́ру
c. Онá правá.
d. Я плóхо себя́ чу́вствую.
e. пить чай с мёдом
f. Мне лу́чше пойти́ домóй.

Body parts and the plural of neuter
nouns and the verb боле́ть (*to be sick*)

The imperfective verbs каза́ться and
чу́вствовать and the modal verb мочь

The verb боле́ть (*to hurt*)
and expressing ailments

Irregular genitive plurals

7. *I feel sick.*

g. мне ка́жется

8. *to drink tea with honey*

h. одева́ться

9. *to get dressed*

i. брать приме́р

10. *to follow (one's) example*

j. де́лать заря́дку

**ANSWER KEY**
1. c; 2. f; 3. j; 4. a; 5. g; 6. b; 7. d; 8. e; 9. h; 10. i

# Grammar Builder 1

▶ 14C Grammar Builder 1 (CD: 5, Track: 33)

## THE IMPERFECTIVE VERBS КАЗА́ТЬСЯ AND ЧУ́ВСТВОВАТЬ AND THE MODAL VERB МОЧЬ

The imperfective verb каза́ться means *to seem*. The phrase мне ка́жется means *it seems to me*. Notice that it's subjectless: the English subject *it* is left out in Russian, and the logical subject, the person who experiences this action, is in the dative case. Literally, the phrase reads *to me (it) seems* (мне ка́жется).

The sentence мне бо́льно (used in Lesson 13) was also subjectless: бо́льно is an adverb that denotes the state of being in pain, so literally this means something like *it's painful to me*—мне бо́льно (dative + adverb).

Мне лу́чше пойти́ домо́й.
*I'd better go home.*

This sentence is also subjectless and works exactly the same way, but with a comparative лу́чше.

The imperfective verb чу́вствовать means *to feel* or, more precisely, *to have a sensation*. However, if you want to express a general state of being (хорошо́,

*mething* and *anything* and negative
pronouns and adverbs

Perfective aspect in
negative sentences

The accusative of personal
pronouns

Imperatives and aspect

плóхо, etc.), rather than a specific sensation, you should add the reflexive particle
себя́ (*self*).

Я хорошó себя́ чу́вствую.
*I feel good.*

Я плóхо себя́ чу́вствую.
*I feel bad.*

Remember that the first в in the verb чу́вствовать is silent. Чу́вствовать is a
Conjugation I verb with the stem ending in –ова. The verbs of this kind are called
ова verbs. All of them have one peculiarity: the suffix –ова– becomes –у(й)– in
the present tense (the й will be absorbed by the following soft vowel: чу́вству(й)
у > чу́вствую). Let's look at its present tense conjugation.

| ЧУ́ВСТВОВАТЬ | |
|---|---|
| *TO FEEL* | |
| я чу́вствую | мы чу́вствуем |
| ты чу́вствуешь | вы чу́вствуете |
| он/она́/онó чу́вствует | они́ чу́вствуют |

The stem reverts to its original form in the past tense: он чу́вствовал, она́
чу́вствовала, онó чу́вствовало, они́ чу́вствовали. Once again, remember to
add себя́ when you're speaking about the way you or other people are feeling.

Как вы себя́ чу́вствуете?
*How are you feeling?*

Я хорошó себя́ чу́вствую.
*I feel good.*

Я плохó себя́ чу́вствую.
*I feel bad.*

Body parts and the plural of neuter
nouns and the verb болéть (*to be sick*)

The imperfective verbs казáться and
чýвствовать and the modal verb мочь

The verb болéть (*to hurt*)
and expressing ailments

Irregular genitive plurals

Я лýчше себя́ чýвствую.

*I feel better.*

Я хýже себя́ чýвствую.

*I feel worse.*

Modal verbs in Russian act in a similar way to those in English and almost always
are followed by an infinitive. Now let's learn the conjugation of the modal verb
мочь (*be able to/can/may*).

| мочь BE ABLE TO/CAN/MAY | |
|---|---|
| я могý | мы мóжем |
| ты мóжешь | вы мóжете |
| он/онá/онó мóжет | они́ мóгут |

Past: мог, моглá, моглó, могли́

Notice the г/ж mutation before the –е endings (the middle forms), but not before
the –у endings (the first and last forms). Also remember the present tense stress
shift here. The modal verb мочь can be used by itself, as in éсли мóжешь (*if you
can*), or with infinitives, as in я могý заболéть (*I may get sick*).

# ✎ Work Out 1

A. Match the phrases below so that they form meaningful and grammatically correct
sentences.

1. Когдá я болéл,

2. Кáждое ýтро

3. Я плóхо себя́ чýвствую,

4. Мне кáжется,

a. поэ́тому мне лýчше пойти́ домóй.

b. и я бýду брать с тебя́ примéр!

c. я пил чай с мёдом.

d. он дéлает заря́дку.

5. Ты молодéц,   e. что я заболéл.

**B. Translate the following sentences into Russian.**

1. *She's right; I'd better go home.*

_____

2. *Just in case, I took her temperature. It was normal.*

_____

3. *I like drinking tea with honey.*

_____

4. *It seems to me that he's gotten sick.*

_____

5. *She's getting dressed.*

_____

**ANSWER KEY**
A. 1. c; 2. d; 3. a; 4. e; 5. b
B. 1. Онá права; мне лýчше пойти домóй. 2. На всякий случай, я измéрил её температýру. Онá былá нормáльная. 3. Я люблю пить чай с мёдом. 4. Мне кáжется, что он заболéл. 5. Онá одевáется.

# Phrase Builder 2
▶ 14C Phrase Builder 2 (CD: 5, Track: 34)

| | |
|---|---|
| у меня сильный нáсморк и кáшель | *I have a very (lit., strong) runny nose and a cough* |
| у меня немнóго болит живóт | *my stomach hurts a little* |
| у меня высóкая температýра | *I have a fever (lit., high temperature)* |
| болéть гриппом | *to be sick with the flu* |

Body parts and the plural of neuter
nouns and the verb боле́ть (*to be sick*)

The imperfective verbs каза́ться and
чу́вствовать and the modal verb мочь

The verb боле́ть (*to hurt*)
and expressing ailments

Irregular genitive plurals

| выпи́сывать—вы́писать реце́пт | *to write a prescription* |
| принима́ть—приня́ть лека́рство | *to take medication* |
| два ра́за в день | *twice a day* |
| по́сле еды́ | *afer meals* |
| до еды́ | *beore meals* |
| во вре́мя еды́ | *wih (during) meals* |
| ка́шель пройдёт | *(the) cough will go away* |
| Поправля́йтесь! | *Get well!* |
| быть у врача́ | *to be at the doctor's (locational)* |
| ходи́ть к врачу́ | *t go to the doctor's (directional)* |

## ✎ Phrase Practice 2

Let's practice the new expressions. Match the English phrases on the left to their
Russian equivalents on the right. Repeat the Russian phrases out loud.

1. *Get well!*      a. два ра́за в день

2. *to take medication*      b. по́сле еды́

3. *twice a day*      c. Поправля́йтесь!

4. *before meals*      d. быть у врача́

5. *after meals*      e. вы́писать реце́пт

6. *with (during) meals*      f. принима́ть лека́рство

7. *to be at the doctor's*      g. во вре́мя еды́

8. *to go to the doctor's*      h. ходи́ть к врачу́

9 *to write (out) a prescription*      i. ка́шель пройдёт

10. *your cough will go away*      j. до еды́

**ANSWER KEY**
1. c; 2. f; 3. a; 4. j; 5. b; 6. g; 7. d; 8. h; 9. e; 10. i

# Grammar Builder 2
▶ 14D Grammar Builder 2 (CD: 6, Track: 1)

## IRREGULAR GENITIVE PLURALS

Look at the phrase два ра́за в день (*two times a day*). The noun раз (*time, occasion*) is irregular: its nominative singular раз coincides with its genitive plural раз (*times, occasions*). This is what this noun looks like when you apply the rule of numbers to it.

| No. sg. | оди́н раз | *one time (once)* |
|---------|----------|-------------------|
| Gen. sg. | два/три/четы́ре ра́за | *two/three/four times* |
| Gen. pl. | пять раз | *five times* |

The question Ско́лько раз в день … ? (*How many times a day … ?*) uses the quantitative word ско́лько and the genitive plural of раз. Two more common nouns follow the same pattern of irregular genitive plurals: челове́к (*person*) and солда́т (*soldier*).

оди́н челове́к, два челове́ка, де́сять челове́к
*one person, two people, ten people*

оди́н солда́т, три солда́та, пятна́дцать солда́т
*one soldier, three soldiers, fifteen soldiers*

Learn the time expressions with the prepositions до, по́сле, во вре́мя. All three are followed by the genitive case:

до еды́ (*before meals*), до пя́тницы (*before Friday*), до обе́да (*before lunch*); по́сле еды́ (*after meals*), по́сле рабо́ты (*after work*), по́сле у́жина (*after*

Body parts and the plural of neuter     The imperfective verbs каза́ться and
nouns and the verb боле́ть (*to be sick*)    чу́вствовать and the modal verb мочь

The verb боле́ть (*to hurt*)          Irregular genitive plurals
and expressing ailments

*dinner*);

во вре́мя еды́ (*during/with meals*), во вре́мя рабо́ты (*during work*), во вре́мя кани́кул (*during the break/vacation*), etc.

## ✎ Work Out 2

Give Russian equivalents to the following English sentences.

1. *I'm sick with the flu.*

   _____

2. *He has a bad cough and a high temperature.*

   _____

3. *I take this medication twice a day after meals.*

   _____

4. *They often go to the doctor's.*

   _____

5. *I have a stomachache.*

   _____

6. *Take (inform.) this medication and your cough will go away. Get well!*

   _____

7. *She was at the doctor's yesterday.*

   _____

**ANSWER KEY**

1. Я боле́ю гри́ппом. 2. У него́ си́льный ка́шель и высо́кая температу́ра. 3. Я принима́ю э́то лека́рство два ра́за в день по́сле еды́. 4. Они́ ча́сто хо́дят к врачу́. 5. У меня́ боли́т живо́т. 6. Прими́ э́то лека́рство, и ка́шель пройдёт. Поправля́йся! 7. Она́ вчера́ была́ у врача́.

## ✎ Drive It Home

Now, let's do more practice on the irregular plurals of раз (*time*) and челове́к (*person*). Fill in the blanks with the correct form of one of these nouns and repeat the entire Russian sentence out loud.

1. Они́ бы́ли в Москве́ два _____.

2. Он ходи́л к врачу́ пять _____.

3. Я ви́дела его́ оди́н _____.

4. Пожа́луйста, принима́йте лека́рство три _____ в день.

5. Ско́лько _____ вы отдыха́ли в Еги́пте?

6. В моём о́фисе рабо́тает со́рок _____.

7. Ско́лько _____ заболе́ли гри́ппом?

8. На остано́вке авто́буса бы́ло два _____.

**ANSWER KEY**

1. ра́за; 2. раз; 3. раз; 4. ра́за; 5. раз; 6. челове́к; 7. челове́к; 8. челове́ка

## How Did You Do?

Let's see how you did in this lesson. You should know how to:

☐ Say that one is right or wrong. (Still unsure? Go back to page 206.)

☐ Use more reflexive verbs. (Still unsure? Go back to page 208.)

☐ Express uncertainty and ability. (Still unsure? Go back to page 210.)

The verb боле́ть (*to hurt*)                                    Irregular genitive plurals
and expressing ailments

☐ Talk more about sickness and health. (Still unsure? Go back to page 211.)

☐ Use some irregular genitive plurals. (Still unsure? Go back to page 213.)

## ✎ Word Recall

Now it's time to review some words, phrases, and constructions from the earlier
lessons. Read the English sentence first, then fill in the blanks, and finally, repeat
the Russian sentence out loud.

1. *I have a very (lit., strong) runny nose.*

    У меня́ _____.

2. *Sometimes, I visit (lit., go as a guest to) my grandmother.*

    Иногда́ я хожу́ _____.

3. *My daughter is twelve years old.*

    Мое́й до́чери _____.

4. *My wife works as a doctor in a hospital.*

    Моя́ жена́ рабо́тает _____.

5. *We have four bedrooms.*

    У нас четы́ре _____.

6. *They have a dacha in the country/suburbs.*

    У них есть да́ча _____.

7. *Their dacha is a house with all the conveniences.*

    Их да́ча—э́то дом _____.

8. *Do they have hot water?*

    У них есть _____?

*mething* and *anything* and negative
pronouns and adverbs

Perfective aspect in
negative sentences

The accusative of personal
pronouns

Imperatives and aspect

9. *They don't have children.*

   У них _____.

10. *How is he doing?*

    Как _____?

**ANSWER KEY**

1. си́льный на́сморк; 2. в го́сти к мое́й ба́бушке; 3. двена́дцать лет; 4. врачо́м в больни́це;
5. спа́льни; 6. за́ городом; 7. со все́ми удо́бствами; 8. горя́чая вода́; 9. нет дете́й; 10. у него́ дела́

# Lesson 15: Sentences

Добро́ пожа́ловать ещё раз! *Welcome once again!*

In this lesson, you'll learn how to:

☐ Say that you went or will go to the doctor's.

☐ Discuss taking medication.

☐ Discuss what's bothering you.

☐ Talk more about aches and pains.

☐ Use indefinite and definite adverbs and pronouns.

☐ Use negative adverbs and pronouns.

☐ Use animate pronouns in the accusative case.

Гото́вы? Тогда́ начнём! **Ready? Then, let's begin!**
Let's get started with some words and phrases.

Body parts and the plural of neuter          The imperfective verbs каза́ться and
nouns and the verb боле́ть (to be sick)       чу́вствовать and the modal verb мочь

The verb боле́ть (to hurt)                              Irregular genitive plurals
and expressing ailments

## Sentence Builder 1

▶ 15A Sentence Builder 1 (CD: 6, Track: 2)

| | |
|---|---|
| Я изме́рил(а) температу́ру. | *I took (my) temperature.* |
| Я ходи́л(а) к врачу́. | *I went to the doctor's (and I'm back).* |
| Я пошёл/пошла́ к врачу́. | *I set out to the doctor (and I'm still away).* |
| Я ходи́л(а) в апте́ку. | *I went to the pharmacy (and I'm back).* |
| Я пошёл/пошла́ в апте́ку. | *I set out to the pharmacy (and I'm still away).* |
| Ты что́-нибудь принима́ешь от температу́ры? | *Are you taking anything for the fever (temperature)?* |
| Нет, я ничего́ не принима́ю. | *No, I'm not taking anything.* |
| Да, я что́-то купи́л в апте́ке. | *Yes, I bought something at the pharmacy.* |
| Ты никогда́ не боле́ешь. | *You're never sick.* |
| Одева́йся тепле́е, а то ты просту́дишься. | *Dress warmer, or else you'll catch a cold.* |
| Я бу́ду брать с тебя́ приме́р! | *I'll follow your example!* |

## Take It Further 1

The aspect of the verb изме́рил(а) in the sentence я изме́рил(а) температу́ру
(*I've taken my temperature*) is perfective because you took the temperature once,
but also because taking the temperature was the result of your getting sick. The
imperfective я ме́рил(а) температу́ру would mean that you either took your
temperature many times, as in когда́ я боле́л(а), я ме́рил(а) температу́ру
пять раз в день (*when I was sick, I took my temperature five times a day*), or that

you were taking your temperature continuously for a certain period of time, as in я ме́рил(а) температу́ру пять мину́т (*I took my temperature for five minutes*).

Keep in mind the multidirectional verb ходи́ть. Я ходи́л(а) к врачу́ (*I went to the doctor*) implies two things at once: 1) that you went to the doctor's, and 2) that you're back now. On the other hand, я пошёл/пошла́ к врачу́ (*I went to the doctor*) means *I set out to the doctor's and I'm not back yet.* The verb пойти́ is perfective, and it always denotes the beginning of a new motion, one's setting out. Its vehicular counterpart is пое́хать: Я пое́хал(а) в Москву́ (*I set out for Moscow [by vehicle]*).

# ✎Sentence Practice 1

Read the English sentence first, then fill in the blank and repeat the entire Russian sentence out loud.

1. *Are you taking anything for the fever (temperature)?*

   Ты_____ от температу́ры?

2. *Yes, I bought something in the pharmacy.*

   Да, я _____ в апте́ке.

3. *I went to the pharmacy.*

   Я ходи́л _____.

4. *You're never sick.*

   Ты _____ не боле́ешь.

5. *I'll follow your example!*

   Я бу́ду _____ с тебя́ _____.

Body parts and the plural of neuter  | The imperfective verbs каза́ться and
nouns and the verb боле́ть (*to be sick*)  | чу́вствовать and the modal verb мочь

The verb боле́ть (*to hurt*)  | Irregular genitive plurals
and expressing ailments

6. *Dress warmer, or else you'll catch a cold.*

   Одева́йся _____, а то ты _____.

7. *I went to the doctor's.*

   Я ходи́л _____.

8. *I set out to the doctor's.*

   Я _____ к врачу́.

   **ANSWER KEY**

   1. что́-нибудь принима́ешь; 2. что́-то купи́л; 3. в апте́ку; 4. никогда́; 5. брать, приме́р; 6. теплее, просту́дишься; 7. к врачу́; 8. пошёл

# Grammar Builder 1

▶ 15B Grammar Builder 1 (CD: 6, Track: 3)

## *SOMETHING* AND *ANYTHING* AND NEGATIVE PRONOUNS AND ADVERBS

Now let's look at the sentence Ты что́-нибудь принима́ешь от температу́ры? (*Are you taking anything for the fever?*). In Russian, you can add the indefinite, unstressed particle –нибудь to any interrogative pronoun, and you will have an indefinite pronoun or adverb: кто́-нибудь, что́-нибудь, ка́к-нибудь, когда́-нибудь, где́-нибудь, etc. For example, что́-нибудь means either *anything* or *something*. The indefinite pronouns/adverbs with –нибудь are often used in questions and/or in the future tense given that they denote something indefinite.

Ты что́-нибудь хо́чешь?
*Do you want anything? (question)*

Я что́-нибудь куплю́ в апте́ке.
*I'll buy something at the pharmacy. (future tense)*

*mething* and *anything* and negative
pronouns and adverbs

Perfective aspect in
negative sentences

The accusative of personal
pronouns

Imperatives and aspect

When this *something* or *anything* is more definite (but still indeterminate), you should make indefinite pronouns or adverbs with the particle –то: ктó-то, чтó-то, кáк-то, когдá-то, гдé-то, etc. These should normally be used in affirmative statements in the past or present tense. Careful: You should not simply identify –нибудь with the English *anything* and –то with *something* since there are too many instances that fall outside of this analogy. Instead, you should understand these Russian particles on their own terms.

Он чтó-то покупáет в аптéке.
*He's buying something in the pharmacy. (affirmative, present)*

Он кудá-то пошёл.
*He went somewhere. (affirmative, past)*

And finally, as opposed to English, these Russian indefinite pronouns and adverbs can't be used in the negative. Instead, you should replace them with the special negative pronouns/adverbs.

| никтó | *no one* |
|-------|----------|
| никáк | *in no way* |
| никогдá | *never* |
| нигдé | *nowhere* |
| ничегó | *nothing (rather than* ничтó) |

These negative ни–pronouns/adverbs must be accompanied by the negative particle не. Technically, this is not a double negation, even if it may look so, because ни is not a negation in Russian but merely a negative particle that must be used only along with the real negation, that is, with не. Here are some examples.

Я ничегó не принимáю.
*I'm not taking anything.*

**Unit 4** Lesson 15: Sentences       221

Body parts and the plural of neuter
nouns and the verb боле́ть (*to be sick*)

The imperfective verbs каза́ться and
чу́вствовать and the modal verb мочь

The verb боле́ть (*to hurt*)
and expressing ailments

Irregular genitive plurals

Я ничего́ не хочу́.
*I don't want anything.*

Ты никогда́ не боле́ешь.
*You never get sick.*

Никто́ не зна́ет, чем он боле́ет.
*No one knows what he is sick with.*

Он нигде́ не был.
*He hasn't been anywhere.*

Я ника́к не пойму́, о чём вы говори́те.
*I can't in any way understand what you're talking about.*

# ✎ Work Out 1

A. Rewrite the following sentences using either ходи́ть or пойти́ in the past tense.
Remember also to replace locations with direction!

1. Мой муж был у врача́.

_____

2. Мой муж сейча́с у врача́.

_____

3. Они́ бы́ли в апте́ке у́тром.

_____

4. Мы бы́ли в магази́не.

_____

*nething* and *anything* and negative
pronouns and adverbs

Perfective aspect in
negative sentences

The accusative of personal
pronouns

Imperatives and aspect

5. Моя́ жена́ сейча́с на рабо́те.

_____

B. Translate the following questions into Russian and then answer them in the
   positive and in the negative. Use indefinite pronouns or adverbs in your answers.

1. *Did you (inform.) buy anything in the pharmacy?*

_____

2. *Do you (form.) take anything for a cough?*

_____

3. *Did she live anywhere in Russia?*

_____

4. *Do they want anything?*

_____

5. *Will we go anywhere tonight?*

_____

**ANSWER KEY**
**A. 1.** Мой муж ходи́л к врачу́. **2.** Мой муж пошёл к врачу́. **3.** Они́ ходи́ли в апте́ку у́тром.
**4.** Мы ходи́ли в магази́н. **5.** Моя́ жена́ пошла́ на рабо́ту.
**B. 1.** Ты что́-нибудь купи́л в апте́ке? Да, я что́-то купи́л в апте́ке. Нет, я ничего́ не купи́л
в апте́ке. **2.** Вы что́-нибудь принима́ете от ка́шля? Да, я что́-то принима́ю от ка́шля. Нет,
я ничего́ не принима́ю от ка́шля. **3.** Она́ жила́ где́-нибудь в Росси́и? Да, она́ жила́ где́-то в
Росси́и. Нет, она́ нигде́ не жила́ в Росси́и. **4.** Они́ хотя́т что́-нибудь? Да, они́ что́-то хотя́т.
Нет, они́ ничего́ не хотя́т. **5.** Мы пойдём куда́-нибудь ве́чером? Да, мы пойдём куда́-то
ве́чером. Нет, мы никуда́ не пойдём ве́чером.

Body parts and the plural of neuter     The imperfective verbs каза́ться and
nouns and the verb боле́ть (*to be sick*)    чу́вствовать and the modal verb мочь

The verb боле́ть (*to hurt*)           Irregular genitive plurals
and expressing ailments

## Sentence Builder 2

▶ 15C Sentence Builder 2 (CD: 6, Track: 4)

| Что вас беспоко́ит? | What's bothering you? |
|---|---|
| У меня́ три́дцать во́семь и пять по Це́льсию. | My temperature is thirty-eight point five Celsius (101.3 F). |
| Воспале́ния лёгких нет. | It's not pneumonia. (lit., No pneumonia.) |
| Мне бо́льно ка́шлять. | It hurts (me) to cough. |
| Мне бо́льно ходи́ть. | It hurts (me) to walk. |
| Мне бо́льно дыша́ть. | It hurts (me) to breathe. |
| У вас, наве́рное, грипп. | You probably have the flu. |
| Сейча́с мно́гие боле́ют гри́ппом. | Many (people) are sick with the flu now. |
| Че́рез пять дней всё пройдёт. | Everything will go away in five days. |
| Дней че́рез пять вы вы́здоровеете. | You'll recover in about five days. |

## Take It Further 2

▶ 15D Take It Further 2 (CD: 6, Track: 5)

Russians use the centigrade scale of temperature. Temperature data is thus quoted по Це́льсию (*according to the Celsius scale*) rather than по Фаренге́йту (*according to the Fahrenheit scale*). So, the normal body temperature is generally considered to be 36,6 C° (97.8 F). Notice that Russians write their decimal fractions with a comma rather than with a dot. So *36.6* is 36,6 in Russian. This is pronounced as три́дцать шесть и шесть, where и (*and*) stands for the decimal point. The preposition че́рез + accusative means *after* or *in,* as in the phrase че́рез пять дней (*in five days/after five days*). It denotes a gap in time after which something happens; in other words, not until this time passes, something can happen. The time period that follows this preposition is in the accusative if it's singular: че́рез неде́лю (*in a week/a week later/not until a week from now*), че́рез ме́сяц (*in a month/after a month/not until a month from now*). If the

*nething* and *anything* and negative
pronouns and adverbs

Perfective aspect in
negative sentences

The accusative of personal
pronouns

Imperatives and aspect

phrase has a numeral, it should follow the Rule of Numbers: че́рез две неде́ли
(*in two weeks*), че́рез пять неде́ль (*in five weeks*), etc.

When you say пять неде́ль (*five weeks*), you're being exact. One of the ways
to express approximation in Russian is to reverse the numeral and the noun.
For example, неде́ль пять means *about five weeks* or *approximately five weeks*.
Remember, if the phrase has a preposition, the preposition goes between the
reversed noun and the numeral: неде́ль че́рез пять means *approximately in five
weeks*. Note that this method of approximating is reserved for colloquial contexts
and would not be appropriate in formal contexts.

---

## ✎ Sentence Practice 2

Read the English sentence first, then fill in the blank and repeat the entire Russian
sentence out loud.

1. *Many (people) are sick with the flu now.*

   Мно́гие сейча́с _____.

2. *You probably have the flu.*

   У вас, _____, грипп.

3. *Everything will go away in three days.*

   _____ всё пройдёт.

4. *You'll get better in about five days.*

   Дней че́рез пять вы _____.

5. *It's not pneumonia. (lit., No pneumonia.)*

   _____ нет.

Body parts and the plural of neuter
nouns and the verb боле́ть (*to be sick*)

The imperfective verbs каза́ться and
чу́вствовать and the modal verb мочь

The verb боле́ть (*to hurt*)
and expressing ailments

Irregular genitive plurals

6. *It hurts (me) to cough.*

Мне бо́льно _____.

7. *It hurts (me) to walk.*

Мне бо́льно _____.

8. *It hurts (me) to breath.*

Мне бо́льно _____.

9. *What's bothering you?*

Что вас _____?

10. *My temperature is 38.5 Celsius.*

У меня́ три́дцать во́семь и пять _____.

### ANSWER KEY
1. боле́ют гри́ппом; 2. наве́рное; 3. Че́рез пять дней; 4. вы́здоровеете; 5. Воспале́ния лёгких; 6. ка́шлять; 7. ходи́ть; 8. дыша́ть; 9. беспоко́ит; 10. по Це́льсию

## Grammar Builder 2
▷ 15E Grammar Builder 2 (CD: 6, Track: 6)

### THE ACCUSATIVE OF PERSONAL PRONOUNS

The imperfective verb беспоко́ить is Conjugation II. It means *to trouble, to bother, to concern* (lit., *to disquiet,* since бес– is *without/dis* in Russian and покой is *rest*). The thing that bothers you is the grammatical subject of the sentence and must be in the nominative case.

Меня́ беспоко́ит моё здоро́вье.
*My health is bothering me.*

*nething* and *anything* and negative
pronouns and adverbs

Perfective aspect in
negative sentences

The accusative of personal
pronouns

Imperatives and aspect

Его́ беспоко́ят зу́бы.

*His teeth are bothering him.*

Notice that the person who's being troubled is in the accusative case. However, the accusative coincides with the genitive for animate masculine singular nouns— that is, for the nouns denoting male human beings and animals, as well as all animate plurals (masculine and feminine). So, you should say Ива́на беспоко́ит го́рло (*Ivan is bothered by his throat* or, literally, *his throat is bothering Ivan*); меня́ беспоко́ит ка́шель ([*this*] *cough is bothering me*); мою́ жену́ беспоко́ит на́сморк (*a runny nose is bothering my wife*), etc. The personal pronouns are the same in the accusative and genitive.

|       | ACCUSATIVE | GENITIVE |
|-------|------------|----------|
| я     | меня́       | меня́     |
| ты    | тебя́       | тебя́     |
| он/но́ | его́        | его́      |
| оа́    | её         | её       |
| мы    | нас        | нас      |
| вы    | вас        | вас      |
| они́   | их         | их       |

Что тебя́ беспоко́ит?

*What's bothering you?*

Её беспоко́ит высо́кая температу́ра.

*A high fever/temperature is bothering her.*

Нас беспоко́ит его́ здоро́вье.

*His health concerns us.*

As you already know, the negated nouns need to be in the genitive of negation in Russian. This is why воспале́ния in воспале́ния лёгких нет is in the genitive case. You should follow this rule whenever you negate anything.

**Unit 4** Lesson 15: Sentences

Body parts and the plural of neuter
nouns and the verb болéть (*to be sick*)

The imperfective verbs казáться and
чýвствовать and the modal verb мочь

The verb болéть (*to hurt*)
and expressing ailments

Irregular genitive plurals

У меня́ нет врéмени.
*I don't have time.*

У негó нет жены́.
*He doesn't have a wife.*

У неё нет дéнег.
*She doesn't have money.*

All the things one doesn't have should be in the genitive of negation. The past tense of нет is нé было.

У меня́ нé было врéмени.
*I didn't have time.*

У негó нé было жены́.
*He didn't have a wife.*

У неё нé было денег.
*She didn't have money.*

It is always fixed in the same singular neuter form не было, so it doesn't agree with anything else in the sentence. The future form of нет is не бýдет; it is equally fixed for all persons and things: у меня́ не бýдет врéмени, у негó не бýдет жены́, у неё не бýдет дéнег. In addition, remember that the personal pronouns егó, её, and их add an н– in the genitive case after prepositions, such as у: у негó, у неё, у них.

*mething* and *anything* and negative
pronouns and adverbs

Perfective aspect in
negative sentences

The accusative of personal
pronouns

Imperatives and aspect

# ✎ Work Out 2

A. Что вас беспокóит? (*What is bothering you?*) Say that these symptoms are bothering the following people. Remember to make the verb agree in number with the subject and put the people in the accusative where necessary!

1. я, нáсморк

   _____

2. мой муж, высóкая температýра

   _____

3. моя́ сестрá, больнóе гóрло

   _____

4. вы, больнáя ногá

   _____

5. ты, больные зубы

   _____

B. Fill in the blanks by restating the first sentences in the negative. Remember to keep the same tense as in the first sentence and use the genitive of negation.

1. У неё былá высóкая температýра.

   У неё _____.

2. У вас бýдет нáсморк.

   У вас _____.

3. У них есть врéмя.

   У них _____.

Body parts and the plural of neuter
nouns and the verb боле́ть (*to be sick*)

The imperfective verbs каза́ться and
чу́вствовать and the modal verb мочь

The verb боле́ть (*to hurt*)
and expressing ailments

Irregular genitive plurals

4. У тебя́ есть хоро́шее лека́рство.

У тебя́ _____.

5. У него́ бу́дет ка́шель.

У него́ _____.

**ANSWER KEY**
A. 1. Меня́ беспоко́ит на́сморк. 2. Моего́ му́жа беспоко́ит высо́кая температу́ра. 3. Мою́ сестру́
беспоко́ит больно́е го́рло. 4. Вас беспоко́ит больна́я нога́. 5. Тебя́ беспоко́ят больны́е зу́бы.
B. 1. не́ было высо́кой температу́ры; 2. не бу́дет на́сморка; 3. нет вре́мени; 4. нет хоро́шего
лека́рства; 5. не бу́дет ка́шля

# ✎ Drive It Home

Now, let's do more practice on the indefinite and negative pronouns and
adverbs with particles –то, –нибудь, and ни—не … Fill in the blanks with the
correct indefinite or negative pronoun/adverb following the English prompts in
parentheses and then repeat the entire Russian sentence out loud.

1. Его́ _____ беспоко́ит? (*anything*)

2. Да, его́ _____ беспоко́ит. (*something*)

3. Нет, его́ _____ беспоко́ит. (*nothing*)

4. Ты _____ был в Росси́и? (*ever*)

5. Да, я _____ был в Росси́и. (*at some point in time*)

6. Нет, я _____ в Росси́и. (*never*)

7. Она́ _____ рабо́тает? (*anywhere*)

8. Да, она́ _____ рабо́тает. (*somewhere*)

9. Нет, она́ _____ рабо́тает. (*nowhere*)

10. Они́ _____ боле́ют? (*with anything*)

*mething* and *anything* and negative
pronouns and adverbs

Perfective aspect in
negative sentences

The accusative of personal
pronouns

Imperatives and aspect

11. Да, они́ _____ боле́ют. (*with something*)

12. Нет, они́ _____ боле́ют. (*with nothing*)

13. Вы _____ принима́ете от ка́шля? (*anything*)

14. Да, я _____ принима́ю от ка́шля. (*something*)

15. Нет, я _____ принима́ю от ка́шля. (*nothing*)

16. Он _____ ходи́л вчера́? (*anywhere*)

17. Да, он _____ ходи́л вчера́. (*somewhere*)

18. Нет, он _____ ходи́л вчера́. (*nowhere*)

**ANSWER KEY**

1. что́-нибудь; 2. что́-то; 3. ничего́ не; 4. когда́-нибудь; 5. когда́-то; 6. никогда́ не был; 7. где́-нибудь; 8. где́-то; 9. нигде́ не; 10. чём-нибудь; 11. чём-то; 12. ниче́м не; 13. что́-нибудь; 14. что́-то; 15. ничего́ не; 16. куда́-нибудь; 17. куда́-то; 18. никуда́ не

# How Did You Do?

Let's see how you did in this lesson. You should know how to:

☐ Say that you went or will go to the doctor's. (Still unsure? Go back to page 217.)

☐ Discuss taking medication. (Still unsure? Go back to page 218.)

☐ Use indefinite and definite adverbs and pronouns. (Still unsure? Go back to page 220.)

☐ Use negative adverbs and pronouns. (Still unsure? Go back to page 221.)

☐ Discuss what's bothering you. (Still unsure? Go back to page 223.)

☐ Talk more about aches and pains. (Still unsure? Go back to page 223.)

☐ Use animate pronouns in the accusative case. (Still unsure? Go back to page 226.)

Body parts and the plural of neuter
nouns and the verb боле́ть (*to be sick*)

The imperfective verbs каза́ться and
чу́вствовать and the modal verb мочь

The verb боле́ть (*to hurt*)
and expressing ailments

Irregular genitive plurals

# ✎ Word Recall

Now it's time to review some words, phrases, and constructions from earlier
lessons. Read the English sentence first, then fill in the blanks, and finally, repeat
the Russian sentence out loud.

1. *She was at the doctor's twice.*

   Она́ _____ ходи́ла _____ .

2. *I'm not feeling well today.*

   Я пло́хо _____ сего́дня.

3. *It seems to me that I'm sick.*

   Мне _____ , что я заболе́ла.

4. *You can catch a cold.*

   Вы _____ простуди́ться.

5. *I have a headache.*

   У меня́ _____ .

6. *He has a normal temperature.*

   У него́ _____ .

7. *My daughter was born on the seventeenth of September.*

   Моя́ дочь родила́сь _____ .

8. *There are many excellent restaurants in the center of the city.*

   В це́нтре го́рода есть _____ .

9. *I'm sure you'll like this film.*

   Я уве́рена, что _____ .

*mething* and *anything* and negative
pronouns and adverbs

Perfective aspect in
negative sentences

The accusative of personal
pronouns

Imperatives and aspect

10. *We like to walk (go on foot).*

   Мы лю́бим _____ .

   **ANSWER KEY**

   1. два ра́за, к врачу́; 2. себя́ чу́вствую; 3. ка́жется; 4. мо́жете; 5. боли́т голова́; 6. норма́льная температу́ра; 7. семна́дцатого сентября́; 8. мно́го отли́чных рестора́нов; 9. тебе́ понра́вится э́тот фильм; 10. ходи́ть пешко́м

# Lesson 16: Conversations

Добро́ пожа́ловать на заключи́тельный уро́к четвёртой главы́!
*Welcome to the final lesson of Unit 4!*

In this lesson, you'll learn how to:

☐ Ask and answer questions in the doctor's office.

☐ Use invitations and commands in Russian.

☐ Use aspect with imperatives.

☐ Use negative imperatives.

☐ Express frustration or failure with negative perfective verbs.

Гото́вы? Тогда́ начнём! *Ready? Then, let's begin!*
Let's get started with Conversation 1.

## ◖ Conversation 1

▶ 16A Conversation 1 (CD: 6, Track: 7- Russian; Track 8- Russian and English)

Sergey is not feeling well. He's talking about it to his girlfriend, Zhenya.

Же́ня:         Приве́т, Серёжа! Как у тебя́ дела́?

**Unit 4** Lesson 16: Conversations        233

Body parts and the plural of neuter
nouns and the verb болéть (*to be sick*)

The imperfective verbs казáться and
чýвствовать and the modal verb мочь

The verb болéть (*to hurt*)
and expressing ailments

Irregular genitive plurals

| | |
|---|---|
| Сергéй: | Всё нормáльно, тóлько мне кáжется, что я заболéл. У меня́ с вéчера боли́т головá и гóрло, и я себя́ плóхо чýвствую. |
| Жéня: | У тебя́ есть температýра? |
| Сергéй: | Не знáю, я не мéрил. |
| Жéня: | А ты чтó-нибудь принимáешь? |
| Сергéй: | Нет, ничегó. Я ещё не ходи́л ни к врачý, ни в аптéку. |
| Жéня: | Сходи́ на вся́кий слýчай. А сейчáс иди домóй, если мóжешь, и пей чай с мёдом. |
| Сергéй: | Да, ты правá. Мне лýчше пойти́ домóй. |
| Жéня: | И одевáйся теплéе, а то ты ещё бóльше простýдишься. |
| Сергéй: | Хорошó. Вот ты, Жень, молодéц! Ты никогдá не болéешь! |
| Жéня: | Это потомý, что я занимáюсь спóртом, по утрáм дéлаю заря́дку и плáваю. |
| Сергéй: | Я послéдую твоемý примéру! |

| | |
|---|---|
| *Zhenya:* | *Hey, Seryozha! How are you doing?* |
| *Sergey:* | *Everything is alright, except that I'm probably (it seems to me) getting sick. I've had a headache and a sore throat since last night, and I'm not feeling well.* |
| *Zhenya:* | *Do you have a fever/temperature?* |
| *Sergey:* | *I don't know. I didn't take it.* |
| *Zhenya:* | *Are you taking anything?* |
| *Sergey:* | *(No), nothing. I haven't gone to the doctor's or the pharmacy yet.* |
| *Zhenya:* | *Go, just in case. And go home now, if you can, and drink tea with honey.* |
| *Sergey:* | *You're right. I'd better go home.* |
| *Zhenya:* | *And dress warmer, or else you'll get even sicker.* |
| *Sergey:* | *All right. But look at you, Zhenya! You never get sick!* |
| *Zhenya:* | *This is because I play sports, exercise in the morning, and swim.* |
| *Sergey:* | *I'll follow your example!* |

*mething* and *anything* and negative
pronouns and adverbs

Perfective aspect in
negative sentences

The accusative of personal
pronouns

Imperatives and aspect

# Take It Further 1

▶ 16B Take It Further 1 (CD: 6, Track: 9)

Notice the verb есть in Zhenya's question У тебя́ есть температу́ра? (*Do you
have a fever/temperature?*). As we've discussed earlier, есть is there because
Sergey may or may not have high temperature. If the fact that Sergey had a fever
had already been established, and Zhenya inquired whether Sergey had a high
fever or a moderate one, then there would be no есть in the question. It would be
У тебя́ высо́кая температу́ра? (*Do you have a high fever?*).

In the sentence я ещё не ходи́л ни к врачу́, ни в апте́ку, the conjunction ни
… ни means *neither … nor*. Notice that, as with the negative pronouns никто́,
ничего́, никогда́, нигде́, etc., the negative particle ни is not enough for the
negation; it has to be coupled with the real negation, the negative particle не: не
ходи́л.

Notice the agreement in the sentence у меня́ с ве́чера боли́т голова́ и го́рло.
The verb боли́т is singular, because it agrees with the closest subject, the noun
голова́, which is singular. Alternatively, in more formal discourse, you could
make the verb agree with both subjects, thus, making it plural: У меня́ боля́т
голова́ и го́рло.

The verb пла́вать is another motion verb. It means *to swim* as well as *to sail*.
This verb is multidirectional. This is why Zhenya uses it for the general action:
я пла́ваю (*I swim*) (–ай type, Conjugation I). Its unidirectional counterpart is
плыть. Like the verb жить (*to live*), плыть is a Conjugation I verb with a –в
stem: я плыву́, ты плывёшь, они́ плыву́т; он плыл, она́ плыла́, они́ плы́ли.
Я плыву́ means *I'm swimming/sailing right now*.

Body parts and the plural of neuter
nouns and the verb боле́ть (*to be sick*)

The imperfective verbs каза́ться and
чу́вствовать and the modal verb мочь

The verb боле́ть (*to hurt*)
and expressing ailments

Irregular genitive plurals

# ✏ Conversation Practice 1

Let's practice now. Match the following English phrases and sentences on the left to their Russian equivalents on the right. Repeat the Russian sentence out loud.

1. *How are you doing?*

2. *Everything is alright.*

3. *I'm probably (it seems to me) getting sick.*

4. *I didn't take (my) temperature.*

5. *I haven't gone to the doctor's yet.*

6. *Go to the doctor's just in case.*

7. *You're right.*

8. *Dress warmer.*

9. *I play sports and swim.*

10. *I'll follow your example.*

a. Я не ме́рил температу́ру.

b. Сходи́ на вся́кий слу́чай к врачу́.

c. Одева́йся тепле́е.

d. Ты права́.

e. Я после́дую твоему́ приме́ру.

f. Я занима́юсь спо́ртом и пла́ваю.

g. Как у тебя́ дела́?

h. Мне ка́жется, что я заболе́л.

i. Я ещё не ходи́л к врачу́.

j. Всё норма́льно.

**ANSWER KEY**
1. g; 2. j; 3. h; 4. a; 5. i; 6. b; 7. d; 8. c; 9. f; 10. e

# Grammar Builder 1

▶ 16C Grammar Builder 1 (CD: 6, Track: 10)

## PERFECTIVE ASPECT IN NEGATIVE SENTENCES

By default, negative sentences in Russian require the imperfective aspect.

Я не ме́рил(а) температу́ру.
*I didn't take my temperature.*

Я не ходи́л(а) к врачу́.
*I didn't go to the doctor's.*

*omething* and *anything* and negative
pronouns and adverbs

Perfective aspect in
negative sentences

The accusative of personal
pronouns

Imperatives and aspect

However, this general rule is broken when the negated action defies one's
expectations. The negative perfective implies a failure to complete an action.

Я не изме́рил(а) температу́ру.
*I haven't taken my temperature. (I was supposed to, expected to, but never did.)*

Я не пошёл/пошла́ к врачу́.
*I haven't gone to the doctor's. (I was supposed to, expected to, but never did.)*

# ✎ Work Out 1

Fill in the blanks with correct perfective or imperfective verb. The explanations
in parentheses will help you with your choice of aspect after negation!

1. *I didn't go the doctor. (Why should I?)*

   Я _____ к врачу́. (ходи́л—пошёл)

2. *I haven't gone to the doctor's. (Even though you told me to.)*

   Я _____ к врачу́. (ходи́л—пошёл)

3. *She hasn't bought the medicine. (Although I specifically had asked her to!)*

   Она́_____лека́рство. (покупа́ла—купи́ла)

4. *He didn't get sick for the entire winter. (He's a healthy guy.)*

   Он _____ всю зи́му. (боле́л—заболе́л)

5. *He hasn't gotten sick. (Although everybody around him was sick.)*

   Он _____. (боле́л—заболе́л)

6. *We didn't take any medication. (Because we didn't have any.)*

   Мы _____ лека́рства. (принима́ли—при́няли)

**ANSWER KEY**

1. не ходи́л; 2. не пошёл; 3. не купи́ла; 4. не болéл; 5. не заболéл; 6. не принимáли

## Conversation 2

▶ 16D Conversation 2 (CD: 6, Track: 11- Russian; Track: 12- Russian and English)

Natalia has symptoms of the flu and goes to see the doctor. Listen to their conversation.

| | |
|---|---|
| Врач: | Здрáвствуйте, проходи́те, сади́тесь! Что вас беспокóит? |
| Натáлья: | Я уже два дня плóхо себя́ чýвствую. У меня́ высóкая температýра—38,5. |
| Врач: | Что у вас боли́т? |
| Натáлья: | У меня́ си́льный нáсморк и кáшель, и немнóго боли́т живóт. |
| Врач: | Открóйте, пожáлуйста, рот и скажи́те: «А-а». |
| Натáлья: | «А-а … ». |
| Врач: | Гóрло немнóго крáсное. Поверни́тесь, пожáлуйста, спинóй, я вас сейчáс послýшаю. Дыши́те … Не дыши́те … Так. Хорошó. Лёгкие чи́стые. Воспалéния лёгких нет. |
| Натáлья: | Да, но мне бóльно кáшлять. |
| Врач: | У вас, навéрное, грипп. Сейчáс мнóгие болéют гри́ппом. Я вам вы́пишу рецéпт. Принимáйте лекáрство два рáза в день пóсле еды́. Дней чéрез пять кáшель пройдёт, и вы вы́здоровеете. |
| Натáлья: | Большóе спаси́бо. До свидáния. |
| Врач: | Всегó хорóшего, поправля́йтесь! |

| | |
|---|---|
| *Doctor:* | *Hello, come in, have a seat. What's bothering you?* |
| *Natalia:* | *I've felt bad for two days. I've had a high temperature of 38.5 (Celsius).* |
| *Doctor:* | *What is hurting you?* |
| *Natalia:* | *I have a (severe) runny nose and cough, and a little stomach pain.* |

*mething* and *anything* and negative
pronouns and adverbs

Perfective aspect in
negative sentences

The accusative of personal
pronouns

Imperatives and aspect

| Doctor: | *Open your mouth please, and say "Ah."* |
| Natalia: | *Ah …* |
| Doctor: | *Your throat is a little red. Turn your back to me, please. I'll listen to your lungs now. Breathe … don't breathe … So, okay. Your lungs are clear. It's not pneumonia (lit., No pneumonia).* |
| Natalia: | *Yes, but it hurts to cough.* |
| Doctor: | *You probably have the flu. Many (people) are sick with the flu right now. I'll write you a prescription. Take the medication twice a day after meals. You'll have this cough for about five days, and then you'll be back to normal.* |
| Natalia: | *Thank you so much. Good-bye.* |
| Doctor: | *All the best, get well!* |

## Take It Further 2

Culturally, imperatives are much more common in Russian than in English. Instead of saying *would you please* or *will you please*, Russians use command forms—*do it* or *don't do it, please!* This is perfectly polite and culturally appropriate provided that you choose the correct imperative. In fact, the roundabout English requests may be considered too vague and even sneaky!

## ✎Conversation Practice 2

Let's practice now. Match the following English phrases and sentences on the left with their Russian equivalents on the right. Repeat the Russian sentence out loud.

1. *Hello, come in, have a seat.*
2. *What's bothering you?*
3. *I have a high fever.*
4. *I have a severe runny nose.*
5. *Open your mouth please.*

a. У меня́ си́льный на́сморк.
b. Что вас беспоко́ит?
c. Откро́йте, пожа́луйста, рот.
d. Мне бо́льно ка́шлять.
e. Я пло́хо себя́ чу́вствую два дня.

Body parts and the plural of neuter
nouns and the verb боле́ть (*to be sick*)

The imperfective verbs каза́ться and
чу́вствовать and the modal verb мочь

The verb боле́ть (*to hurt*)
and expressing ailments

Irregular genitive plurals

6. *Turn around please.*

f. Здра́вствуйте, проходи́те, сади́тесь.

7. *It hurts (me) to cough.*

g. У меня́ высо́кая температу́ра.

8. *I've felt sick/bad for two days.*

h. Всего́ хоро́шего, поправля́йтейсь!

9. *Take the medication twice a day after meals.*

i. Поверни́тесь, пожа́луйста.

10. *All the best, get well!*

j. Принима́йте лека́рство два ра́за в день по́сле еды́.

**ANSWER KEY**
1. f; 2. b; 3. g; 4. a; 5. c; 6. i; 7. d; 8. e; 9. j; 10. h

# Grammar Builder 2

▶ 16E Grammar Builder 2 (CD: 6, Track: 13)

## IMPERATIVES AND ASPECT

The imperative is used for commands, requests, invitations, and prohibitions. Different from English, in Russian there are singular and plural imperative forms. In order to form Russian imperatives, you need to follow a few simple rules.

1. If you hear the sound "й" anywhere in the conjugation ending, you can stop right there—this is your basic imperative form. For example, in я рабо́таю, you can hear (but can't see!) the sound "й" in the end of the stem before the grammatical ending: рабо́та[йу] = ю. Consequently, your imperative is рабо́тай in the singular informal, and рабо́тайте in the plural or respectful form.

2. If the conjugated forms don't have the sound "й" before their endings, they will have a consonant. Look at the first person singular (я живу́, я бу́ду) and notice the difference in stress: я живу́ has an end stress, whereas я бу́ду is stressed on the stem. This difference determines their imperatives.

mething and *anything* and negative
pronouns and adverbs

Perfective aspect in
negative sentences

The accusative of personal
pronouns

Imperatives and aspect

a. If the 1st person singular of a given verb has an end stress, its imperative will end in a stressed и: я живу́ > живи́/живи́те (*live!*);

b. if the 1st person singular has stem stress, the imperative ends in the soft sign: я бу́ду > будь/бу́дьте (*be!* as in будь здоро́в, *be healthy/take care*).

Conjugation I verbs keep their mutation in the imperatives: я пишу́; ты пи́шешь–пиши́! (*Write!*)

Conjugation II verbs don't keep their mutations anywhere but in the first person singular; this goes for the imperatives as well: я люблю́; ты лю́бишь > люби́! or люби́те (*Love!*)

One rare exception to the rule in 2b above: if the conjugation stem ends in two consonants, then the imperative ending is always an и regardless of the stress. For example, the verb *to remember* is по́мнить. The first person conjugation, я по́мню, has two consonants, м and н, in the end of the stem; consequently, the imperative is по́мни(те) regardless of its stem stress.

The reflexive endings, –ся and –сь, don't interfere with the above rules. You simply add them to the formed imperative. As always, add –ся after consonants (including the й) and –сь after vowels (поправля́йся, поправля́йтесь). Irregular verbs also have irregular imperatives.

| IRREGULAR VERBS | IMPERATIVE |
|---|---|
| дать<br>*to give* | да́й(те) |
| есть<br>*to eat* | е́шь(те) |

You'll learn more about the imperative of дать in the following unit.

Body parts and the plural of neuter
nouns and the verb болеть (*to be sick*)

The imperfective verbs казаться and
чувствовать and the modal verb мочь

The verb болеть (*to hurt*)
and expressing ailments

Irregular genitive plurals

You also need to consider the choice of aspect in the imperatives. Choose the imperfective imperatives when you presume that your command is expected. This will happen in polite invitations because they imply, "Of course, you should know that you're welcome!"

For example, you say to a visitor, Здравствуйте, проходите, садитесь! (*Hello [lit., be healthy!], come in, have a seat!*). These imperatives clearly imply that the addressee should expect such a welcome. On the contrary, when you ask for or command something that the other person wasn't supposed to know or expect, you should use perfective imperatives. Only perfective imperatives are polite in real commands, requests, or favors.

Пожалуйста, откройте окно!
*Please open the window!*

The perfective here implies that I realize that you weren't supposed to open the window without my explicit request.

Negative imperatives are mostly imperfective—consider it a default setting. However, the common exceptions to this pattern are не забудь(те) (*don't forget*), не упади(те) (*don't fall/watch your step*), не скажи(те) (*don't say that*), не опоздай(те) (*don't be late*), and не заболей(те) (*don't get sick*). They usually follow the initial warning смотри(те)! (*watch out!/make sure you don't*) and have an accusatory connotation (i.e. *I think that you just might!*).

Смотри(те) не забудь(те)!
*Make sure you don't forget!*

Смотри(те) не заболей(те)!
*Make sure you don't get sick!*

*mething* and *anything* and negative
pronouns and adverbs

Perfective aspect in
negative sentences

The accusative of personal
pronouns

Imperatives and aspect

Смотри́(те) не упади́(те)!
*Make sure you don't fall!*

# ✎ Work Out 2

A. Write singular and then plural commands based on the following infinitive
phrases. Don't change the aspect! Then, repeat the entire command out loud.

1. не боле́ть

sg. _____

pl. _____

2. де́лать заря́дку

sg. _____

pl. _____

3. принима́ть лека́рство

sg. _____

pl. _____

4. вы́писать реце́пт

sg. _____

pl. _____

5. занима́ться спо́ртом

sg. _____

pl. _____

6. любить меня́

    sg. _____

    pl. _____

7. купи́ть проду́кты

    sg. _____

    pl. _____

8. не покупáть лекáрства

    sg. _____

    pl. _____

9. измéрить температýру

    sg. _____

    pl. _____

10. сказáть прáвду

    sg. _____

    pl. _____

B. Read the English sentence first, then fill in the blanks with the correct form of imperfective or perfective imperative. Make the imperatives formal where asked to.

1. *Please buy me tea. (form.)*

    Пожáлуйста, _____ мне чай.

2. *Don't take this medication! (form.)*

    _____ э́то лекáрство!

3. *Tell me, what's your name? (inform.)*

   _____ мне, как тебя зову́т?

4. *Open your mouth, please. (form.)*

   _____ рот, пожа́луйста.

5. *Please come in. (form.)*

   Пожа́луйста,_____.

6. *Get well! (form.)*

   _____!

7. *Dress warmer (inform.)*

   _____ тепле́е.

8. *Eat please! (form.)*

   _____, пожа́луйтста!

**ANSWER KEY**

A. 1. не боле́й, не боле́йте; 2. де́лай заря́дку, де́лайте заря́дку; 3. принима́й лека́рство, принима́йте лека́рство; 4. вы́пиши реце́пт, вы́пишите реце́пт; 5. занима́йся спо́ртом, занима́йтесь спо́ртом; 6. люби́ меня́, люби́те меня́; 7. купи́ проду́кты, купи́те проду́кты; 8. не покупа́й лека́рства, не покупа́йте лека́рства; 9. изме́рь температу́ру, изме́рьте температу́ру; 10. скажи́ пра́вду, скажи́те пра́вду

B. 1. купи́те; 2. Не принима́йте; 3. Скажи́; 4. Откро́йте; 5. проходи́те; 6. Поправля́йтесь; 7. Одева́йся; 8. Е́шьте

## 🌐 Culture Note

You may have noticed that Sergey in Conversation 1 called Же́ня "Жень." This is a colloquial vocative form. The vocative case is the case for nouns being addressed by the speaker. It no longer exists in Russian, except for a few idiomatic and very old expressions, such as Бо́же мой! (*My God!*) or Го́споди! (*Oh, Lord!/Oh, God!*). These are the vocative form of the nouns Бог (*God*) and Госпо́дь (*the Lord*). In colloquial speech, every Russian first name that ends in a vowel (male or female)

Body parts and the plural of neuter
nouns and the verb боле́ть (*to be sick*)

The imperfective verbs каза́ться and
чу́вствовать and the modal verb мочь

The verb боле́ть (*to hurt*)
and expressing ailments

Irregular genitive plurals

can be shortened if you're addressing the person by his/her name directly. So, if
your friend's name is Же́ня, you can directly call her or him Жень; Ми́ша may
be addressed as Миш; Серёжа—Серёж; Ле́на—Лен; Та́ня—Тань; Ира—Ир;
etc. However, remember that these vocative short forms are not nicknames and
should be used only colloquially when you address the person directly and when
you know a person well.

## ✎ Drive It Home

Now, let's drive home negative perfective verbs when they mean frustration or
failure to accomplish an action one was supposed to have done. Read the English
sentence first, then fill in the blanks with the negative perfective verb (provided
in parentheses), and finally repeat the entire sentence out loud.

1. Он не _____ э́то лека́рство. (*buy*)

2. Мы не _____ к врачу́. (*go on foot*)

3. Врач не _____ нам реце́пт. (*prescribe, write out*)

4. Она́ не _____ температу́ру. (*take, measure*)

5. Вы не _____ пра́вду. (*say*)

6. Он не _____ че́рез неде́лю. (*get better*)

7. Ты не _____ моему́ приме́ру. (*follow*)

8. Она́ не _____ . (*get sick*)

**ANSWER KEY**
1. купи́л; 2. пошли́; 3. вы́писал; 4. изме́рила; 5. сказа́ли; 6. попра́вился; 7. после́довал; 8. заболе́ла

mething and *anything* and negative
pronouns and adverbs

Perfective aspect in
negative sentences

The accusative of personal
pronouns

Imperatives and aspect

## How Did You Do?

Let's see how you did in this lesson. You should know how to:

☐ Express frustration or failure with negative perfective verbs. (Still unsure? Go back to page 236.)

☐ Ask and answer questions in the doctor's office. (Still unsure? Go back to page 237.)

☐ Use invitations and commands in Russian. (Still unsure? Go back to page 240.)

☐ Use aspect with imperatives. (Still unsure? Go back to page 240.)

☐ Use negative imperatives. (Still unsure? Go back to page 242.)

## ✎ Word Recall

Now it's time to review some words, phrases, and constructions from the earlier lessons. Read the English sentence first, then fill in the blanks, and finally, repeat the Russian sentence out loud.

1. *His temperature is thirty eight point five Celsius.*

   У него́ температу́ра три́дцать во́семь и пять _____.

2. *In about five days, you'll get better.*

   _____ вы вы́здоровеете.

3. *For how much time (how long) did you live in Russia?*

   _____ вы жи́ли в Росси́и?

4. *What time is it now?*

   _____ сейча́с _____?

Body parts and the plural of neuter
nouns and the verb боле́ть (*to be sick*)

The imperfective verbs каза́ться and
чу́вствовать and the modal verb мочь

The verb боле́ть (*to hurt*)
and expressing ailments

Irregular genitive plurals

5. *It's three o'clock in the afternoon.*

   Сейча́с _____.

6. *I'm finishing work at five thirty.*

   Я зака́нчиваю рабо́ту _____.

7. *I'll buy a washer in the spring.*

   Я куплю́ _____ весно́й.

8. *She is married.*

   Она́ _____.

9. *My wife is from California.*

   Моя́ жена́ _____.

10. *She's staying home now with our younger daughter.*

    Она́ сейча́с _____ с на́шей _____ до́черью.

    **ANSWER KEY**
    1. по Це́льсию; 2. Дней че́рез пять; 3. Ско́лько вре́мени; 4. Ско́лько, вре́мени; 5. три часа́ дня;
    6. в пять часо́в три́дцать мину́т; 7. стира́льную маши́ну; 8. за́мужем; 9. из Калифо́рнии;
    10. сиди́т до́ма, мла́дшей

Don't forget to practice and reinforce what you've
learned by visiting **www.livinglanguage.com/
languagelab** for flashcards, games, and quizzes!

# Unit 4 Quiz

## Контро́льная рабо́та №4

Now let's review. In this section you'll be tested on what you've learned in Unit 4. Once you've completed it, score yourself to see how well you've done. If you find that you need to go back and review, please do so before continuing on to the final unit of *Intermediate Russian*.

Let's get started!

A. Fill in the blanks using the correct form of the verb *to feel*. Pay attention to the tense and person of the conjugated verb.

1. Я сего́дня плохо́ _____ .

2. Она́ плохо́ _____ в пя́тницу.

3. Как вы сейча́с_____ ?

4. Спаси́бо, мы сейча́с _____ лу́чше.

5. Всю про́шлую неде́лю он хорошо́ _____ .

B. Say what's hurting these people. Use the information in parentheses and remember to make the verb agree with the number of the aching body part.

1. У меня́ весь день _____ . (*feet, present*)

2. У моего́ дру́га неде́лю _____ . (*teeth, past*)

3. У Никола́й ча́сто _____ . (*head, present*)

4. У меня́ ре́дко _____ . (*stomach, present*)

5. Вчера у него _____. (throat, past)

C. Write how many times per day, week, or year these people do the following things.

1. Я принима́ю лека́рство _____ в день. (three times)

2. Она ме́рит температу́ру _____ в день. (five times)

3. Я хожу́ в спорти́вный зал _____ в неде́лю. (six times)

4. Он де́лает заря́дку _____ в день. (once)

5. Мы отдыха́ем на мо́ре _____ в год. (twice)

D. Fill in the blanks using the correct form of the indefinite or definite pronoun or adverb, –нибудь or –то.

1. У вас _____ есть от ка́шля?

2. Она мне _____ сказа́ла, но я не по́мню, что.

3. Вы _____ были в Росси́и?

4. Он _____ рабо́тает, но я не зна́ю, где.

5. Мы _____ пойдём в суббо́ту.

E. Fill in the blanks using the correct negative pronoun and negation.

1. Я _____ был в Росси́и. (never)

2. Она _____ принима́ет от ка́шля. (nothing)

3. Он сейча́с _____ рабо́тает. (nowhere)

4. Мы _____ пойдём в суббо́ту. (nowhere)

5. _____ пришёл к нам в го́сти. (no one)

F. Fill in the blanks using the correct form of the imperative given in parentheses in English.

1. _____ мне, пожалуйста, это лека́рство. (*buy, sg.*)

2. _____ нам, пожалуйста, пра́вду. (*tell, pl.*)

3. _____, пожалуйста! (*come in, pl.*)

4. _____, пожалуйста, суп. (*eat, sg.*)

5. _____ мне, пожалуйста, это лека́рство. (*prescribe, pl.*)

**ANSWER KEY**

**A.** 1. себя чу́вствую; 2. себя чу́вствовала; 3. себя боле́ли чу́вствуете; 4. себя чу́вствуем; 5. себя чу́вствовал

**B.** 1. боля́т но́ги; 2. болели зу́бы; 3. боли́т голова́; 4. боли́т живо́т; 5. боле́ло го́рло

**C.** 1. три раза; 2. пять раз; 3. шесть раз; 4. раз; 5. два раза

**D.** 1. что́-нибудь; 2. что́-то; 3. когда́-нибудь; 4. где́-то; 5. куда́-нибудь

**E.** 1. никогда́ не; 2. ничего́ не; 3. нигде́ не; 4. никуда́ не; 5. Никто́ не

**F.** 1. Купи́; 2. Скажи́те; 3. Проходи́те; 4. Ешь; 5. Вы́пишите

# How Did You Do?

Give yourself a point for every correct answer, then use the following key to tell whether you're ready to move on:

**0–7 points:** It's probably a good idea to go back through the lesson again. You may be moving too quickly, or there may be too much "down time" between your contact with Russian. Remember that it's better to spend 30 minutes with Russian three or four times a week than it is to spend two or three hours just once a week. Find a pace that's comfortable for you, and spread your contact hours out as much as you can.

**8–12 points:** You would benefit from a review before moving on. Go back and spend a little more time on the specific points that gave you trouble. Re-read the Grammar Builder sections that were difficult, and do the Work Outs one more time. Don't forget about the online supplemental practice material, either. Go to **www.livinglanguage.com/languagelab** for games and quizzes that will reinforce the material from this unit.

**13–17 points:** Good job! There are just a few points that you might consider reviewing before moving on. If you haven't worked with the games and quizzes on **www.livinglanguage.com/languagelab**, please give them a try.

**18–20 points:** Great! You're ready to move on to the next unit.

|  |  |
|--|--|
|  |  |

points

# Unit 5:
## Talking on the Phone

Поздравля́ем с оконча́нием четвёртой главы́ и нача́лом пя́той!
*Congratulations on the completion of Unit 4 and the beginning of Unit 5!*

# Lesson 17: Words

In this lesson, you'll review some of the old words and expressions and also learn how to:

☐ Use various Russian verbs denoting speaking.

☐ Use Russian terms for friendship.

☐ Use basic telephone vocabulary.

☐ Use various Russian verbs denoting meeting.

Гото́вы? Тогда́ начнём! *Ready? Then, let's begin!*
Let's get started with some words and phrases.

## Word Builder 1

▶ 17A Word Builder 1 (CD: 6, Track: 14)

| слу́шать *(imperf., conj. I, –ай)* | *to listen* |
|---|---|
| слы́шать *(imperf., conj. II, –а2)* | *to hear* |

| говори́ть *(imperf., conj.II, –и)* | to speak, to talk |
| сказа́ть *(perf., conj. I, –а)* | to say |
| говори́ть по-ру́сски/по-англи́йски | to speak Russian/English |
| говори́ть по телефо́ну | to talk on the phone |
| разгова́ривать *(imperf., conj. I, –ай)* | to converse, to chat, to talk |
| разгово́р | conversation |
| догова́риваться *(conj. I)*—договори́ться *(conj. II)* о встре́че с юри́стом | to agree (mutually) about a meeting with a lawyer |
| встреча́ть *(conj. I)*—встре́тить дру́га *(conj. II)* встреча́ться *(conj. I)*—встре́титься с дру́гом *(conj. II)* | to meet a friend/to meet with a friend |
| делова́я встре́ча | business meeting |
| би́знес-ланч | business lunch |
| послеза́втра | the day after tomorrow |
| позавчера́ | the day before yesterday |

## Take It Further 1

▶ 17B Take It Further 1 (CD: 6, Track: 15)

The verbs догова́риваться—договори́ться mean *to agree mutually*. You should differentiate them from the verbs соглаша́ться—согласи́ться meaning *to consent*. For example, the sentence они́ договори́лись встре́титься ве́чером means *they agreed to meet in the evening (and it was a mutual decision)*, as opposed to она́ согласи́лась встре́титься с ним ве́чером, which means *she consented to meet with him in the evening (because he insisted)*. It is common to use the perfective verb договори́ться in the past plural form договори́лись when you mean to say affirmatively *yes, okay*, or *agreed*.

You should also be careful to differentiate between the verbs встреча́ть(ся) — встре́тить(ся) and знако́мить(ся) — познако́мить(ся). Although all of them mean *to meet,* the second pair знако́миться — познако́миться stands for making one's acquaintance for the first time, while the first pair встреча́ться — встре́титься is used for all other encounters. When these verbs are transitive, that is, when the action they denote is directed at another party, they drop the reflexive particle —ся: я встре́тил вас у метро́ (*I met you by the metro),* я познако́мил вас с ним (*I introduced you to him*); whereas мы познако́мились на рабо́те means *we met (became acquainted) at work.* In addition, the imperfective verb встреча́ться colloquially means *to date someone:* они́ встреча́ются (*they're dating*).

---

## ✎ Word Practice 1

Let's practice these words. Match the English words on the left with their Russian equivalents on the right. Repeat the Russian words out loud.

| | |
|---|---|
| 1. *conversation* | a. разгова́ривать |
| 2. *to speak (imperf.)* | b. би́знес-ланч |
| 3. *to say (perf.)* | c. встреча́ться |
| 4. *to converse (imperf.)* | d. договори́ться |
| 5. *business meeting* | e. встре́титься |
| 6. *business lunch* | f. сказа́ть |
| 7. *to meet (imperf.)* | g. позавчера́ |
| 8. *to meet (perf.)* | h. делова́я встре́ча |
| 9. *to agree (perf.)* | i. разгово́р |
| 10. *the day before yesterday* | j. говори́ть |

**ANSWER KEY**
1. i; 2. j; 3. f; 4. a; 5. h; 6. b; 7. c; 8. e; 9. d; 10. g

To speak and to listen

Russian time expressions and irregular
endings in the prepositional case

Expressing friendship in
russian

The verbs уйти́ (to leave), прийти́ (
arrive) and дава́ть—дать (to give)

## Grammar Builder 1

▶ 17C Grammar Builder 1 (CD: 6, Track: 16)

### TO SPEAK AND TO LISTEN

Let's learn three verbs for *to speak* in Russian: говори́ть, сказа́ть, and
разгова́ривать. The first one, говори́ть, is an imperfective Conjugation II verb
with the stem ending in an –и. It has no alternations or stress shifts. Its past tense
is also regular: говори́л, говори́ла, говори́ло, говори́ли. This verb denotes a
physical act of speaking. For example, you can speak гро́мко (*loudly*), бы́стро
(*fast*), or ти́хо (*softly*). You can also speak foreign languages: говори́ть по-ру́сски
(*speak Russian*), or говори́ть по-англи́йски (*speak English*).

*To talk on the phone* is говори́ть по телефо́ну.

Он говори́т то́лько по-ру́сски.
*He speaks only Russian.*

Я пло́хо говорю́ по-англи́йски.
*I speak English poorly.*

Мы говори́м по телефо́ну.
*We are speaking on the phone.*

The Conjugation I verb сказа́ть is perfective; it has the а–stem and the з/ж
mutation throughout the entire future tense paradigm, as well as a stress shift.
Its conjugation is similar to the verb писа́ть (*to write*), except that писа́ть
has the с/ш mutation. The past tense of сказа́ть is regular: сказа́л, сказа́ла,
сказа́ло, сказа́ли. This verb means *to say something specific and complete* rather
than *to speak continuously*. When you ask for directions in Russian or any other
information, you typically introduce your request with the following common
phrase:

Дава́й(те) (*Let's*)

Short form adjectives
and comparatives

Telephone grammar

The modal word до́лжен
(*should*), aspect and context

Скажи́те, пожа́луйста …
*Tell (me) please …*

The third verb is разгова́ривать. It's imperfective, Conjugation I with the stem ending in ива(й). It conjugates exactly like ай– verbs, e.g., рабо́тать. The verb разгова́ривать means *to have a conversation*.

Они́ у́жинали в рестора́не и разгова́ривали.
*They were having dinner at a restaurant and talked/conversed.*

The verbs слу́шать and слы́шать correspond to the English verbs *to listen* and *to hear*. Both are imperfective. Слу́шать is Conjugation I with the ай–stem (like рабо́тать); it takes a direct object in the accusative case.

Вы слу́шаете му́зыку?
*Do you listen to music?*

Слы́шать is Conjugation II and belongs to a special subtype. Its stem ends in an –a like in писа́ть, but, as opposed to all a–type verbs which are Conjugation I, слы́шать is Conjugation II. So, its stem should be qualified as a2–stem. Most verbs of this subtype have a husher before the last –a in their stems: слы-ш-а-. This is how they can be recognized and distinguished from regular a–verbs that belong to Conjugation I.

 Before we go on, let's briefly summarize what you need to know about Conjugation II. Only three types of verb stems belong to Conjugation II: e–verbs (e.g., виде-ть), и–verbs (e.g., говори-ть), and a2–verbs with preceding hushers (e.g., слыша-ть). All other Russian stems are Conjugation I. If a Conjugation II verb has a mutation, it occurs only in the first person singular form: я ви́жу, ты ви́дишь, они́ ви́дят, etc. Conjugation II verbs have the endings –ат/ят in the third person plural. All Conjugation II forms (in the present/future tense) have an и in the ending except for the first person singular and third person plural forms.

# ✎ Work Out 1

A. Read the English sentence first, then fill in the blanks using the correct verb, and finally repeat the Russian sentence out loud.

1. *You speak Russian too fast.*

   Ты _____ сли́шком быстро.

2. *What did you (fem.) say? I (masc.) didn't hear.*

   Что ты _____? Я не _____.

3. *They conversed at a restaurant.*

   Они́ _____ в рестора́не.

4. *He spoke on the phone with his wife.*

   Он _____ с жено́й.

5. *I (masc.) conversed with/talked to his daughter.*

   Я _____ с его́ до́черью.

6. *We agreed to meet the day after tomorrow, on Friday.*

   Мы _____ встре́титься послеза́втра, в пя́тницу.

B. Fill in the blanks choosing the right verb *to meet* from the following list: встре́тить, встреча́ться, or познако́миться. Remember to make the verb agree with its subject.

1. Ру́сские партнёры _____ америка́нского бизнесме́на в аэропорту́ вчера́ ве́чером.

2. —Отку́да вы его́ зна́ете? —Мы _____ на делово́й встре́че про́шлым ле́том.

Дава́й(те) (Let's)

Short form adjectives
and comparatives

Telephone grammar

The modal word до́лжен
(should), aspect and context

3. За́втра все ме́неджеры _____ днём на би́знес-ланче.

4. У тебя́ есть брат? Я хочу́ _____ с ним.

5. Приходи́ ко мне в го́сти. Я тебя́ _____ о́коло метро́.

6. По́сле рабо́ты мы всегда́ _____ в э́том кафе́.

**ANSWER KEY**

A. 1. говори́шь по-ру́сски; 2. сказа́ла, слы́шал; 3. разгова́ривали; 4. говори́л по телефо́ну;
5. разгова́ривал; 6. договори́лись

B. 1. встре́тили; 2. встреча́лись; 3. встреча́ются; 4. познако́миться; 5. встре́чу; 6. встреча́емся

# Word Builder 2

▶ 17D Word Builder 2 (CD: 6, Track: 17)

| | |
|---|---|
| к сожале́нию | *unfortunately* |
| знако́мый/знако́мая/знако́мые (*male/female/plural*) | *acquaintance/acquaintances* |
| друг/друзья́ | *(close) friend/friends* |
| звони́ть—позвони́ть (*conj. II; –и*) дру́гу | *to call/to make a phone call to a friend* |
| перезвони́ть (кому́?) | *to call back (lit., re-call) (whom?)* |
| телефо́нный звоно́к | *phone call* |
| телефо́н | *phone, phone number* |
| но́мер телефо́на | *phone number* |
| но́мер | *hotel room* |
| дома́шний телефо́н | *home phone, home phone number* |
| моби́льный телефо́н | *cell phone, cell phone number* |
| спра́шивать (*conj. I; –ай*)—спроси́ть (*conj. II; –и*) | *to ask* |

## Take It Further 2

▶ 17E Take It Further 2 (CD: 6, Track: 18)

The noun телефо́н denotes a *physical phone* or a *phone number,* so the phrase
како́й у вас телефо́н most often means *what's your phone number* but it can
also be used to ask what brand of phone you have. The full Russian phrase
for *phone number* is телефо́нный но́мер or но́мер телефо́на. The phrase
моби́льный телефо́н means either *cell phone* (the object) or *cell phone number*;
дома́шний телефо́н usually stands for *home phone number.* So it's common to
say перезвони́(те) мне на моби́льный/дома́шний телефо́н (*call me back on
my cell/home phone*); notice the use of the accusative case after the preposition на
(на дома́шний телефо́н/на рабо́ту/дом, etc.). The colloquial or slang terms for
*cell phone* in Russian are: моби́льный, моби́льник, моби́ла, тру́бка, труба́. The
verb звони́ть—позвони́ть belongs to Conjugation II; it has the и-stem without
mutations or stress shifts. It means *to call /to make a phone call.* Note that it takes
the dative case (not the accusative): позвони́(те) мне (*call me*). Перезвони́ть
means to call back, literally *to re-call.* It's common to say я перезвоню́ попо́зже
(*I'll call back later*), or перезвони́(те) попо́зже ([*you*] *call back later*).

## ✎ Word Practice 2

Let's practice these words. Match the English words on the left to their Russian
equivalents on the right. Repeat the Russian words out loud.

1. *close friends*

2. *acquaintance (male)*

3. *acquaintance (female)*

4. *phone number*

5. *cell phone (number)*

6. *to ask (imperf.)*

7. *to ask (perf.)*

a. позвони́ть дру́гу

b. но́мер телефо́на

c. спроси́ть

d. друзья́

e. но́мер

f. знако́мый

g. телефо́нный звоно́к

Давáй(те) (*Let's*)

Short form adjectives
and comparatives

Telephone grammar

The modal word дóлжен
(*should*), aspect and context

8. *phone call*

h. спрáшивать

9. *to make a phone call to a friend (perf.)*

i. знакóмая

10. *hotel room*

j. мобúльный телефóн

**ANSWER KEY**
1. d; 2. f; 3. i; 4. b; 5. j; 6. h; 7. c; 8. g; 9. a; 10. e

# Grammar Builder 2
▶ 17F Grammar Builder 2 (CD: 6, Track: 19)

## EXPRESSING FRIENDSHIP IN RUSSIAN

The Russian word друг denotes a closer relationship than its English counterpart *friend*. Друг can be translated more accurately as *close friend*. Memorize the irregular plural друзья́ (*friends*). Also, keep in mind that друг usually doesn't imply a romantic relationship (though it can be used to indirectly refer to someone as one's boyfriend.) The Russian language doesn't really have a standard neutral word for *boyfriend*. All of its possible equivalents are stylistically marked in Russian. For example, молодóй человéк (*lit., young man*) is somewhat euphemistic and old-fashioned—parents sometimes use this word to refer to boyfriends of their daughters; пáрень (*lit., youth, guy*) is more neutral but some would say a bit folksy; бойфренд (*boyfriend*), recently borrowed from English, is trendy and foreign.

The situation is slightly better for the word *girlfriend*. Russians do have a standard term, дéвушка (*lit., girl, young lady*) with the restrictions that first, it applies only to young girls and second, it is distinguished from the regular word, *young lady*, only by the context. Alternatively, there is also a new borrowing гéрлфренд (*girlfriend*). Note that the phrase э́то моя́ дéвушка means *this is my girlfriend*, and not *this is my girl*. The Russian term подрýга (*female friend*) usually refers to a female friend of a female and doesn't normally indicate a romantic relationship, unless in jest.

For a less close friendship, Russians use знакóмый, the equivalent of the English *acquaintance*. As you can see, знакóмый is a substantivized adjective;

consequently, it has adjectival endings: знако́мая for a *female friend*, and знако́мые for the plural form.

Это мой друг.
*This is my friend. (This is my boyfriend.)*

Это моя́ де́вушка.
*This is my girlfriend.*

Это мой знако́мый.
*This is my acquaintance.*

 **Tip!**

Use mnemonic devices for the words and expressions that are hard to remember or differentiate. It doesn't matter how silly or personal you make them. In fact, the sillier or more striking they are, the better you'll remember them! For example, to make a distinction between слу́шать (*to listen*) and слы́шать (*to hear*), think of the phrase слу́шать му́зыку (*listen to music*) where you have assonance (repeated vowels) in the three у. This way, you'll remember that the у in the root stands for music and for listening. Take time to create your own mnemonic devices and they will help you remember many Russian expressions and grammar points!

## ✎ Work Out 2

A. Find the appropriate Russian term for the following definitions of your friend. Choose one of the following: друг, подру́га, знако́мый, знако́мая, де́вушка, бо́йфренд, гёрлфренд.

1. You're a female and you have a good friend who's also a female.

Давай(те) (*Let's*)

Short form adjectives
and comparatives

Telephone grammar

The modal word до́лжен
(*should*), aspect and context

2. You're a male and you have a good male friend.

_____

3. Your acquaintance is a male.

_____

4. You're a "trendy" female and you have a boyfriend.

_____

5. You're a female and your acquaintance is a female.

_____

6. You're a young male and you have a girlfriend of your age.

_____

B. Как сказа́ть по-ру́сски? Translate the following sentences into Russian.

1. *Call (inform.) me on (my) cell phone.*

_____

2. *This is my home phone number.*

_____

3. *He called me back on my home phone number.*

_____

4. *Her friends call me every day.*

_____

5. *Your (form.) acquaintances didn't call me back.*

_____

*To speak* and *to listen*

Russian time expressions and irregular
endings in the prepositional case

Expressing friendship in
russian

The verbs уйти (*to leave*), прийти (
*arrive*) and давать—дать (*to give*)

6. *Call (form.) me back at work tomorrow after lunch.*

---

**ANSWER KEY**
A. 1. подру́га; 2. друг; 3. знако́мый; 4. бойфренд; 5. знако́мая; 6. де́вушка
B. 1. Позвони́ мне на моби́льный телефо́н. 2. Это мой дома́шний телефо́н. 3. Он мне
перезвони́л на дома́шний телефо́н. 4. Её друзья́ звоня́т мне ка́ждый день. 5. Ва́ши
знако́мые не перезвони́ли мне. 6. Перезвони́те мне на рабо́ту за́втра по́сле обе́да.

## ✎ Drive It Home

Now, let's do more practice on the different forms of the phrase *to call someone on
the phone* (звони́ть по телефо́ну + dative). Read the English sentence first, then
fill in the blanks with the correct phrase, and finally, repeat the entire Russian
sentence out loud.

1. *He often calls me on the phone.*

   Он ча́сто _____ по телефо́ну.

2. *Yesterday, he called (perf.) me at 12 at night.*

   Вчера́ он _____ в двена́дцать часо́в но́чи.

3. *Please call me the day after tomorrow.*

   Пожа́луйста, _____ послеза́втра.

4. *Please call her back a little later.*

   Пожа́луйста, _____ попо́зже.

5. *Thank you, I'll call him back a little later.*

   Спаси́бо, я _____ попо́зже.

6. *We called (perf.) him on his cell phone.*

   Мы _____ на _____.

Давáй(те) (*Let's*)

Short form adjectives
and comparatives

Telephone grammar

The modal word дóлжен
(*should*), aspect and context

7. *We called (imperf.) him at home but he wasn't at home.*

Мы _____ домóй, но егó нé бы́ло дóма.

8. *What's your home phone number? I'll call you tonight.*

Какóй ваш _____? Я _____

сегóдня вéчером.

**ANSWER KEY**

1. звони́т мне; 2. позвони́л мне; 3. позвони́те мне; 4. перезвони́те ей; 5. перезвоню́ ему; 6. позвони́ли ему, моби́льный; 7. звони́ли ему; 8. домáшний телефóн, позвоню́ вам

## How Did You Do?

Let's see how you did in this lesson. You should know how to:

☐ Use various Russian verbs denoting speaking. (Still unsure? Go back to page 256.)

☐ Use Russian terms for friendship. (Still unsure? Go back to page 259.)

☐ Use basic telephone vocabulary. (Still unsure? Go back to page 259.)

☐ Use various Russian verbs denoting meeting. (Still unsure? Go back to page 261.)

## ✎ Word Recall

Now it's time to review some words, phrases, and constructions from the earlier lessons. Read the English sentence first, then fill in the blanks, and finally, repeat the Russian sentence out loud.

1. *Take (inform.) this medication every day.*

_____ э́то _____ кáждый день.

2. *Did they buy anything at the pharmacy?*

Они́ _____ в аптéке?

Expressing friendship in russian

3. *Is anything bothering you?*

   Вас чтó-нибудь _____?

4. *No, nothing's bothering me.*

   Нет, _____ беспокóит _____.

5. *Did you go (fem.) to the doctor's?*

   Ты _____ к врачу́?

6. *On Monday(s), Wendesday(s), and Friday(s), I go to the gym.*

   _____ я хожу́ в

   спорти́вный зал.

7. *I buy groceries and cook by myself.*

   Я _____ и _____.

8. *After work, I like to ride (my) bike.*

   Пóсле рабóты я люблю́ _____.

9. *Do you (inform.) play sports?*

   Ты _____?

10. *Yes, I swim in the swimming pool.*

   Да, я _____ в бассéйне.

**ANSWER KEY**

1. Принима́й, лека́рство; 2. чтó-нибудь купи́ли; 3. беспокóит; 4. ничегó не, меня́; 5. ходи́ла; 6. В понеде́льник, сре́ду и пя́тницу; 7. сам покупа́ю проду́кты, готóвлю; 8. ката́ться на велосипе́де; 9. занима́ешься спóртом; 10. пла́ваю

# Lesson 18: Phrases

Добро́ пожа́ловать ещё раз! *Welcome once again!*

In this lesson, you'll learn how to:

☐ Use basic time expressions in Russian.

☐ Use some irregular nouns in the prepositional case of location.

☐ Use some basic phrases for telephone etiquette.

☐ Talk about arriving and leaving in Russian.

☐ Use the irregular verb *to give* in Russian.

Гото́вы? Тогда́ начнём! *Ready? Then, let's begin!*

Let's get started with some useful phrases.

## Phrase Builder 1

▶ 18A Phrase Builder 1 (CD: 6, Track: 20)

| договори́ться о встре́че | to set up a meeting (lit., agree about a meeting) |
|---|---|
| гла́вный о́фис фи́рмы | main office of the firm/company |
| штаб-кварти́ра фи́рмы | company's headquarters |
| в про́шлый понеде́льник | last Monday |
| на э́той неде́ле | this week |
| в бу́дущем/сле́дующем ме́сяце | next month |
| в бу́дущем/сле́дующем году́ | next year |

*To speak* and *to listen*

Russian time expressions and irregular
endings in the prepositional case

Expressing friendship in
russian

The verbs уйти (*to leave*), прийти (
*arrive*) and давать—дать (*to give*)

| в пе́рвой полови́не дня | *in the morning (lit., in the first half of the day)* |
| во второ́й полови́не дня | *in the afternoon (lit., in the second half of the day)* |
| в неформа́льной обстано́вке | *informally (lit., in an informal setting)* |
| у себя́ в кабине́те | *at one's own office* |
| С прие́здом! | *Welcome! (lit., With arrival!)* |
| Как (вы) долете́ли? | *How was (your) flight?* |

## Take It Further 1

When Russians make appointments, they often refer to the morning part of the day, before lunch, as пе́рвая полови́на дня, literally, *(the) first half (of the) day*. The afternoon part of the work day is втора́я полови́на дня, literally, *(the) second half (of the) day*. Remember that you need to use these time expressions with the prepositional case: в пе́рвой полови́не дня, во второ́й полови́не дня.

Notice the reflexive personal pronoun себя́ in the phrase: у себя́ в кабине́те (*in his own office*). This pronoun refers to the subject of the sentence. It stays in the same form regardless of the grammatical person of the subject. So you should say: он у себя́ в кабине́те, она́ у себя́ в кабине́те, я у себя́ в кабине́те, etc. Literally, the phrase он у себя́ в кабине́те means *he is at his (own) office*. This is the most idiomatic way of expressing this idea in Russian.

## ✎ Phrase Practice 1

Let's practice the new expressions. Match the English phrases on the left with their Russian equivalents on the right. Repeat the Russian phrases out loud.

1. *last Monday*                    a. в пе́рвой полови́не дня

Давáй(те) (*Let's*)

Short form adjectives
and comparatives

Telephone grammar

The modal word дóлжен
(*should*), aspect and context

| | |
|---|---|
| 2. *last week* | b. С приéздом! |
| 3. *next month* | c. у себя́ в кабинéте |
| 4. *next year* | d. в прóшлый понедéльник |
| 5. *in the first half of the day* | e. Как вы долетéли? |
| 6. *in the second half of the day* | f. в слéдующем году́ |
| 7 *Welcome (lit., with arrival)!* | g. на прóшлой недéле |
| 8. *How was (your) flight?* | h. договори́ться о встрéче |
| 9. *at one's own office* | i. во вторóй полови́не дня |
| 10. *set up a meeting* | j. в бу́дущем мéсяце |

**ANSWER KEY**
1. d; 2. g; 3. j; 4. f; 5. a; 6. i; 7. b; 8. e; 9. c; 10. h

# Grammar Builder 1

▶ 18B Grammar Builder 1 (CD: 6, Track: 21)

## RUSSIAN TIME EXPRESSIONS AND IRREGULAR ENDINGS IN THE PREPOSITIONAL CASE

When you need *to set up a meeting* (договори́ться о встрéче), you need to use time expressions in order to say *when* (когда́). Russian time expressions are different from the English ones, and you can't just translate them word for word. They also don't conform to one general rule. Yet they aren't random either. Let's notice certain patterns among Russian time expressions—they'll help you remember and use them properly. You already know how to say in the morning, in the afternoon, in the evening, and at night in Russian; how to say on a given day of the week; and how to say on a given date. Now, consider the following rules of thumb:

if the time unit is less than a week, use the preposition в with the accusative case: в пя́тницу (*on Friday*), в э́ту мину́ту (*this minute*), в э́тот день (*this/that day*), etc;

*To speak* and *to listen*

Russian time expressions and irregular
endings in the prepositional case

Expressing friendship in
russian

The verbs уйти (*to leave*), прийти
*arrive*) and дава́ть—дать (*to give*

if the time unit is a week, use the preposition на with the prepositional case: на э́той неде́ле (*this week*), на про́шлой неде́ле (*last week*), на бу́дущей неде́ле (*next week*), etc;

if the time unit is more than a week, use the preposition в with the prepositional case: в э́том ме́сяце (*this month*), в бу́дущем году́ (*next year*), в про́шлом ве́ке (*in the last century*), etc.

The adjectives бу́дущий (*next*), сле́дующий (*next* or *the next*), or про́шлый (*last* or *past*) are commonly used with the above time expressions. But remember to make them agree with the nouns they modify!

Did you notice the irregular prepositional ending у in the phrase в бу́дущем году́? This ending occurs in a limited number of Russian masculine one syllable nouns in the prepositional case only after the prepositions denoting *location* (в or на). These nouns end in a hard consonant, and their locative ending у is always stressed. Look at the following chart.

| бе́рег (*from the OldSlavonic* брег) | на берегу́ | *shore, on the shore* |
|---|---|---|
| глаз | в глазу́ | *eye, in the eye* |
| год | в году́ | *year, in the year* |
| лес | в лесу́ | *forest/woods, in the woods* |
| мост | на мосту́ | *bridge, on the bridge* |
| нос | на носу́ | *nose, on the nose* |
| порт | в порту́ | *port, at the port* |
| ряд | в ряду́ | *row, in the row* |

Note that the phrase в углу́ means *in the corner (of a room)*; the phrase на углу́ means *at the corner (of a street)*.

| сад  | в садý          | garden/orchard, in the garden |
| угол | в углý/на углý  | corner, in the corner/at the corner |
| час  | в часý          | hour, in the hour |
| шкаф | в шкафý         | cabinet/dresser/cupboard, in the cabinet/dresser/cupboard |

Note that the phrase в углý means *in the corner (of a room)*; the phrase на углý means *at the corner (of a street)*.

# ✎ Work Out 1

A. Когдá вы встрéтились или встрéтитесь с вáшим дрýгом? (*When did you meet or will you meet with your friend?*) Complete the sentences below by filling in the blanks with the time expressions in parentheses.

1. Мы встречáлись два рáза _____. (*last year*)

2. Вы встрéтитесь с дирéктором _____. (*this week*)

3. Онú встречáются на бúзнес-ланч _____. (*this Wednesday*)

4. Я встрéчусь с вáшим знакóмым _____.

    (*next week*)

5. Ты с ним встречáешься _____. (*next year*)

6. Мы бóльше не бýдем встречáться _____. (*this month*)

*To speak* and *to listen*

Russian time expressions and irregular
endings in the prepositional case

Expressing friendship in
russian

The verbs уйти (*to leave*), прийти (
*arrive*) and давать—дать (*to give*)

**B.** Как сказа́ть по-ру́сски? Translate the following sentences into Russian.

1. *The director is in his office.*

   _____

2. *We arranged a meeting in an informal setting.*

   _____

3. *Welcome! How was your flight?*

   _____

4. *They will meet in the main office of the firm in the second half of the day.*

   _____

5. *I will meet you (form.) at the corner of the street.*

   _____

**ANSWER KEY**

A. 1. в про́шлом году́; 2. на э́той неде́ле; 3. в сре́ду; 4. на сле́дующей неде́ле; 5. в сле́дующем
году́; 6.в э́том ме́сяце

B. 1. Дире́ктор у себя́ в кабине́те. 2. Мы договори́лись встре́титься в неформа́льной
обстано́вке. 3. С прие́здом! Как вы долете́ли? 4. Они́ встре́тятся в гла́вном о́фисе фи́рмы во
второ́й полови́не дня. 5. Я встре́чу вас на углу́ у́лицы.

# Phrase Builder 2

▶ 18C Phrase Builder 2 (CD: 6, Track: 22)

| Алло́!/Алле́! | Hello! (only when you pick up the phone) |
|---|---|
| Отку́да вы звони́те? | Where are you calling from? |
| звони́ть—позвони́ть из гости́ницы | to call from a hotel |
| остана́вливаться (*conj. I,* –ай)—останови́ться (*conj. II,* –и) в гости́нице | to stay in a hotel |

Intermediate Russian

Давай(те) (*Let's*)

Short form adjectives
and comparatives

Telephone grammar

The modal word до́лжен
(*should*), aspect and context

| уйти́ (*perf.*) в магази́н | to leave for a store |
| прийти́ (*perf.*) домо́й | to come home |
| верну́ться (*perf., conj. I, –ну*) домо́й | to come back/return home |
| да́йте мне, пожа́луйста, ваш телефо́н | give me your phone number please |
| дава́ть—дать (*irregular*) | to give |
| запи́сывать—записа́ть телефо́н | to write down the phone number |
| ждать—подожда́ть (*conj. I, –а*) звонка́ | to wait for a phone call |

## Take It Further 2

▶ 18D Take It Further 2 (CD: 6, Track: 23)

The verbs ждать—подожда́ть (*to wait for*) are regular. They belong to Conjugation I with the а–stem. However, as opposed to their English counterpart which uses a preposition *for*, the Russian verbs take a direct object in the accusative case: я жду А́ню (*I'm waiting [for] Anya*), ты ждёшь дире́ктора (*you're waiting [for] the director* [notice the animate form!]), они́ подожду́т меня́ (*they will wait [for] me*), etc. Also remember that the imperative form of this verb is usually perfective in Russian: подожди́(те) меня́ (*wait [for] me*). The genitive звонка́ (*call*) in the phrase ждать звонка́ is idiomatic; it comes from the somewhat outdated genitive partitive case. It means *waiting for any kind of phone call* as opposed to *waiting for a more specific phone call*: ждать звоно́к. However, this distinction is not strong in modern Russian so both forms are fully interchangeable.

*To speak* and *to listen*

**Russian time expressions and irregular endings in the prepositional case**

Expressing friendship in
russian

The verbs уйти́ (*to leave*), прийти́
*arrive*) and дава́ть—дать (*to give*

## ✎ Phrase Practice 2

Let's practice the new expressions. Match the English phrases on the left with
their Russian equivalents on the right. Repeat the Russian phrases out loud.

1. *give me your phone number*       a. останови́ться в гости́нице

2. *to write down the phone number*  b. Отку́да вы звони́те?

3. *to come home*                    c. звони́ть из гости́ницы

4. *to come back home*               d. записа́ть телефо́н

5. *to stay in a hotel*              e. ждать звонка́

6. *Where are you calling from?*     f. дава́ть

7. *to call from a hotel*            g. уйти́ в магази́н

8. *to wait for a phone call*        h. верну́ться домо́й

9. *to leave for a store*            i. да́йте мне ваш телефо́н

10. *to give*                        j. прийти́ домо́й

**ANSWER KEY**
1. i; 2. d; 3. j; 4. h; 5. a; 6. b; 7. c; 8. e; 9. g; 10. f

## Grammar Builder 2

▶ 18E Grammar Builder 2 (CD: 6, Track: 24)

### THE VERBS УЙТИ́ (*TO LEAVE*), ПРИЙТИ́ (*TO ARRIVE*), AND ДАВА́ТЬ—ДАТЬ (*TO GIVE*)

Let's look at the perfective motion verbs уйти́ and прийти́. Both denote a
pedestrian action rather than a vehicular one. The verb уйти́ means *to leave a
place on foot*; the verb прийти́ means *to arrive on foot*. Both verbs can also denote
a movement within the city limits (even including vehicular ones!) when the mode
of transport is irrelevant, but it's important that the activity is a local one. Thus, the
sentence они́ приду́т ко мне в го́сти (*they will come over to my house*) doesn't
necessarily mean that they will walk. It merely implies that we live in the same
city, and they'll visit me locally; the mode of their transport stays unidentified

Давай(те) (*Let's*)

Short form adjectives
and comparatives

Telephone grammar

The modal word до́лжен
(*should*), aspect and context

and irrelevant. Remember that, since both verbs are perfective, they don't have a present tense. This is how these verbs are conjugated in the future tense.

| УЙТИ́ | |
|---|---|
| *TO LEAVE A PLACE ON FOOT* | |
| я уйду́ | мы уйдём |
| ты уйдёшь | вы уйдёте |
| он/она́/оно́ уйдёт | они́ уйду́т |

| ПРИЙТИ́ | |
|---|---|
| *TO ARRIVE ON FOOT* | |
| я приду́ | мы придём |
| ты придёшь | вы придёте |
| он/она́/оно́ придёт | они́ приду́т |

The prefix у– means *away from*; the prefix при– means *to*. Notice how the stem ид– in the verb идти́ mutates when these prefixes are added to it: у-йд-у and при-д-у; and in the infinitives: у-й-ти and при-й-ти.

These verbs need to be contrasted with the verbs вы́йти (*to leave, to exit*) and войти́ (*to enter*). These two verbs describe shorter movements, ones that emphasize a physical exiting and entering rather than just leaving a place or arriving at it. The verb вы́йти is often used when a specific time of leaving is mentioned, and when the person is expected to be back. For example, you should say я вы́шел/вы́шла из до́ма в во́семь часо́в утра́ (*I left home at eight o'clock in the morning*), because the action happened at a specific time, and you will also be back by the end of the day.

The verb уйти́ denotes *to leave* as a more radical departure, such as *for the day* or *for good*. For example, you should say он ушёл с рабо́ты в пять часо́в ве́чера (*he left work at five p.m.*), regardless of the specific time в пять часо́в (*five p.m*) being mentioned because he *left for the day*. Moreover, the phrase он ушёл с рабо́ты in a different context can mean *he quit his job*.

The past tense forms of these verbs are predictable if you remember the past tense of the verb идти́ (шёл, шла, шло, шли): ушёл/ушла́, пришёл/пришла́, вы́шел/вы́шла (the prefix вы– is always stressed in perfective verbs!), etc.

The phrases прийти́ домо́й (to *come home*) and верну́ться домо́й (to *return home*) are synonymous. Notice that, because of the movement toward home, the adverb домо́й is in the directional form (домо́й) rather than its locative form (до́ма).

Now let's look at the verbs дава́ть/дать (*to give*), which are irregular in both the imperfective and perfective forms.

| ДАВА́ТЬ TO GIVE, IMPERF. | |
|---|---|
| я даю́ | мы даём |
| ты даёшь | вы даёте |
| он/она́/оно́ даёт | они́ даю́т |

Past: дава́л, дава́ла, дава́ло, дава́ли

| ДАТЬ TO GIVE, PERF. | |
|---|---|
| я дам | мы дади́м |
| ты дашь | вы дади́те |
| он/она́/оно́ даст | они́ даду́т |

Past: дал, дала́, дало́, да́ли

The past tenses are regular for both verbs: дава́л, дава́ла, дава́ло, дава́ли and дал, дала́, дало́, да́ли (though notice the slightly irregular feminine/neuter stress shift for дала́/дало́). Дава́й(те) is the imperfective imperative; the perfective imperative is дай(те).

Давай(те) (*Let's*)

Short form adjectives
and comparatives

Telephone grammar

The modal word до́лжен
(*should*), aspect and context

Дава́ть/дать take the accusative case for direct object and the dative for indirect object (the recipient of the action).

Да́йте мне (*dat.*), пожа́луйста, ваш телефо́н (*acc.*).
*Give me your telephone number, please.*

# ✎ Work Out 2

A. Fill in the blanks using the correct form of the motion verb given in parentheses. Pay attention to the conjugation, agreement, and tense!

1. Я _____ из до́ма в де́вять часо́в утра́. (*left/exited*)

2. Она́ _____ домо́й по́сле рабо́ты ве́чером. (*will come*)

3. Сего́дня я _____ с рабо́ты в шесть часо́в ве́чера. (*will leave*)

4. Мы _____ из такси́ и _____ в гла́вный о́фис фи́рмы. (*exited, entered*)

5. Я перезвони́л ей, когда́ она́ _____ на рабо́ту. (*came*)

B. Give Russian equivalents to the following English sentences.

1. *I'll call you (form.) from the hotel.*

_____

2. *Give (inform.) me, please, your phone number. I'll write it down.*

_____

3. *Wait (pl.) for him! He'll come in a minute.*

_____

To speak *and* *to listen*

Russian time expressions and irregular
endings in the prepositional case

Expressing friendship in
russian

The verbs уйти (*to leave*), прийти (
*arrive*) and давать—дать (*to give*)

4. *We'll stay in a hotel in the center of the city.*

_____

5. *When will you (form.) return home?*

_____

**ANSWER KEY**
A. 1. ушёл; 2. придёт; 3. уйду; 4.вы́шли, вошли́; 5. пришла́
B. 1. Я позвоню́ вам из гости́ницы. 2. Дай мне, пожа́луйста, твой но́мер телефо́на. Я его́
запишу́. 3. Подожди́те его́! Он придёт че́рез мину́ту. 4. Мы остано́вимся в гости́нице в
це́нтре го́рода. 5. Когда́ вы вернётесь домо́й?

## ✎ Drive It Home

Now, let's do more practice on the time expressions. Fill in the blanks with the
correct form of one of these phrases in parentheses and then repeat the entire
Russian sentence out loud.

1. Мои́ друзья́ прие́дут _____. (*next week*)

2. Мои́ друзья́ прие́дут _____. (*next year*)

3. Мои́ друзья́ прие́дут _____. (*this month*)

4. Мои́ друзья́ прие́дут _____. (*this week*)

5. Мои́ друзья́ прие́хали _____. (*last week*)

6. Мои́ друзья́ прие́хали _____. (*last month*)

7. Мои́ друзья́ прие́хали _____. (*last year*)

8. Мои́ друзья́ прие́дут _____. (*on Wednesday*)

9. Мои́ друзья́ прие́дут _____. (*on Saturday*)

Давáй(те) (*Let's*)

Short form adjectives
and comparatives

Telephone grammar

The modal word дóлжен
(*should*), aspect and context

**ANSWER KEY**

1. на слéдующей недéле; 2. в слéдующем годý; 3. в э́том мéсяце; 4. на э́той недéле; 5. на прóшлой недéле; 6. в прóшлом мéсяце; 7. в прóшлом годý; 8. в срéду; 9. в суббóту

# How Did You Do?

Let's see how you did in this lesson. You should know how to:

☐ Use basic time expressions in Russian. (Still unsure? Go back to page 269.)

☐ Use some irregular nouns in the prepositional case of location. (Still unsure? Go back to page 269.)

☐ Use some basic phrases for telephone etiquette. (Still unsure? Go back to page 272.)

☐ Talk about arriving and leaving in Russian. (Still unsure? Go back to page 274.)

☐ Use the irregular verb *to give* in Russian. (Still unsure? Go back to page 276.)

# ✎ Word Recall

Now it's time to review some words, phrases, and constructions from the earlier lessons. Read the English sentence first, then fill in the blanks, and finally, repeat the Russian sentence out loud.

1. *How are you feeling today?*

   Как вы _____ сегóдня?

2. *I'm feeling well.*

   Я _____ хорошó.

3. *She can help you today.*

   Онá _____ вам помóчь сегóдня.

*To speak* and *to listen*

Russian time expressions and irregular
endings in the prepositional case

Expressing friendship in
russian

The verbs уйти́ (*to leave*), прийти́ (
*arrive*) and дава́ть—дать (*to give*)

4. *I can buy you groceries tomorrow.*

   Я _____ купи́ть вам _____ за́втра.

5. *Good job!*

   _____!

6. *It seems to me that I'm getting sick.*

   Мне _____, что я заболе́ла.

7. *I have a headache.*

   У меня́ _____ голова́.

8. *My ears are hurting.*

   У меня́ _____ уши.

9. *I'm well settled (masc.) in my new apartment.*

   Я хорошо́ _____ в мое́й но́вой кварти́ре.

10. *She went to Moscow in 1999.*

    Она́ _____ в Москву в ты́сяча девятьсо́т_____

    _____ году́.

**ANSWER KEY**
1. себя́ чу́вствуете; 2. чу́вствую себя́; 3. мо́жет; 4. могу́, проду́кты; 5. Молоде́ц; 6. ка́жется;
7. боли́т; 8. боля́т; 9. устро́ился; 10. е́здила, девяно́сто девя́том

Давай(те) (*Let's*)

Short form adjectives
and comparatives

Telephone grammar

The modal word до́лжен
(*should*), aspect and context

# Lesson 19: Sentences

Добро́ пожа́ловать ещё раз! Welcome once again!

In this lesson, you'll review some of the old words and expressions and also learn how to:

☐ Say *let's do something* in Russian.

☐ Say that someone *isn't, wasn't,* or *won't be* somewhere.

☐ Use essential expressions for telephone etiquette.

Гото́вы? Тогда́ начнём! *Ready? Then, let's begin!*
Let's get started with some useful phrases.

## Sentence Builder 1

▶ 19A Sentence Builder 1 (CD: 6, Track: 25)

| | |
|---|---|
| Я вас слу́шаю. | *I'm listening to you. (form., used instead of "hello")* |
| Здра́вствуйте, э́то говори́т Ива́н Петро́в. | *Hello, this is Ivan Petrov speaking.* |
| Вас беспоко́ит Ива́н Петро́в. | *Ivan Petrov calling (formal; lit., Ivan Petrov is disturbing you.)* |
| Соедини́те меня́, пожа́луйста, с Алекса́ндром Васи́льевичем. | *Connect me, please, with Aleksandr Vasilievich. (Transfer me, please, to Aleksandr Vasilievich.)* |
| Подожди́те, пожа́луйста, одну́ мину́ту. | *Just a minute, please (lit., Wait, please, for one minute.)* |

| Одну́ мину́точку. | One minute. |
|---|---|
| Я звоню́, что́бы договори́ться о на́шей встре́че. | I'm calling in order to set up our meeting (lit., to agree about our meeting). |
| Я вас бу́ду ждать за́втра у себя́ в кабине́те. | I'll wait for you tomorrow in my office. |
| Мы мо́жем встре́титься за́втра в любо́е вре́мя. | We can meet any time tomorrow. |
| Дава́йте встре́тимся в пя́тницу, в де́сять часо́в утра́. | Let's meet on Friday, at 10 a.m. |
| Дава́йте вме́сте пойдём на обе́д/ ланч/би́знес-ланч. | Let's go have lunch together. |
| Дава́йте продо́лжим разгово́р в неформа́льной обстано́вке. | Let's continue (this) conversation in an informal setting. |

## Take It Further 1

▶ 19B Take It Further 1 (CD: 6, Track: 26)

The neologism ланч (*lunch*) is mostly used for a business lunch in Russian, which is often just another expression for a *prix fixe* afternoon meal in a restaurant. Обе́д (*lunch*) is the word for a more traditional midday meal.

The Russian что́бы + *infinitive* is equivalent to the English expression *in order to* + *infinitive*. The sentence я звоню́, что́бы договори́ться о на́шей встре́че means *I'm calling in order to set up our meeting*. As in English, both clauses refer to the same subject: I'm calling and I'm trying to set up a meeting. So just as in English, you can leave out что́бы (*in order to*) in colloquial speech and simply say я звоню́ договори́ться о на́шей встре́че (*I'm calling to set up our meeting*). The following infinitive is often perfective because you do something *in order to* accomplish it.

Здра́вствуйте, э́то говори́т + *nominative,* Вас беспоко́ит + *nominative,* or соедини́те меня́, пожа́луйста, с + *instrumental* are more formal expressions in Russian phone etiquette. It's not customary to introduce oneself when calling someone at home. However, people do so in formal situations. The elliptic phrases одну́ мину́ту or одну́ мину́точку/мину́тку are in the accusative case because the imperative подожди́(те) (*wait for*) is implied. So the full sentence would be: Пожа́луйста, подожди́те одну́ мину́ту! (*Please wait for one minute!*). It's common and idiomatic to leave out подожди́те, пожа́луйста in the situations when you ask somebody to wait for a moment. You can also replace the noun мину́та in the accusative case with other nouns in the accusative that denote intervals of time: мину́точка/мину́тка (*little minute*), секу́нда (*second*)/ секу́ндочка (*little second*), etc. So you can equally say: одну́ мину́ту or одну́ мину́точку, одну́ секу́нду, or одну́ секу́ндочку.

## ✎Sentence Practice 1

Let's practice the new sentences. Match the English phrases on the left with their Russian equivalents on the right. Repeat the Russian phrases out loud.

1. *I'll wait for you tomorrow in my office.*

2. *Let's meet on Friday.*

3. *Let's meet at 10 a.m.*

4. *Just a minute please.*

5. *This is Ivan Petrov speaking.*

6. *I'm listening.*

7. *I'm calling to set up our meeting.*

a. Одну́ мину́ту, пожа́луйста.

b. Э́то говори́т Ива́н Петро́в.

c. Я звоню́, что́бы договори́ться о на́шей встре́че.

d. в неформа́льной обстано́вке

e. Я вас слу́шаю.

f. Дава́йте встре́тимся в пя́тницу.

g. Мы мо́жем встре́титься за́втра в любо́е вре́мя.

8. *We can meet any time tomorrow.*

h. Дава́йте продо́лжим наш разгово́р.

9. *Let's continue our conversation.*

i. Дава́йте встре́тимся в де́сять часо́в утра́.

10. *in an informal setting*

j. Я вас бу́ду ждать за́втра у себя́ в кабине́те.

**ANSWER KEY**
1. j; 2. f; 3. i; 4. a; 5. b; 6. e; 7. c; 8. g; 9. h; 10. d

# Grammar Builder 1

▶ 19C Grammar Builder 1 (CD: 6, Track: 27)

## ДАВА́Й(ТЕ) (*LET'S*)

Now, let's learn one more way of expressing commands in Russian. Besides standard imperatives, you can also use the inclusive command that starts with *let's*. It consists of two parts: first, the imperative дава́й(те), and then, either the imperfective infinitive or the 1st person plural form of a perfective verb. This is how you should make your choice of aspect. If what you're suggesting is an expected, continuous, or recurrent action, you should use the imperfective infinitive after дава́й(те).

Дава́йте обе́дать!
*Let's have lunch! (i.e., let's go ahead and have lunch, the one you've been expecting to have).*

Дава́й всегда́ встреча́ться в це́нтре!
*Let's always meet downtown! (всегда́ marks a recurrent action and calls for the imperfective aspect)*

Дава́й(те) (*Let's*)

Short form adjectives
and comparatives

Telephone grammar

The modal word до́лжен
(*should*), aspect and context

However, if what you're suggesting is a perfective singular action—one that requires a change of state and is relatively new to the context—you need to have the perfective verb in the first person plural.

Дава́йте встре́тимся в це́нтре!

*Let's meet downtown! (i.e., let's this time do something different and meet downtown)*

Дава́й пойдём в кино́!

*Let's go to the movies! (i.e., let's get out of the house and go to the movies instead)*

The expression пойдём (*let's go*), which you learned in Unit 1, is an elliptic command; дава́йте пойдём (*let's go*) is a full expression. Notice that for the elliptic form—and only for this elliptic command (*let's) go (on foot)*—there exists the plural elliptic form: Пойдёмте!

# ✎ Work Out 1

A. Fill in the blanks with the appropriate Russian forms of the English verbs in parentheses.

1. Дава́йте _____ в теа́тр сего́дня ве́чером. (*go*)

2. Дава́йте завтра́ _____ с дире́ктором в гла́вном о́фисе
   фи́рмы. (*meet*)

3. Дава́й всегда́ _____ её по́сле рабо́ты. (*wait for*)

4. Не уходи́! Дава́й _____ на́ших друзе́й. (*wait for*)

5. Дава́йте иногда́ _____ в э́том рестора́не. (*have lunch*)

To speak and to listen

Russian time expressions and irregular
endings in the prepositional case

Expressing friendship in
russian

The verbs уйти (to leave), прийти (
arrive) and давать—дать (to give)

6. Дава́й сего́дня не пойдём в на́шу столо́вую, а _____ в э́том

   кафе́. (have lunch)

7. Он ещё не пришёл?! Дава́йте _____ ему́. (call)

B. Как сказа́ть по-ру́сски? Translate the following sentences into Russian.

1. *Hello, this is Mike speaking.*

   _____

2. *Please connect me with the director.*

   _____

3. *Just a minute.*

   _____

4. *Let's continue this conversation in the restaurant. (form.)*

   _____

5. *Let's set up a meeting. (inform.)*

   _____

6. *I'm waiting for you in my office. (form.)*

   _____

7. *Will you wait for me? We'll go have lunch together. (inform.)*

   _____

**ANSWER KEY**

A. 1. пойдём; 2. встре́тимся; 3. ждать; 4. подождём; 5, обе́дать; 6. пообе́даем; 7. позвони́м
B. 1. Здра́вствуйте, э́то говори́т Майк. 2. Соедини́те меня́, пожа́луйста, с дире́ктором.
3. Одну́ мину́ту/мину́точку. 4. Дава́йте продо́лжим э́тот разгово́р в рестора́не. 5. Дава́й
договори́мся о встре́че. 6. Я жду вас у себя́ в кабине́те. 7. Ты подождёшь меня́? Мы вме́сте
пойдём пообе́даем.

Давай(те) (*Let's*)

Short form adjectives
and comparatives

Telephone grammar

The modal word до́лжен
(*should*), aspect and context

## Sentence Builder 2

▶ 19D Sentence Builder 2 (CD: 6, Track: 28)

| | |
|---|---|
| Здра́вствуйте! Позови́те, пожа́луйста, Ива́на. | *Hello! May I speak to Ivan please?* |
| К сожале́нию, его́ нет до́ма. | *Unfortunately, he's not home.* |
| Кто его́ спра́шивает? | *(May I ask) who's calling? (lit., Who is asking for him?)* |
| Куда́ вы звони́те? | *What place are you trying to reach?* |
| Вы не туда́ попа́ли. | *You have the wrong number. (lit., You didn't hit there. You missed.)* |
| Вы оши́блись но́мером. | *You have the wrong number. (lit., You made a mistake in the phone number.)* |
| Что ему́ переда́ть? | *May I take a message? (lit., What [should I] pass to him?)* |
| Переда́йте, пожа́луйста, что звони́л Ива́н. | *Tell (him) please that Ivan called.* |
| Обяза́тельно переда́м. | *I certainly will (tell him that).* |
| Он вам перезвони́т с моби́льного телефо́на. | *He'll call you back from (his) cell phone.* |
| Он вам перезвони́т, когда́ вернётся домо́й. | *He'll call you back when he returns.* |

## Take It Further 2

Позови́(те), пожа́луйста, + *name in the accusative case* is the most common polite way of asking for a person on the phone. The shorter expression, Мо́жно Никола́я, is often considered too casual and familiar. Don't hesitate to use imperatives for requests in Russian as in Позови́(те), пожа́луйста! They are perfectly courteous when you choose the right aspect!

*To speak* and *to listen*

Russian time expressions and irregular
endings in the prepositional case

Expressing friendship in
russian

The verbs уйти́ (*to leave*), прийти́ (
*arrive*) and дава́ть—дать (*to give*)

There are two ways of saying *you have the wrong number* in Russian. You can say
вы не туда́ попа́ли, which literally means *you didn't hit there,* or you can say
вы ошиблись но́мером, which literally means *you made a mistake in the phone
number.* Both are equally idiomatic and you can use them interchangeably.

## ✎ Sentence Practice 2

Let's practice the new sentences. Match the English phrases on the left to their
Russian equivalents on the right. Repeat the Russian phrases out loud.

| | |
|---|---|
| 1. *He is not home.* | a. Куда́ вы звони́те? |
| 2. *Who's calling?* | b. Что ему переда́ть? |
| 3. *What place are you trying to reach?* | c. Обяза́тельно переда́м. |
| 4. *unfortunately* | d. Он вам перезвони́т. |
| 5. *May I take a message?* | e. Его́ нет до́ма. |
| 6. *Tell him that Ivan called.* | f. Позови́те, пожа́луйста, Ива́на. |
| 7. *I'll certainly tell (him).* | g. к сожале́нию |
| 8. *He'll call you back.* | h. с моби́льного телефо́на |
| 9. *from his cell phone* | i. Переда́йте, пожа́луйста, что звони́л Ива́н. |
| 10. *May I speak to Ivan please?* | j. Кто его́ спра́шивает? |

**ANSWER KEY**
1. e; 2. j: 3. a; 4. g; 5. b; 6. i; 7. c; 8. d; 9. h; 10. f

Давай(те) (*Let's*)

Short form adjectives
and comparatives

Telephone grammar

The modal word до́лжен
(*should*), aspect and context

# Grammar Builder 2

▶ 19F Grammar Builder 2 (CD: 6, Track: 29)

## TELEPHONE GRAMMAR

Notice the genitive of negation in the seemingly simple sentence, Его́ нет
до́ма (*he's not home*). This sentence reads literally *it's none of him at home*.
Consequently, the missing person needs to be put in the genitive case—the genitive
of negation. Нет in the past tense becomes не́ бы́ло; it always stays the same in
the past because it agrees with the implied subject *it*. Notice that не́ receives an
accent, which is not customary for one-syllable words. That is because не́ бы́ло is
pronounced as one word, that is, with one primary accent which is on не́.

Его́ не́ бы́ло до́ма.
*He wasn't home.*

Её не́ бы́ло до́ма.
*She wasn't home.*

Их не́ бы́ло до́ма.
*They weren't home.*

Similarly, the future form is always не бу́дет.

Его́ не бу́дет до́ма.
*He won't be home.*

Её не бу́дет до́ма.
*She won't be home.*

*To speak* and *to listen*

Russian time expressions and irregular
endings in the prepositional case

Expressing friendship in
russian

The verbs уйти (*to leave*), прийти (*to
arrive*) and дава́ть—дать (*to give*)

Их не бу́дет до́ма.
*They won't be home.*

If you call a person, you should use the dative case (кому́? *to whom?*) after the
Russian verb звони́ть:

Я звоню́ Ива́ну.
*I'm calling Ivan.*

Кому́ вы звони́те?
*Who are you calling?*

But if you call an office, a company, or any other organization, you should use the
accusative of direction (куда́? *where to?*) with the appropriate preposition в or на:

Я звоню́ в университе́т.
*I'm calling the university.*

Я звоню́ на по́чту.
*I'm calling the post office.*

Куда́ вы звони́те?
*Where are you calling?*

In order to *take a message* or *leave a message,* Russians use one verb переда́ть,
which literally means *to pass* or *to give.*

Что ему́ переда́ть?
*May I take a message?*

When you want someone to take a message, simply use the perfective imperative.

Дава́й(те) (*Let's*)

Short form adjectives
and comparatives

Telephone grammar

The modal word до́лжен
(*should*), aspect and context

Переда́йте, пожа́луйста, что звони́л Ива́н.
*Tell [him/her] that Ivan called please.*

Notice that the subject Ива́н in the subordinate clause is at the end of the clause.
However, if this subject is a pronoun, you should place it before the verb.

Переда́йте, пожа́луйста, что я звони́л(а).
*Tell [him/her] that I called please.*

# ✎ Work Out 2

A. Кого́ нет до́ма? (*Who is not home?*) Say that the following people *aren't, weren't,*
and *won't be* at the given locations at the times given in parentheses. Remember
to use the genitive of negation!

1. дире́ктор (*in the main office*)

   _____ (*present*)

   _____ (*past*)

   _____ (*future*)

2. она́ (*at home*)

   _____ (*present*)

   _____ (*past*)

   _____ (*future*)

3. я (*at work*)

   _____ (*present*)

   _____ (*past*)

   _____ (*future*)

*To speak* and *to listen*

Russian time expressions and irregular
endings in the prepositional case

Expressing friendship in
russian

The verbs уйти́ (*to leave*), прийти́ (
*arrive*) and дава́ть—дать (*to give*)

4. наш америка́нский партнёр (*in Moscow*)

_____ (*present*)

_____ (*past*)

_____ (*future*)

5. мы (*at the meeting*)

_____ (*present*)

_____ (*past*)

_____ (*future*)

6. твой знако́мый (*at home*)

_____ (*present*)

_____ (*past*)

_____ (*future*)

B. Как сказа́ть по-ру́сски? **Rewrite the following conversation in Russian.**

1. *Hi! May I please speak to Natasha?*

_____

2. *Hi! Unfortunately, she's not home.*

_____

3. *(May I ask) who's calling?*

_____

4. *This is her friend, Mike, speaking.*

_____

Давáй(те) (*Let's*)

Short form adjectives
and comparatives

Telephone grammar

The modal word дóлжен
(*should*), aspect and context

5.  *May I take a message?*

_____

6. *Please tell her I called.*

_____

7. *She'll call you back when she returns.*

_____

**ANSWER KEY**
A. 1. Дирéктора нет в глáвном óфисе. Дирéктора нé было в глáвном óфисе. Дирéктора не бýдет в глáвном óфисе. 2. Её нет дóма. Её нé было дóма. Её не бýдет дóма. 3. Меня нет на рабóте. Меня нé было на рабóте. Меня не бýдет на рабóте. 4. Нáшего америкáнского партнёра нет в Москвé. Нáшего америкáнского партнёра нé было в Москвé. Нáшего америкáнского партнёра не бýдет в Москвé. 5. Нас нет на встрéче. Нас нé было на встрéче. Нас не бýдет на встрéче. 6. Твоегó знакóмого нет дóма. Твоегó знакóмого нé было дóма. Твоегó знакóмого не бýдет дóма.
B. 1. Здрáвствуйте! Позовите, пожáлуйста, Натáшу. 2. Здрáвствуйте! К сожалéнию, её нет дóма. 3. А кто её спрáшивает? 4. Э́то говорит её друг Майк. 5. Что ей передáть? 6. Пожáлуйста, передáйте, что я звонил. 7. Онá вам перезвонит, когдá вернётся.

# ✎ Drive It Home

Now, let's do more practice on the conjugation of the verb давáть—дать (*to give*). Fill in the blanks with the correct form of this verb then repeat the entire Russian sentence out loud.

1. Они всегдá _____ мой телефóн. (*imperf.*)

2. Вы всегдá _____ мой телефóн. (*imperf.*)

3. Я всегдá _____ ваш телефóн. (*imperf.*)

4. Ты всегдá _____ мой телефóн. (*imperf.*)

5. Он _____ мне их телефóн зáвтра. (*perf.*)

6. Ты _____ мне их телефóн зáвтра. (*perf.*)

7. Я _____ тебе их телефóн зáвтра. (*perf.*)

8. Вы _____ мне их телефóн зáвтра. (*perf.*)

9. Они _____ мне их телефóн зáвтра. (*perf.*)

10. Мы _____ вам их телефóн зáвтра. (*perf.*)

**ANSWER KEY**
1. даю́т; 2. даёте; 3. даю́; 4. даёшь; 5. даст; 6. дашь; 7. дам; 8. дади́те; 9. даду́т; 10. дади́м

# How Did You Do?

Let's see how you did in this lesson. You should know how to:

☐ Say *let's do something* in Russian. (Still unsure? Go back to page 284.)

☐ Say that someone *isn't*, *wasn't*, or *won't be* somewhere. (Still unsure? Go back to page 289.)

☐ Use essential expressions for telephone etiquette. (Still unsure? Go back to page 289.)

# Word Recall

Now it's time to review some words, phrases, and constructions from the earlier lessons. Listen to the English sentence first, then fill in the blanks, and finally, repeat the Russian sentence out loud.

1. *My things are in the closet.*

   Мой вéщи _____.

2. *We stayed (perf.) in a new hotel.*

   Мы _____ в нóвой гости́нице.

Давай(те) (Let's)

Short form adjectives
and comparatives

Telephone grammar

The modal word до́лжен
(should), aspect and context

3. *He met (for the first time) her parents yesterday.*

    Вчера́ он _____.

4. *We are meeting at the corner of the street.*

    Мы встреча́емся _____ у́лицы.

5. *Do you (form.) speak German?*

    Вы говори́те _____?

6. *Please come in, have a seat.*

    Пожа́луйста, _____.

7. *I never eat meat.*

    Я _____ мя́са.

8. *Would you (form.) like (do you want) anything for breakfast?*

    Вы хоти́те_____?

9. *Please open (form.) the window.*

    Пожа́луйста, _____ окно́.

10. *Every evening, I swim in the pool.*

    Ка́ждый ве́чер я _____.

**ANSWER KEY**

1. в шкафу́; 2. останови́лись; 3. познако́мился с её роди́телями; 4. на углу́; 5. по-неме́цки;
6. проходи́те, сади́тесь; 7. никогда́ не ем; 8. что́-нибудь на за́втрак; 9. откро́йте; 10. пла́ваю в
бассе́йне

# Lesson 20: Conversations

Поздравля́ем с после́дним уро́ком после́дней главы́ э́того ку́рса!
*Congratulations on reaching the final lesson of the Intermediate course!*

In this lesson, you'll put all of the new words and expressions into two typical phone conversations and learn how to:

☐ Leave a message and set up a meeting.

☐ Use short adjectives and participles in all three tenses.

☐ Use some short and compound comparatives.

☐ Ask for the person you need on the telephone.

☐ Use the modal verb *should* in Russian.

Гото́вы? Тогда́ начнём! *Ready? Then, let's begin!*
Let's get started with Conversation 1.

## ⓒ Conversation 1
▶ 20A Conversation 1 (CD: 6, Track: 30- Russian; Track: 31- Russian and English)

Kim Brighton, an American businessperson, is calling her business partner, the director of a Russian company, GosEnergo, Aleksandr Vasilievich Rubliov. She is calling his Moscow office in order to make an appointment with him. First, she speaks with his office assistant who then connects her with the director.

Секрета́рь:  Штаб-кварти́ра фи́рмы «ГосЭне́рго» слу́шает.

Давáй(те) (*Let's*)

Short form adjectives
and comparatives

Telephone grammar

The modal word дóлжен
(*should*), aspect and context

| | |
|---|---|
| Г-жа Брáйтон: | Здрáвствуйте. Это говори́т Ким Брáйтон, америкáнский партнёр вáшей фи́рмы. Соедини́те меня́, пожáлуйста, с Алексáндром Васи́льевичем. |
| Секретáрь: | Здрáвствуйте, госпожá Брáйтон. Вы óчень хорошó говори́те по-рýсски. Вы звони́те из Амéрики? |
| Г-жа Брáйтон: | Нет, я сейчáс в Москвé. |
| Секретáрь: | Однý минýточку. Я вас сейчáс соединю́ с дирéктором. |
| Г-н Рублёв: | Я вас слýшаю. |
| Г-жа Брáйтон: | Здрáвствуйте, господи́н Рублёв. Вас беспокóит Ким Брáйтон. Я ужé в Москвé. |
| Г-н Рублёв: | Здрáвствуйте, госпожá Брáйтон. Рад вас слы́шать! С приéздом! Как вы устрóились? |
| Г-жа Брáйтон: | Спаси́бо. Я прекрáсно устрóилась. Я звоню́, чтóбы договори́ться о нáшей встрéче. Когдá у вас бýдет врéмя на э́той недéле? |
| Г-н Рублёв: | Мы мóжем встрéтиться зáвтра в любóе врéмя пóсле обéда. Я тáкже свобóден в пя́тницу в пéрвой полови́не дня. Когдá вам удóбнее? |
| Г-жа Брáйтон: | Давáйте встрéтимся в пя́тницу, в 10 часóв утрá, в глáвном óфисе вáшей фи́рмы на Цветнóм бульвáре. |
| Г-н Рублёв: | Óчень хорошó. А пóсле деловóй встрéчи давáйте вмéсте пойдём на ланч и продóлжим разговóр в неформáльной обстанóвке. |
| Г-жа Брáйтон: | Договори́лись. До встрéчи. |
| Г-н Рублёв: | Всегó харóшего. Я бýду вас ждать у себя́ в кабинéте послезáвтра, в пя́тницу, в дéсять. |

| | |
|---|---|
| *Secretary:* | *The headquarters of GosEnergo (lit., is listening).* |
| *Ms. Brighton:* | *Hello. This is Kim Brighton speaking, an American partner of your company. Connect me please with Aleksandr* |
| *Secretary:* | *Hello, Ms. Brighton. You speak Russian very well. Are you calling from America?* |

**Unit 5** Lesson 20: Conversations

*To speak* and *to listen*

Russian time expressions and irregular
endings in the prepositional case

Expressing friendship in
russian

The verbs уйти́ (*to leave*), прийти́ (
*arrive*) and дава́ть—дать (*to give*)

| Ms. Brighton: | No, I'm in Moscow now. |
|---|---|
| Secretary: | Just a minute. I'll transfer you to the director. |
| Mr. Rubliov: | Hello (lit., I'm listening). |
| Ms. Brighton: | Hello, Mr. Rubliov. Kim Brighton speaking (lit., disturbing you). I'm already in Moscow. |
| Mr. Rubliov: | Hello, Ms. Brighton. Glad to hear (from) you! Welcome! Are you well settled? |
| Ms. Brighton: | Thank you. I'm very comfortable (lit., I'm very well settled). I'm calling in order to set up our meeting. When will you have time this week? |
| Mr. Rubliov: | We can meet any time tomorrow after lunch. I'm also free on Friday in the morning (lit., in the first half of the day). What's more convenient for you? |
| Ms. Brighton: | Let's meet on Friday at 10 a.m. in the main office of your company on Tsvetnoy Boulevard. |
| Mr. Rubliov: | Very well. And after the business meeting, let's have lunch together and continue our conversation in an informal setting. |
| Ms. Brighton: | Agreed. See you (lit., until the meeting)! |
| Mr. Rubliov: | All the best. I'll be waiting for you in my office the day after tomorrow, on Friday, at ten o'clock. |

## Take It Further 1

▶ 20B Take It Further 1 (CD: 6, Track: 32)

The English adverb *also* has three equivalents in Russian: то́же, та́кже, and ещё. You already know two of them. То́же means *too,* when one subject is compared to another: Мой друг лю́бит о́перу, и я то́же люблю́ о́перу. (*My friend likes opera, and I like opera too.*) Here, то́же (*also/too*) means *as compared to* my friend or *likewise.* Ещё means *in addition to,* when it introduces a new item to a list of things. For example, if you say я люблю́ о́перу, и ещё я люблю́ бале́т (*I like opera and also I like ballet*), it's understood that the same subject likes opera and ещё, *in addition* to it, ballet. But there's one more possibility. Notice how Mr.

Rubliov says in the conversation: Я тáкже свобóден в пя́тницу (*I'm also free on Friday*). Тáкже doesn't differentiate between the two meanings above and stands for *in addition to* as well as for *likewise*. Тáкже is characteristic of more formal speech, so you wouldn't normally use it when speaking with friends. Mr. Rubliov is being formal with his American partner; therefore, his choice of тáкже instead of ещё is justified.

# ✎Conversation Practice 1

Now let's practice some of the phrases and sentences from the conversation above. Read the English sentence first, then fill in the blanks, and finally repeat the Russian sentence out loud.

1. *Hi. This is Kim Brighton speaking.*

   Здрáвствуйте. _____ Ким Брайтон.

2. *Are you calling from America?*

   Вы _____?

3. *I'm glad to hear (from) you.*

   Я _____.

4. *I'm very well settled.*

   Я _____.

5. *When will you have time this week?*

   Когдá у вас _____?

6. *We can meet any time tomorrow after lunch.*

   Мы _____ за́втра _____

   _____.

7. *I'm also free on Friday before noon.*

   Я _____ в пя́тницу _____

   _____.

8. *When is it more convenient for you?*

   Когда́ _____?

9. *Let's meet in the main office of your company.*

   _____ в гла́вном о́фисе ва́шей фи́рмы.

10. *Agreed. Until then.*

   _____. До встре́чи.

### ANSWER KEY

1. Это говори́т; 2. звони́те из Аме́рики; 3. рад вас слы́шать; 4. прекра́сно устро́илась; 5. бу́дет вре́мя на э́той неде́ле; 6. мо́жем встре́титься, в любо́е вре́мя по́сле обе́да; 7. та́кже свобо́ден, в пе́рвой полови́не дня, 8. вам удо́бнее; 9. Дава́йте встре́тимся; 10. Договори́лись

## Grammar Builder 1

▶ 20C Grammar Builder 1 (CD: 6, Track: 33)

### SHORT FORM ADJECTIVES AND COMPARATIVES

In Russian, there are short form adjectives and long form adjectives, for example, свобо́ден (short form) and свобо́дный (long form). Below we will look at some ways in which short form adjectives differ from long form adjectives. It should be noted that in conversational Russian, long forms are preferred, with some exceptions, one of which is рад (*glad*) shown in the sentence below.

Давáй(те) (*Let's*)

Short form adjectives
and comparatives

Telephone grammar

The modal word дóлжен
(*should*), aspect and context

Я рад вас слы́шать.
*I'm glad to hear you.*

Short form adjectives are used as predicates only. They need to match the gender of their subjects. Masculine subjects require the masculine (zero) ending in their predicates (он рад); feminine subjects require the feminine –а/я ending (онá рáда); plural subjects should be matched with the plural ending –ы/и (они́ рáды). As always, the verb *to be* is left out in the present tense. In the past and future, it reappears in appropriate forms: он был рад/он бýдет рад, онá былá рáда/онá бýдет рáда, они́ бы́ли рáды/они́ бýдут рáды. Let's look at another example.

Я свобóден/свобóдна в пя́тницу.
*I'm free on Friday.*

Here, свобóден/свобóдна is also a short adjective. So you should say: он свобóден, онá свобóдна, они́ свобóдны, он был свобóден, он бýдет свобóден, etc. Notice the fleeting е before all vowel endings. The short adjective зáнят (*busy*) works the same way as рад: он зáнят, онá занятá, онó зáнято, они́ зáняты.

Now, let's learn how to form Russian comparatives. Удóбнее (*more convenient/ comfortable*) is an example of a standard Russian comparative adjective, one that ends in –ee. Take a look at a few common standard comparatives below.

| ADJECTIVE | ENGLISH | COMPARATIVE | ENGLISH |
|---|---|---|---|
| нóвый | *new* | новéе | *newer* |
| стáрый | *old* | старéе | *older* |
| краси́вый | *pretty* | краси́вее | *prettier* |
| интерéсный | *interesting* | интерéснее | *more interesting* |
| холóдный | *cold* | холоднéе | *colder* |

**Unit 5** Lesson 20: Conversations

*To speak* and *to listen*

Russian time expressions and irregular
endings in the prepositional case

Expressing friendship in
russian

The verbs уйти́ (*to leave*), прийти́ (*to
arrive*) and дава́ть—дать (*to give*)

Some comparatives have only one –е in the end preceded by a mutated consonant (except in the example большо́й, in which there is no mutation). Take a look at the following common comparatives of this type.

| ADJECTIVE | ENGLISH | COMPARATIVE | ENGLISH |
|-----------|---------|-------------|---------|
| большо́й | *big* | бо́льше | *bigger* |
| ма́ленький | *small* | ме́ньше | *smaller* |
| дорого́й | *expensive* | доро́же | *more expensive* |
| дешёвый | *cheap* | деше́вле | *cheaper* |
| бли́зкий | *close* | бли́же | *closer* |

Like in English, the Russian adjectives хоро́ший (*good*) and плохо́й (*bad*) have irregular comparative forms лу́чше (*better*) and ху́же (*worse*). If you have trouble remembering the correct comparative form (or if this form doesn't exist), you can always use a compound comparative which consists of бо́лее (*more*) or ме́нее (*less*) and a regular adjective. So, instead of saying нове́е (*newer*), you can say бо́лее но́вый (*more new*) and, by analogy, ме́нее но́вый (*less new*). The easiest way to introduce the object of comparison is by the conjunction чем (*than*) always preceded by a comma.

Это кафе́ деше́вле, чем рестора́н.
*This café is cheaper than the restaurant.*

And finally, comparatives can be used in the adverbial function, that is, they can modify actions.

Он живёт бли́же.
*He lives closer.*

However, as opposed to English, Russian simple comparatives can't directly modify nouns! For example, you can say in English *I live in a newer house;* in order to say it in Russian, you need to use a compound comparative, or an adjective with the comparative word *more*.

Я живý в бóлее нóвом дóме.

*I live in a newer house.*

We'll come back to the question of comparatives in Unit 1 of *Advanced Russian*.

# ✎ Work Out 1

A. Restate the following sentences in the past and in the future tense.

1. Он рад меня́ ви́деть.

_____

2. Вы свобóдны в пя́тницу пóсле обéда?

_____

3. Онá зáнята в пéрвой полови́не дня.

_____

4. Я свобóден в пять часóв вéчера.

_____

5. Мои́ друзья́ рáды пойти́ со мной на ланч.

_____

B. Restate the following sentences using comparatives.

1. Эта кни́га интерéсная.

_____

2. Мне удóбно с вáми встрéтиться пóсле обéда.

_____

**3.** Он жил близко от работы.

_____

**4.** Продукты в этом магазине дорогие.

_____

**5.** Мы остановились в новой гостинице.

_____

**6.** Он хорошо говорит по-русски.

_____

**7.** Этот ресторан был дешёвый.

_____

**ANSWER KEY**

**A. 1.** Он был рад меня видеть. Он будет рад меня видеть. **2.** Вы были свободны в пятницу после обеда? Вы будете свободны в пятницу после обеда? **3.** Она была занята в первой половине дня. Она будет занята в первой половине дня. **4.** Я был свободен в пять часов вечера. Я буду свободен в пять часов вечера. **5.** Мои друзья были рады пойти со мной на ланч. Мои друзья будут рады пойти со мной на ланч.
**B. 1.** Эта книга интереснее. **2.** Мне удобнее с вами встретиться после обеда. **3.** Он жил ближе к работе. **4.** Продукты в этом магазине дороже. **5.** Мы остановились в более новой гостинице. **6.** Он лучше говорит по-русски. **7.** Этот ресторан был дешевле.

## Conversation 2

20D Conversation 2 (CD: 6, Track: 34- Russian; Track: 35- Russian and English)

Kelly, an American visitor to Russia, is trying to reach her Russian acquaintance, Nastya. Unfortunately, Nastya isn't home. Her husband, Vasilii, picks up the phone and talks to Kelly.

Василий:    Аллё!
Келли:      Здравствуйте! Позовите, пожалуйста, Настю.

Да&#769;вай(те) (*Let's*)

Short form adjectives
and comparatives

Telephone grammar

The modal word до&#769;лжен
(*should*), aspect and context

| Васи&#769;лий: | Здра&#769;вствуйте! К сожале&#769;нию, её нет до&#769;ма. А кто её спра&#769;шивает? |
| Ке&#769;лли: | Это говори&#769;т её америка&#769;нская знако&#769;мая Ке&#769;лли. Я сейча&#769;с в Росси&#769;и и звоню&#769; из гости&#769;ницы. Когда&#769; она&#769; бу&#769;дет до&#769;ма? |
| Васи&#769;лий: | На&#769;стя ушла&#769; в магази&#769;н, но уже&#769; ско&#769;ро должна&#769; прийти&#769;. |
| Ке&#769;лли: | Хорошо&#769;. Переда&#769;йте ей, пожа&#769;луйста, что я звони&#769;ла. |
| Васи&#769;лий: | Обяза&#769;тельно переда&#769;м. Или вот что, да&#769;йте мне, пожа&#769;луйста, ваш телефо&#769;н в гости&#769;нице. На&#769;стя перезвони&#769;т вам или с моби&#769;льного телефо&#769;на, или когда&#769; вернётся домо&#769;й. |
| Ке&#769;лли: | Хорошо&#769;. Запи&#769;сывайте. Телефо&#769;н гости&#769;ницы 137–77–91. Я останови&#769;лась в но&#769;мере 1017. |
| Васи&#769;лий: | Спаси&#769;бо. Я всё записа&#769;л. |
| Ке&#769;лли: | До свида&#769;ния. Я бу&#769;ду ждать её звонка&#769;. |
| Васи&#769;лий: | Всего&#769; хоро&#769;шего. |

| *Vasilii:* | *Hello!* |
| *Kelly:* | *Hello! May I speak to Nastya?* |
| *Vasilii:* | *Hi! Unfortunately, she's not home. May I ask who is calling?* |
| *Kelly:* | *This is her American acquaintance, Kelly, calling. I'm in Russia now, and I'm calling from the hotel. When will she be back?* |
| *Vasilii:* | *Nastya left for the store, but she should come back soon.* |
| *Kelly:* | *Okay. Please let her know that I called.* |
| *Vasilii:* | *Certainly, I will. Or, you know what? Give me your phone number at the hotel. Nastya will call you back either from her cell phone or when she comes home.* |
| *Kelly:* | *Okay. Write it down. The hotel phone number is 137–77–91. I am in Room 1017.* |
| *Vasilii:* | *Thank you. I've written everything down.* |
| *Kelly:* | *Good-bye. I'll be waiting for her phone call.* |
| *Vasilii:* | *Take care.* |

## Take It Further 2

Notice that Vasilii says **аллё** when he first picks up the phone. Although it sounds like a hello, this is not a greeting of any kind that you might use on the street; it's just a signal that he answered the phone, and the person on the other line can speak up. **Аллё** or **алло́** are equivalent to the more formal **я слу́шаю**, as used in Conversation 1. They are the most common ways of answering the phone. The actual greeting follows in the next two lines. Kelly says **здра́вствуйте** (*hello*), and Vasilii responds with his own greeting. The caller is considered polite when he or she begins with an actual greeting: **здра́вствуйте**.

## ✎ Conversation Practice 2

Now let's practice some of the phrases and sentences from the conversation above. Read the English sentence first, then fill in the blanks, and finally repeat the Russian sentence out loud.

1. *May I speak to Nastya?*

   _____, пожа́луйста, _____.

2. *Unfortunately, she is not home.*

   _____, _____ нет до́ма.

3. *Nastya left for the store.*

   На́стя _____.

4. *She should come back soon.*

   Она́ ско́ро _____ прийти́.

5. *Please let her know that I called.*

   _____, пожа́луйста, что я звони́ла.

6. *I certainly will (let her know).*

   _____ передáм.

7. *Nastya will call you back from her cell phone.*

   Настя _____ с мобильного телефóна.

8. *Nastya will call you when she comes back home.*

   Настя позвонит вам, когдá _____ _____ .

9. *I'm staying in Room 1017.*

   Я _____ тысяча семнáдцать.

10. *I'll be waiting for her phone call.*

    Я _____ её звонкá.

    **ANSWER KEY**
    1. Позовите, Настю; 2. К сожалéнию, её; 3. ушлá в магазин; 4. должнá; 5. Передáйте ей;
    6. Обязáтельно; 7. перезвонит вам; 8. вернётся домóй; 9. остановилась в нóмере; 10. бýду
    ждать

# Grammar Builder 2

▶ 20E Grammar Builder 2 (CD: 6, Track: 36)

## THE MODAL WORD ДÓЛЖЕН (*SHOULD*), ASPECT AND CONTEXT

Take a look at the example of the modal word должен (*should*):

Онá скóро должнá прийти.
*She should be back soon.*

Дóлжен (*should*) is a short adjective. You should use it on two occasions. First, when you need to express *necessity*.

Я до́лжен/должна́ договори́ться о встре́че.
*I have to set up a meeting.*

In this case, до́лжен (as opposed to other modal words) implies a deeply felt necessity. Second, when you need to express that something is probable, as in:

Она́ должна́ по́мнить вас.
*She should remember you.*

The phrase она́ ско́ро должна́ прийти́ is of the second kind.

Notice the imperfective aspect of звони́ла in the sentence переда́йте ей, пожа́луйста, что я звони́ла. Regardless of the fact that Kelly called once and got through (at least to Nastya's husband), the aspect of звони́ла is still imperfective, because it denotes an action taken out of the immediate context, out of causes and consequences, and, in a way, out of immediate temporality. It becomes a mere statement of fact. In other words, it's irrelevant when exactly she called, or what her phone call related to. She just happened to have called.

Let's consider another example. If you say that you read «Война́ и мир» (*War and Peace*) in the past, what aspect should you use? You can say either я чита́л/а «Войну́ и мир» or я прочита́л/а «Войну́ и мир». It's crucial to understand that in both situations you read it once and to the end. However, the decision depends on the connection of this statement with the greater context. The perfective statement я прочита́л «Войну́ и мир» implies that I was supposed to have read it (let's say, it was on my syllabus at school), and I did. In other words, it focuses on the act of reading as a result of something (e.g. it being on my syllabus). The imperfective я чита́л «Войну́ и мир» doesn't imply any prior obligation or expectation that I do so (I just happened to have read it at one point in time); thus, it becomes a mere statement of the fact.

Давай(те) (*Let's*)

Short form adjectives
and comparatives

Telephone grammar

The modal word **должен**
(*should*), aspect and context

Я читáл(а) «Войнý и мир».

*I read* War and Peace.

Я прочитáл(а) «Войнý и мир».

*I read* War and Peace.

Notice also the imperfective aspect of the imperative записывайте. It is imperfective because it doesn't introduce a new notion into the context: Kelly knows that Vasilii wants to have her phone number (he just said so), so she gives him a "go ahead" to write it down. Therefore, her imperative is imperfective.

However, when he originally asked for her phone number, he used the perfective aspect.

Дáйте мне ваш телефóн в гостúнице.

*Give me your number at the hotel.*

Here, he is suggesting something radically new to the context. Remember that Russian imperatives are perfective when they command a totally new action, a change of state. On the other hand, as you already know, most invitations are imperfective in Russian because they imply the generally shared understanding of a welcome.

Пожáлуйста, приходúте в гóсти!

*Please come to see us!*

Садúтесь.

*Have a seat.*

Ешьте!

*Eat! (Go ahead and enjoy your meal!)*

To speak and to listen

Russian time expressions and irregular
endings in the prepositional case

Expressing friendship in
russian

The verbs уйти (to leave), прийти (
arrive) and давать—дать (to give)

Пейте!

*Drink! (Please have a drink!)*


# ✎ Work Out 2

A. Что вы должны сделать? (*What do you have to do?*) Fill in the blanks with the
correct form of the modal verb должен (*should/have to*), Then restate the same
sentences in the past tense and repeat both out loud.

1. Мы _____ позвонить в главный офис.

   _____

2. Моя дочь _____ вернуться домой после обеда.

   _____

3. Моя жена _____ передать им привет.

   _____

4. Мой знакомый _____ перезвонить вам на домашний телефон.

   _____

5. Мои друзья _____ ждать вашего звонка.

   _____

B. Fill in the blanks by choosing the correct aspect of the verb in parentheses. Before
making your choice, consider the greater context either implied or suggested in
English.

1. Я _____ в этой гостинице. (останавливался—

   остановился: *at one point in time in the past*).

2. _____ мне, пожалуйста ваш домашний телефон. (давайте—дайте:

   *I'm making a request*)

3. _____ мне, пожалуйста, на мобильный.

   (перезванивайте—перезвоните: *I'm making a request*)

4. Ты хочешь позвонить? Пожалуйста, _____! (звони—позвони: *I see*

   *that you'd like to make a phone call*)

5. _____, пожалуйста, Наташу! (зовите—позовите: *this is my*

   *request*)

6. Вы хотите записать мой телефон? Пожалуйста, _____.

   (записывайте—запишите: *the person is ready to do so*)

**ANSWER KEY**

A. 1. должны, Мы должны были позвонить в главный офис. 2. должна, Моя дочь должна была вернуться домой после обеда. 3. должна, Моя жена должна была передать им привет. 4. должен, Мой знакомый должен был перезвонить вам на домашний телефон. 5. должны, Мои друзья должны были ждать вашего звонка.

B. 1. останавливался; 2. Дайте; 3. Перезвоните; 4. звони; 5. Позовите; 6. записывайте

## ✎ Drive It Home

Now, let's drive home some short comparatives that you've learned so far. Read the English sentence first, then fill in the blanks with the negative perfective verb (provided in parentheses), and finally repeat the entire sentence out loud.

1. *This car is newer than mine.*

   Эта машина_____, чем моя.

2. *Moscow is older than St. Petersburg.*

   Москва _____, чем Санкт-Петербург.

3. *The center is prettier than the suburbs.*

   Центр _____, чем при́город.

4. *This book is more interesting.*

   Эта кни́га _____.

5. *It's colder in the winter than in the spring.*

   Зимо́й _____, чем весно́й.

6. *Her house is bigger.*

   Её дом _____.

7. *This restaurant is more expensive.*

   Этот рестора́н _____.

8. *This hotel is better.*

   Эта гости́ница _____.

9. *The metro is closer that the bus.*

   Метро́ _____, чем авто́бус.

10. *Groceries are cheaper in this supermarket.*

    Проду́кты _____ в э́том суперма́ркете.

    **ANSWER KEY**
    1. нове́е; 2. старе́е; 3. краси́вее; 4. интере́снее; 5. холодне́е; 6. бо́льше; 7. доро́же; 8. лу́чше; 9. бли́же; 10. деше́вле

Давай(те) (*Let's*)

Short form adjectives
and comparatives

Telephone grammar

The modal word дóлжен
(*should*), aspect and context

## How Did You Do?

Let's see how you did in this lesson. You should know how to:

☐ Leave a message and set up a meeting. (Still unsure? Go back to page 296.)

☐ Use short adjectives and participles in all three tenses. (Still unsure? Go back to page 300.)

☐ Use some short and compound comparatives. (Still unsure? Go back to page 301.)

☐ Ask for the person you need on the telephone. (Still unsure? Go back to page 304.)

☐ Use the modal verb *should* in Russian. (Still unsure? Go back to page 307.)

## ✎ Word Recall

Now it's time to review some words and constructions from the earlier lessons. Match the English sentences on the left with their Russian equivalents on the right and repeat the Russian sentences out loud.

1. *He is not home.*

2. *You got the wrong number.*

3. *He's in his (own) office.*

4. *They had dinner in a café and conversed.*

5. *What did you just say?*

6. *Take this medication after meals.*

a. Он у себя́ в кабинéте.

b. Принимáйте э́то лекáрство пóсле еды́.

c. Вы вы́здоровеете дней чéрез пять.

d. Онá родилáсь в Росси́и.

e. Егó нет дóма.

f. Что вы тóлько что сказáли?

7. *He has a severe cough.*

8. *You'll get better in about five days.*

9. *She was born in Russia.*

10. *It's two twenty five now.*

g. Вы оши́блись но́мером.

h. Сейча́с два часа́ два́дцать пять мину́т.

i. Они́ у́жинали в кафе́ и разгова́ривали.

j. У него́ си́льный ка́шель.

**ANSWER KEY**

1. e; 2. g; 3. a; 4. i; 5. f; 6. b; 7. j; 8. c; 9. d; 10. h

Don't forget to practice and reinforce what you've learned by visiting **www.livinglanguage.com/languagelab** for flashcards, games, and quizzes!

# Unit 5 Quiz

Контро́льная рабо́та №5

Congratulations on reaching the final quiz in the Intermediate Course! Let's review what you've learned in Unit 5. Once you've completed it, score yourself to see how well you've done. If you find that you need to go back and review, please do so before continuing on to the first unit of the Advanced Course.
Let's get started!

A. Fill in the blanks using the correct equivalent of the verb *to meet*. The tense and aspect of the verb are given in the parentheses.

1. Вчера́ ве́чером мы пе́рвый раз _____ с его́ роди́телями. (*perf., past*)

2. Сего́дня я _____ с жено́й по́сле рабо́ты, и мы идём в теа́тр. (*present*)

3. Мы с друзья́ми всегда́ _____ у метро́. (*present*)

4. Я о́чень хочу́ _____ с твоей сестро́й. (*perf., infinitive*)

5. Роди́тели _____ своего́ сы́на в аэропорту́. (*imperf., past*)

B. Fill in the blanks with the correct form of the verb *to come (on foot)* or *to leave (on foot)*. The tense of the verb is indicated in the parentheses.

1. Мои́ друзья́ _____ ко мне в го́сти в шесть часо́в ве́чера. (*future*)

2. Она́ _____ с рабо́ты по́сле обе́да. (*past*)

3. Во ско́лько вы сего́дня _____ домо́й? (*future*)

4. Он _____ в магази́н, но ско́ро вернётся. (*past*)

5. Позвони́ мне с рабо́ты, когда́ ты _____ в о́фис. (*future*)

C. Fill in the blanks with the correct time expression. Follow the prompts in parentheses.

1. Мы отдыха́ли на мо́ре _____. (*last year*)

2. Я всегда́ хожу́ в кино́ _____. (*on Saturday/s*)

3. Они́ о́чень мно́го рабо́тали _____. (*this month*)

4. Я бу́ду занима́ться до́ма _____. (*next week*)

5. _____ была́ прекра́сная пого́да. (*on this/that day*)

D. Fill in the blanks saying that the people in parentheses *aren't, weren't*, or *won't be* at the mentioned places. Pay attention to the tense of each sentence.

1. _____ до́ма вчера́ ве́чером. (он)

2. За́втра _____ в го́роде. (мы)

3. _____ сего́дня _____ на рабо́те. (моя́ жена́)

4. Извини́те, _____ сейча́с до́ма. (Ива́н)

5. _____ в университе́те: она́ заболе́ла. (На́стя)

E. Fill in the blanks using the correct inclusive command *let's do something* given in parentheses. Pay attention to your choice of aspect and form.

1. _____ их по́сле рабо́ты. (*let's wait, sg.*)

2. _____ всегда́ _____ в э́той столо́вой. (*let's have lunch, pl.*)

3. _____ему ве́чером. (*let's call, sg.*)

4. _____ о встре́че в Росси́и. (*let's agree, pl.*)

5. _____ в кино́ за́втра. (*let's go, sg.*)

F. Fill in the blanks using the correct short adjective, or comparative in parentheses.

1. Она́ _____ вас ви́деть. (*will be glad*)

2. Вы _____ по́сле обе́да? (*will be free*)

3. Эта кафе́ _____, чем рестора́н. (*cheaper*)

4. Он _____ весь день на рабо́те. (*was busy*)

5. Эта гости́ница и _____, и _____. (*bigger, newer*)

**ANSWER KEY**

A. 1. познако́мились; 2. встреча́юсь; 3. встреча́емся; 4. познако́миться; 5. встреча́ли

B. 1. приду́т; 2. ушла́; 3. придёте; 4. ушёл; 5. придёшь

C. 1. в про́шлом году́; 2. в суббо́ту; 3. в э́том ме́сяце; 4. на сле́дующей неде́ле; 5. В э́тот день

D. 1. Его́ не́ было; 2. нас не бу́дет; 3. Мое́й жены́; нет; 4. Ива́на нет; 5. На́сти не́ было

E. 1. Дава́й подождём; 2. Дава́йте, обе́дать; 3. Дава́й позвони́м; 4. Дава́йте договори́мся; 5. Дава́й пойдём

F. 1. бу́дет ра́да; 2. бу́дете свобо́дны; 3. деше́вле; 4. был за́нят; 5. бо́льше, нове́е

# How Did You Do?

Give yourself a point for every correct answer, then use the following key to tell whether you need to review Unit 5:

**0–7 points:** It's probably a good idea to go back through the lesson again. You may be moving too quickly, or there may be too much "down time" between your contact with Russian. Remember that it's better to spend 30 minutes with Russian three or four times a week than it is to spend two or three hours just once a week. Find a pace that's comfortable for you, and spread your contact hours out as much as you can.

**8–12 points:** You would benefit from a review before moving on. Go back and spend a little more time on the specific points that gave you trouble. Re-read the Grammar Builder sections that were difficult, and do the Work Outs one more time. Don't forget about the online supplemental practice material, either. Go to **www.livinglanguage.com/languagelab** for games and quizzes that will reinforce the material from this unit.

**13–17 points:** Good job! There are just a few points that you could consider reviewing. If you haven't worked with the games and quizzes on **www. livinglanguage.com/languagelab**, please give them a try.

**18–20 points:** Great! Congratulations! You've completed Intermediate Russian! You're ready to move on to *Advanced Russian*.

points

# Pronunciation Guide

Russian pronunciation will be easy once you learn the rules of pronunciation and reading, which hold true with very few exceptions. It is just as easy to say *ah* as it is to say *oh,* or to say *vast* as it is to say *fast.* But if you pronounce *f* where it should be *v,* or *oh* where it should be *ah,* or *eh* where it should be *ee,* it would be difficult to understand you. Knowing these rules will help you to have a sound picture of the word you are learning and will help you to recognize it when it is spoken by native speakers; you want to understand as well as to speak!

1. Russian spelling is not phonetic. Spelling and sound don't always match up. Many native Russians think it does, but they are wrong!

2. Learn word units. Always try to pronounce pronouns, prepositions, and adjectives together with the words they modify. Note that all words that have more than one syllable are marked with an accent mark. This is done only for the sake of the student. Accent marks will not be found in reading material outside of textbooks, but for the sake of proper pronunciation, it is necessary to memorize the stress in each word.

3. Russian punctuation varies little from that of English in the use of the semicolon, colon, exclamation point, question mark, and period. However, the use of the comma is determined by concrete grammatical rules and generally does not, as in English, indicate a pause in speech or an inversion in word order.  Usually, commas in Russian indicate a new clause whether principle or subordinate; inversions within one clause don't need commas.

4. Many letters represent several sounds. It is important to keep this in mind at the beginning of your study and to acquire the proper reading and pronunciation habits at the very start.

5. The Russian language has twenty consonant letters representing thirty-five consonant sounds, because fifteen of these twenty letters can represent either soft or hard (palatalized or nonpalatalized) sounds.  Three are hard only; three

are soft only including one semi-vowel (or glide). There are ten vowels and one semi-vowel. We discuss palatalization in more detail in *Essential* Lesson 1 Take It Further 3. For now, consider the following.

6. Softness, or palatalization, of consonants is indicated by the vowels: е, ё, и, ю, я, and ь (soft sign). When a consonant is followed by one of these vowels, the consonant is palatalized—i.e., it is soft. In palatalization, the articulation of a consonant in its nonpalatalized form is altered in a specific way: the place and manner of articulation remain the same, but the middle part of the speaker's tongue moves up to the palate and to the front to produce palatalization. Palatalization in the Russian language has particular significance and should therefore be carefully studied, as the meaning of a word changes through palatalization.

## 1. VOWELS

Now that you've looked at the difference between Russian and English on a broad scale, let's get down to the specifics by looking at individual sounds, starting with Russian vowels.

| LETTER | PRONUNCIATION | EXAMPLES |
|---|---|---|
| Aa | *when stressed, like a in father* | а́рмия (*army*), ла́мпа (*lamp*), ма́ло (*little*) |
| | *when unstressed, like a in father, but shorter* | команди́р (*commander*), каде́т (*cadet*) |
| | *otherwise, like the a in sofa* | каранда́ш (*pencil*), магази́н (*store*), аванга́рд (*avant-garde*) |
| Oo | *when stressed, like the o in gone or aw in saw* | он (*he*), до́брый (*kind*) |

| LETTER | PRONUNCIATION | EXAMPLES |
| --- | --- | --- |
| | *when unstressed, either in first place before the stressed syllable or used initially, like the o in sob* | Борис (*Boris*), она́ (*she*), оно́ (*it*), отвеча́ть (*to answer*) |
| | *otherwise, like the a in sofa* | хорошо́ (*well*), пло́хо (*badly*), молоко́ (*milk*) |
| Уу | *like the oo in food* | стул (*chair*), суп (*soup*), у́тро (*morning*), туда́ (*there* ), уро́к (*lesson*), узнава́ть (*to find out*), учи́тель (*teacher*) |
| ы | *similar to the i in sit but more "throaty"* | ты (*you*), мы (*we*), вы (*pl,. you*), мы́ло (*soap*), малы́ (*short adj., small*), столы́ (*tables*), была́ (*she was*) |
| Ээ | *like the e in echo* | э́то (*this*), э́ти (*these*), поэ́т (*poet*), эта́п (*period, stage*) |

The function of the vowels е, ё, и, ю, я, which are preceded by a glide (the sound similar to the final sound in the English word *may*), is the palatalization of the previous consonant, to which they lose the above-mentioned glide. However, when they follow a vowel or soft or hard signs, or when they appear initially, they are pronounced as in the alphabet—i.e., with the initial glide.

| LETTER | PRONUNCIATION | EXAMPLES |
| --- | --- | --- |
| Ее | *when stressed, like the ye in yet; it always palatalizes the preceding consonant, except the letters* ж, ц, *and* ш *(which are always hard)* | нет (*no*), Ве́ра (*Vera, faith*), сесть (*to sit down*) |
| | *when unstressed, like the i in sit* | всегда́ (*always*), сестра́ (*sister*), жена́ (*wife*) |
| | *initially, or after another vowel, with the glide stressed, like ye in yet, or unstressed, like ye* | ей (*to her*), её (*her*), пое́здка (*trip*) |
| Ёё | *like the yo in yoke; always palatalizes the preceding consonant, except the letters* ж, ц, *and* ш *(which are always hard) and is always stressed* | мёд (*honey*), тётя (*aunt*), ёлка (*fir tree*), моё (*my*), ещё (*yet, still*) |
| Ии | *like ee in beet; always palatalizes the preceding consonant, except the letters* ж, ц, *and* ш *(which are always hard)* | си́ла (*strength*), Ли́за (*Liza*), никогда́ (*never*), иногда́ (*sometimes*) |
| | *after the letters* ж, ц, *and* ш, *like the Russian sound* ы | ши́на (*tire*), жи́ть (*live*) |

| LETTER | PRONUNCIATION | EXAMPLES |
|---|---|---|
| Йй | *like the y in boy* | мой (*my*), пойти́ (*to go*), споко́йно (*quietly*), Нью-Йо́рк (*New York*) |
| Юю | *in the middle of a word, like oo in food; it always palatalizes the preceding consonant* | Лю́ба (*Lyuba*), люблю́ (*I love*), люби́ть (*to love*) |
| | *when used initially, it retains its glide and is pronounced like you* | ю́бка (*skirt*), юбиле́й (*jubilee, anniversary*) |
| Яя | *when stressed in the middle of the word, like ya in yacht; it always palatalizes the preceding consonant* | мя́со (*meat*), мая́к (*lighthouse*) |
| | *when unstressed, it is pronounced either like the ee of beet or like the a of sofa if it is the last letter of a word; it always palatalizes the preceding consonant* | тётя (*aunt*), де́сять (*ten*) |
| | *when stressed, like the ya in yacht; when used initially, it retains its glide* | я́блоко (*apple*), янва́рь (*January*) |
| | *when unstressed, like the yi in yippy* | язы́к (*language, tongue*) |

## 2. HARD AND SOFT SIGNS

| LETTER | PRONUNCIATION | EXAMPLES |
|---|---|---|
| ь | *the soft sign; it palatalizes the preceding consonant, allowing the following vowel to retain its glide, and indicates that the preceding consonant is soft when written at the end of a word* | пье́са (*play*), пья́ный (*drunk*), свинья́ (*pig*) |
| ъ | *the hard sign; it indicates that the preceding consonant remains hard and that the following vowel retains its glide* | объём (*volume*), объясня́ть (*explain*) |

## 3. CONSONANTS

Russian consonants, like those in most languages, may be voiced or voiceless. The distinction between voiced and voiceless consonants is based on one aspect of otherwise identical articulation: in voiced consonants, the vocal cords are involved in articulation, while in voiceless consonants, they are not.

| б в г д ж з | (*voiced*) | *b v g d zh z* |
|---|---|---|
| п ф к т ш с | (*voiceless*) | *p f k t sh s* |

When two consonants are pronounced together in Russian, the first one becomes like the second one if it can.

| всё, все, вчера́ | в = *v becomes voiceless; it's pronounced as f* |
|---|---|

| | |
|---|---|
| сде́лать, сдать | c = s becomes voiced; it's pronounced as z |

The preposition в (*in*) is pronounced as *f* before voiceless consonants. В шко́ле (*in school*) is pronounced f shkoh-leh.

Russian consonants can also be soft or hard, i.e., palatalized or nonpalatalized. Exceptions are the consonants ж, ш, and ц, which are always hard and ч, щ, and й (the glide), which are always soft.

These rules seem complicated, but it is much easier to learn them in the beginning and to start reading and speaking correctly than it is to try to correct erroneous pronunciation later on.

| LETTER | PRONUNCIATION | EXAMPLES |
|---|---|---|
| Бб | *like b in bread* | брат (*brother*), бума́га (*paper*), бага́ж (*baggage*) |
| | *palatalized* | бе́лый (*white*), бино́кль (*binoculars*) |
| | *at the end of a word or before a voiceless consonant, like the p in hip* | ю́бка (*skirt*), зуб (*tooth*), хлеб (*bread*) |
| | *voiceless palatalized* | дробь (*buckshot*), зыбь (*ripple*) |
| Вв | *like the v in very* | ваш (*your*), вот (*here*), вода́ (*water*) |
| | *palatalized* | ве́ра (*faith*), конве́рт (*envelope*), весь (*all*) |

| LETTER | PRONUNCIATION | EXAMPLES |
| --- | --- | --- |
| | *at the end of a word or before a voiceless consonant, like the f in half* | Ки́ев (*Kiev*), в шко́ле (*in school*), вчера́ (*yesterday*), кров (*shelter*) |
| | *voiceless palatalized* | кровь (*blood*) |
| Гг | *like the g in good* | газе́та (*newspaper*), где (*where*), гармо́ния (*harmony*) |
| | *palatalized* | гита́ра (*guitar*), геоме́трия (*geometry*) |
| | *before к, like the Russian к or х (see below)* | легко́ (*lightly, easily*), мя́гко (*softly*) |
| | *between е and о, like the v in victor* | его́ (*his*), ничего́ (*nothing*), сего́дня (*today*) |
| | *at the end of a word, voiceless, like the k in rock* | рог (*horn*), четве́рг (*Thursday*) |
| Дд | *like the d in door* | дом (*house*), родно́й (*kindred*) |
| | *palatalized* | де́рево (*wood*), оди́н (*one*) |
| | *at the end of a word or before a voiceless consonant, like the t in take* | обе́д (*dinner*), подко́ва (*horseshoe*), по́дпись (*signature*) |
| | *voiceless palatalized* | грудь (*breast*) |

| LETTER | PRONUNCIATION | EXAMPLES |
|--------|---------------|----------|
| Жж | *like s in measure* | жар *(heat)*, женá *(wife)*, жить *(to live)*, пожáр *(fire)* |
| | *at the end of a word or before a voiceless consonant, like the sh in shake* | лóжка *(spoon)*, муж *(husband)* |
| | *it always stays hard evern before "soft" vowels* | живóт *(abdomen)*, Жорá *(first name)* |
| Зз | *like the z in zebra* | здáние *(building)*, знать *(to know)* |
| | *palatalized* | зелёный *(green)*, зимá *(winter)* |
| | *at the end of a word or before a voiceless consonant, like the s in sit* | ползти́ *(crawl)*, воз́ *(cart)* |
| Кк | *like the k in kept* | кни́га *(book)*, класс *(class)*, карандáш *(pencil)* |
| | *palatalized* | кéпка *(cap)*, кероси́н *(kerosene)*, Ки́ев *(Kiev)*, кинó *(movie)* |
| | *before a voiced consonant, voiced, like the g in good* | вокзáл *(railroad station)*, экзáмен *(examination)*, к брáту *(to the brother)* |
| Лл | *like the l in look* | лóжка *(spoon)*, лáмпа *(lamp)*, мел *(chalk)* |

| LETTER | PRONUNCIATION | EXAMPLES |
|---|---|---|
| | *palatalized, a bit like the ll in million* | любо́вь (*love*), лёгкий (*light*), мель (*shoal*), боль (*pain*) |
| Мм | *like the m in man* | ма́ма (*mama*), магни́т (*magnet*), дом (*house*), паро́м (*ferry*) |
| | *palatalized* | мя́со (*meat*), ми́на (*mine*) |
| Нн | *like the n in noon* | нос (*nose*), нож (*knife*), балко́н (*balcony*) |
| | *palatalized* | не́бо (*sky*), неде́ля (*week*), ня́ня (*nurse*), конь (*horse*) |
| Пп | *palatalized* | пе́рвый (*first*), письмо́ (*letter*), цепь (*chain*) |
| Рр | *like the r in root* | ру́сский (*Russian*), пара́д (*parade*), пода́рок (*gift*), рука́ (*hand*) |
| | *palatalized* | рис (*rice*), поря́док (*order*), дверь (*door*) |
| Сс | *like the s in see* | сон (*dream*), суп (*soup*), свет (*light*), мясо (*meat*), ма́сло (*butter*) |
| | *palatalized* | се́вер (*north*), село́ (*village*), весь (*all*) |
| | *before a voiced consonant, voiced, like the z in zebra* | сде́лать (*to do*), сгоре́ть (*to burn down*) |

| LETTER | PRONUNCIATION | EXAMPLES |
|---|---|---|
| Тт | like the t in table | табáк (tobacco), тот (that), стол (table), тогдá (then) |
| | palatalized | тень (shade), стенá (wall) |
| | before a voiced consonant, like the d in dark | отдáть (to give away), отгадáть (to guess) |
| Фф | like the f in friend | фáбрика (factory), Фрáнция (France), фарфóр (porcelain) |
| | palatalized | афúша (poster) |
| | before a voiced consonant, like the v in victor | афгáнец (Afghan) |
| Хх | like the ch in loch | тúхо (quietly), хорошó (well), тéхника (technique), блохá (flea) |
| | palatalized | хúна (quinine), хúмия (chemistry) |
| Цц | like the ts in gets | цветóк (flower), цепь (chain), цирк (circus), пациéнт (patient), пéрец (pepper) |
| Чч | before a vowel, like the ch in church; it is always soft even after "hard" vowels | чай (tea), час (hour), чáсто (often), чемодáн (suitcase) |
| | before a consonant, like the sh in shall | что (what), конéчно (of course) |

| LETTER | PRONUNCIATION | EXAMPLES |
|---|---|---|
| Шш | *like the sh in shall* | шаг за ша́гом (*step after step*), ша́хматы (*chess*), ши́на (*tire*), шёлк (*silk*), шерсть (*wool*), ты говори́шь (*you speak (sing.)*) |
| Щщ | *like the shch in fresh cheese; it is always soft even after "hard" vowels* | щека́ (*cheek*), щётка (*brush*), по́мощь (*help*), посеще́ние (*visit*), ща́вель (*sorrel*) |

## 4. SPELLING RULES

All Russian endings fall under two general categories: hard and soft. Hard endings follow hard consonants and soft endings follow soft consonants to maintain vowel correspondence.

| VOWELS IN HARD ENDINGS | VOWELS IN SOFT ENDINGS |
|---|---|
| а | я |
| о | ё |
| у | ю |
| ы | и |
| э | е |

However, an additional complication interferes with this fairly straightforward system and overrides it. This complication is usually referred to as the spelling rule. The spelling rule concerns only eight consonants: four hushers (because they produce a hushing sound)—ж, ш, щ, ч; three gutturals (because they are pronounced in the back of your mouth)—г, к, х; and the letter ц.

All gutturals and all hushers must be followed by the letters: а, у, and и (and never by я, ю, ы)!

Ц is followed by an ы at the end of the word, but by an и in the middle.

All hushers and ц must be followed by either a stressed о or an unstressed е!

Memorize this spelling rule and always keep it in mind along with the above chart! They will take mystery out of the Russian endings and will reduce in half what you otherwise would have to memorize mechanically.

Keep in mind the following points:

- жо and жё, and цэ and це, are pronounced alike.
- цы and ци, шо and шё, and the letters ж, ц, and ш are always hard.
- чо and чё, що and щё, and the letters ч and щ are always soft.

Read these rules over and over again. Listen to the recordings several times. You have learned them not when you have read and understood the rules, but when you can remember and repeat the sounds and words correctly without looking at the book. Master these, and you will speak Russian well.

Five fundamental rules

1. Remember which syllable is stressed; all others will be reduced.

2. Remember that unstressed о is pronounced *ah* in prestressed positions including unstressed positions in the beginning of the word and as a very short sound ə (*schwa*) in all other unstressed positions.

3. Remember that when two consonants are next to each other, the first changes according to the second; all voiced consonants become voiceless at the end of the word (if they can).

4. Remember that unstressed е and я in prestressed syllables are pronounced *eeh*.

5. Remember that the letters е, ё, и, ю, я, and ь palatalize the preceding consonant, unless it has no palatalized counterpart.

6. Remember that the letters е, ё, ю and я lose their initial glide й after consonants, but retain it after vowels, the soft and hard signs (ь and ъ), and in the beginning of the word.

# Grammar Summary

## 1. THE RUSSIAN ALPHABET

| RUSSIAN LETTER | NAME |
|---|---|
| Аа | *ah* |
| Бб | *beh* |
| Вв | *veh* |
| Гг | *geh* |
| Дд | *deh* |
| Ее | *yeh* |
| Ёё | *yoh* |
| Жж | *zheh* |
| Зз | *zeh* |
| Ии | *ee* |
| Йй | *ee krátkoye* |
| Кк | *kah* |
| Лл | *el* |
| Мм | *em* |
| Нн | *en* |
| Оо | *oh, aw* |
| Пп | *peh* |
| Рр | *er* |
| Сс | *es* |
| Тт | *teh* |
| Уу | *oo* |
| Фф | *ef* |
| Хх | *khah* |
| Цц | *tseh* |
| Чч | *cheh* |
| Шш | *shah* |
| Щщ | *shchah* |

| RUSSIAN LETTER | NAME |
|---|---|
| Ы | *i* |
| Ь | *soft sign* |
| Ъ | *hard sign* |
| Ээ | *eh* |
| Юю | *yoo* |
| Яя | *yah* |

## 2. PRONUNCIATION

### VOWELS

The letter a, when stressed, is pronounced like the English *ah*; when unstressed before a stressed syllable, a is pronounced *ah*, but shorter, and in most other positions is given a brief sound, the so called *shwa* sound /ə/ as in the English *but* or *fun*. Like in English, the Russian /ə/ (*shwa*) cannot be stressed.

The letter o, when stressed, is pronounced *oh* or *aw* as in *saw* (spoken with a rounded east coast accent) but it is not a diphthong, that is, it is never pronounced as a long *o* in the English *Oh!* or *Joe*; when unstressed in first place before the stressed syllable or used initially, o is pronounced *ah* (indistinguishable from a), and in all other positions it becomes a *shwa* /ə/ (just like an a).

The letter y is pronounced both stressed and unstressed like the English *oo* in *hook* or *loop*, except that the unstressed y is a bit shorter.

The letter ы doesn't have an exact English equivalent; it is somewhat similar to the *i* sound in *silly*.

The letter э is pronounced like the *eh* in *echo*.

Five vowels—е, ё, и, ю, and я—have a glide (the sound similar to the final sound in the English word *boy* and the Russian й) in front of them. The function of these vowels is the palatalization (softening) of the preceding consonant, to which they lose the above-mentioned glide. However, when they follow a vowel or a soft or hard sign, or when they appear in the initial position in a word, they are pronounced as in the alphabet, i.e., with the initial glide.

The letter и always palatalizes the preceding consonant and is pronounced like the *ee* in *beet*, except when it follows the letters ж, ц, and ш (which are never palatalized); then it is pronounced like the Russian sound ы.

The letter е always palatalizes the consonant that precedes it, except when the consonant is ж, ц, or ш. When stressed, it is pronounced like the *yeh* in *yet*; in unstressed positions it is pronounced like the *ee* in *beet*. In the beginning of a word, it is pronounced with the glide: when stressed, like *yeh*; unstressed, like *yeeh*.

The letter ё always palatalizes the preceding consonant, and is always stressed. It is pronounced *yoh* as in *yawn* (spoken with a rounded east coast accent).

The letter я always palatalizes the preceding consonant; when stressed, it is pronounced *yah,* and when unstressed, it is pronounced like a shortened *ee.* In the initial position, it retains its glide; when stressed, it is pronounced *yah,* and when unstressed, *ee* (after consonants) and *yeeh* (elsewhere).

The letter ю always palatalizes the preceding consonant. It is pronounced *yoo* everywhere exept after consonants where it loses its glide and becomes a "soft" *oo* (like the French *u* in *tu* or the German *ü* in *über*).

The letter ь is called the soft sign; it palatalizes the preceding consonant, allowing the following vowel to retain its glide.

The letter ъ is called the hard sign. It indicates that the preceding consonant remains hard and that the following vowel retains its glide.

The glide й is more a consonant than a vowel: it can never be stressed or form a syllable. It is pronounced like the final sound in *boy*.

## CONSONANTS

As in many languages, most Russian consonants may be voiced or voiceless, and form several pairs.

|  | RUSSIAN | ENGLISH |
|---|---|---|
| voiced | б в г д ж з | *b v g d zh z* |
| voiceless | п ф к т ш с | *p f k t sh s* |

When two consonants are pronounced together, they must both be either voiced or voiceless. In Russian, the second one always remains as it is, and the first one changes accordingly.

| всё, все, вчера́ | в (*v*) pronounced as *f* |
|---|---|
| сделать, сдать | с (*s*) pronounced as *z* |

The preposition в (*in*) is pronounced *f* before a voiceless consonant in the beginning of the next word: В шко́ле is pronounced *f shkoh-leh*. All consonants—except л, м, н, and р—lose their voicing and become voiceless at the end of a word.

All consonants—except ж, ц, ш, ч, щ, and й—can also be either hard or soft (i.e., nonpalatalized or palatalized). They become soft when followed by the letter ё, и, ю, я or ь. ж, ц, and ш are always hard and ч, щ, and й (if we consider it a consonant) are always soft. One more note on pronunciation: the letter г, when appearing between the vowels е/о and о in grammatical endings, is pronounced *v*, as in the word ничего́, никого́.

## 3. GENDER

All Russian nouns, pronouns, adjectives, ordinal numerals, as well as cardinal numerals one and two, and even verbs in the past tense have gender: masculine, feminine, or neuter. There is no gender distinction in the plural.

| | MASCULINE | FEMININE | NEUTER | PLURAL |
|---|---|---|---|---|
| Noun, pronoun, past tense verb endings | hard consonant, ь | а/я | о/е | а/я, ы/и |
| Adjective, ordinal numeral, participle ending | ой/ый/ий | ая/яя | ое/ее | ые/ие |

Note: Pronouns, adjectives, and ordinal numerals always agree in gender and number with the nouns they modify.

## 4. CASES

a. With few exceptions, all nouns, pronouns, and adjectives decline, i.e. change form depending on their function in a sentence. Each declension has six cases.

| Nominative | Кто? Что | *Who? What?* |
|---|---|---|
| Genitive | Кого? Чего? <br> От кого? От чего? <br> У кого? У чего? <br> Без кого? Без чего? | *Whom? What?* <br> *From whom? From what?* <br> *At or by whom/what?* <br> *Without whom/what?* |
| Dative | Кому? Чему? <br> К кому? К чему? | *To whom? To what?* <br> *Toward whom/what?* |

| Accusative | Кого́? Что?<br>Куда́? | Whom? What?<br>Where (direction toward)? |
|---|---|---|
| Instrumental | Кем? Чем?<br>С кем? С чем? | By whom? By what?<br>With whom? With what? |
| Prepositional or<br>Locative | О ком? О чём?<br>В ком? В чём?<br>Где? | About whom/what?<br>In whom? In what?<br>Where (location)? |

b. Overall characteristics of the cases and most used prepositions:

1. The nominative case is used for the subject of the sentence.

2. The genitive case is the case of possession and negation. It is also used with many prepositions, the most common of which are:

| без | without |
|---|---|
| для | for |
| до | up to |
| из | out of |
| о́коло | near, next to |
| от | from |
| по́сле | after |
| у | at or by |

3. The dative case is used in the meaning of *to whom/what*. Prepositions used with the dative case are:

| к | toward |
|---|---|
| по | along |

4. The accusative is the direct object case. It is also used after prepositions denoting direction:

| в | to, into |
|---|---|
| за | behind (direction), for, instead of |
| на | to, into, on (direction) |

5. The instrumental case indicates the manner of action or instrument with which the action is performed; the instrumental of means is used without prepositions. Prepositions used with the instrumental case include:

| с | with (together with, accompaniment) |
|---|---|
| мéжду | between |
| пéред | in front of |
| над | over |
| под | under (location) |
| за | behind (location) |

6. The prepositional or locative case indicates location and is also used when speaking about something or someone. This is the only case which cannot be used without prepositions. The prepositions most frequently used with this case are:

| в | in, at |
|---|---|
| на | on, at |
| о/об | about |
| при | in the presence of, under (the reign of) |

## 5. DECLENSION OF NOUNS

| MASCULINE SINGULAR | Hard: Animate | Hard: Inanimate | Soft: Animate | Soft: Inanimate |
|---|---|---|---|---|
| | *student* | *question* | *inhabitant* | *shed* |
| Nom. | студе́нт | вопро́с | жи́тель | сара́й |
| Gen. | студе́нт-а | вопро́с-а | жи́тел-я | сара́-я |
| Dat. | студе́нт-у | вопро́с-у | жи́тел-ю | сара́-ю |
| Acc. | студе́нт-а | вопро́с | жи́тел-я | сара́й |
| Inst. | студе́нт-ом | вопро́с-ом | жи́тел-ем | сара́-ем |
| Prep. | о студе́нт-е | о вопро́с-е | о жи́тел-е | о сара́-е |

| MASCULINE PLURAL | | | | |
|---|---|---|---|---|
| Nom. | студе́нт-ы | вопро́с-ы | жи́тел-и | сара́-и |
| Gen. | студе́нт-ов | вопро́с-ов | жи́тел-ей | сара́-ев |
| Dat. | студе́нт-ам | вопро́с-ам | жи́тел-ям | сара́-ям |
| Acc. | студе́нт-ов | вопро́с-ы | жи́тел-ей | сара́-и |
| Inst. | студе́нт-ами | вопро́с-ами | жи́тел-ями | сара́-ями |
| Prep. | о студе́нт-ах | о вопро́с-ах | о жи́тел-ях | о сара́-ях |

Notice that the accusative case of animate masculine nouns (and all animate plural nouns) is the same as the genitive, while the accusative of inanimate masculine nouns is the same as the nominative.

| FEMININE SINGULAR | Hard | Soft | |
|---|---|---|---|
| | *room* | *earth* | *family* |
| Nom. | ко́мната | земля́ | семья́ |
| Gen. | ко́мнат-ы |земл-и́ | семь-и́ |
| Dat. | ко́мнат-е | земл-е́ | семь-е́ |
| Acc. | ко́мнат-у | зе́мл-ю | семь-ю́ |
| Inst. | ко́мнат-ой(ою) | земл-ёй(ёю) | семь-ёй(ёю) |

**FEMININE SINGULAR**

|  | Hard | Soft |  |
|---|---|---|---|
|  | *room* | *earth* | *family* |
| Prep. | о ко́мнат-е | о земл-е́ | о семь-е́ |

**FEMININE PLURAL**

| Nom. | ко́мнат-ы | зе́мл-ии | семь-и́ |
|---|---|---|---|
| Gen. | ко́мнат | земе́л-ь | сем-е́й |
| Dat. | ко́мнат-ам | зе́мл-ям | се́мь-ям |
| Acc. | ко́мнат-ы | зе́мл-ии | се́мь-и |
| Inst. | ко́мнат-ами | зе́мл-ями | се́мь-ями |
| Prep. | о ко́мнат-ах | о зе́мл-ях | о се́мь-ях |

**NEUTER SINGULAR**

|  | Hard | Soft |  |
|---|---|---|---|
|  | *window* | *sea* | *wish* |
| Nom. | окно́ | мо́ре | жела́ние |
| Gen. | окн-а́ | мо́р-я | жела́н-ия |
| Dat. | окн-у́ | мо́р-ю | жела́н-ию |
| Acc. | окн-о́ | мо́р-е | жела́н-ие |
| Inst. | окн-о́м | мо́р-ем | жела́н-ием |
| Prep. | об окн-е | о мо́р-е | о жела́н-ии |

**NEUTER PLURAL**

| Nom. | о́кн-а | мор-я́ | жела́н-ия |
|---|---|---|---|
| Gen. | о́к-оон | мор-е́й | жела́н-ий |
| Dat. | о́кн-ам | мор-я́м | жела́н-иям |
| Acc. | о́кн-а | мор-я́ | жела́н-ия |
| Inst. | о́кн-ами | мор-я́ми | жела́н-иями |
| Prep. | об о́кн-ах | о мор-я́х | о жела́н-иях |

*Note: The variants (ою), (ёю), and (ёю) in the instrumental case for feminine singular nouns are poetic, dialectal, or folksy. Also б is added to the preposition о (as in the prepositional case of hard neuter singular nouns) before vowels (excluding the vowels е, ё, я, and ю, which start with the glide й).

## SOME IRREGULAR DECLENSIONS

| SINGULAR | | | | |
|---|---|---|---|---|
| | Masculine | Feminine | | Neuter |
| | *road* | *mother* | *daughter* | *name* |
| Nom. | путь | мать | дочь | и́мя |
| Gen. | пут-и́ | ма́т-ери | до́ч-ери | и́м-ени |
| Dat. | пут-и́ | ма́т-ери | до́ч-ери | и́м-ени |
| Acc. | путь | мать | дочь | и́мя |
| Inst. | пут-ём | ма́т-ерью | до́ч-ерью | и́м-енем |
| Prep. | о пут-и́ | о ма́т-ери | о до́ч-ери | об и́м-ени |

| PLURAL | | | | | |
|---|---|---|---|---|---|
| Nom. | пут-и́ | ма́т-ери | до́ч-ери | им-ена́ | де́т-и |
| Gen. | пут-е́й | мат-ере́й | доч-ере́й | им-ён | дет-е́й |
| Dat. | пут-я́м | мат-еря́м | доч-еря́м | им-ена́м | де́т-ям |
| Acc. | пут-и́ | мат-ере́й | доч-ере́й* | им-ена́ | дет-е́й* |
| Inst. | пут-я́ми | мат-еря́ми | доч-еря́ми | им-ена́ми | дет-ьми́ |
| Prep. | о пут-я́х | о мат-еря́х | о доч-еря́х | об им-ена́х | о де́т-ях |

*Note: Since there is no gender distinction in the plural, the accusative plural of all animate nouns is the same as the genitive plural.

## 6. DECLENSION OF ADJECTIVES

**SINGULAR**

|  | Masc. | Fem. | Neut. | Masc. | Fem. | Neut. |
|---|---|---|---|---|---|---|
|  | ый | ая | ое | ой | ая | ое |
| Nom. | но́вый | но́вая | но́вое | сухо́й | суха́я | сухо́е |
| Gen. | но́в-ого | но́в-ой | но́в-ого | сух-о́го | сух-о́й | сух-о́го |
| Dat. | но́в-ому | но́в-ой | но́в-ому | сух-о́му | сух-о́й | сух-о́му |
| Acc. | *same as nom. or gen.* | но́в-ую | но́в-ое | *same as nom. or gen.* | сух-у́ю | сух-о́е |
| Inst. | но́в-ым | но́в-ой(-ою) | но́в-ым | сух-и́м | сух-о́й(-ою) | сух-и́м |
| Prep. | о но́в-ом | о но́в-ой | о но́в-ом | о сух-о́м | о сух-о́й | о сух-о́м |

**PLURAL**

| Nom. | но́в-ые | сух-и́е |
|---|---|---|
| Gen. | но́в-ых | сух-и́х |
| Dat. | но́в-ым | сух-и́м |
| Acc. | *same as nom. or gen.* | *same as nom. or gen.* |
| Inst. | но́в-ыми | сух-и́ми |
| Prep. | о но́в-ых | о сух-и́х |

|  | **SINGULAR** | | | **PLURAL** |
|---|---|---|---|---|
|  | Masc. | Fem. | Neut. |  |
| NOM. | си́н-ий | си́н-яя | си́н-ее | си́н-ие |
| Gen. | си́н-его | си́н-ей | си́н-его | си́н-их |
| Dat. | си́н-ему | си́н-ей | си́н-ему | си́н-им |
| Acc. | *same as nom. or gen.* | си́н-юю | си́н-ее | *same as nom. or gen.* |
| Inst. | си́н-им | си́н-ей(-ею) | си́н-им | си́н-ими |
| Prep. | о си́н-ем | о си́н-ей | о си́н-ем | о си́н-их |

## 7. DECLENSION OF PRONOUNS

Below are the personal pronouns in their various forms.

| | SINGULAR | | | | |
|---|---|---|---|---|---|
| | 1st person | 2nd person | 3rd person | | |
| | | | MASC. | NEUT. | FEM. |
| Nom. | я | ты | он | оно́ | она́ |
| Gen. | меня́ | тебя́ | его́ | его́ | её |
| Dat. | мне | тебе | ему́ | ему́ | ей |
| Acc. | меня́ | тебя́ | его́ | его́ | её |
| Instr. | мной(-о́ю) | тобо́й(-о́ю) | им | им | ей (е́ю) |
| Prep. | обо мне | о тебе | о нём | о нём | о ней |

| | PLURAL | | | REFLEXIVE |
|---|---|---|---|---|
| | 1st person | 2nd person | 3rd person | Reflexive pronoun (*sing.* *or pl.*) |
| Nom. | мы | вы | они́ | — |
| Gen. | нас | вас | их | себя́ |
| Dat. | нам | вам | им | себе |
| Acc. | нас | вас | их | себя́ |
| Instr. | на́ми | ва́ми | и́ми | собо́й(-о́ю) |
| Prep. | о нас | о вас | о них | о себе |

The various forms of *my* are shown below.

| | SINGULAR | | | PLURAL |
|---|---|---|---|---|
| | Masc. | Fem. | Neut. | All genders |
| Nom. | мой | моя́ | моё | мои́ |
| Gen. | моего́ | моей | моего́ | мои́х |
| Dat. | моему́ | моей | моему́ | мои́м |

|  | SINGULAR | | | PLURAL |
|---|---|---|---|---|
|  | Masc. | Fem. | Neut. | All genders |
| Acc. | same as nom. or gen. | мою | моё | same as nom. or gen. |
| Inst. | мои́м | мое́й(-ею) | мои́м | мои́ми |
| Prep. | о моём | о мое́й | о моём | о мои́х |

Твой (*your, sg.*), свой (*the subject's own*) are declined in the same way.

For the third-person possessive, the genitive case of the personal pronouns is used. It always agrees with the gender and number of the possessor.

| NOMINATIVE | GENITIVE | ENGLISH |
|---|---|---|
| он | его́ | *his* |
| она́ | её | *her* |
| оно́ | его́ | *its* |
| они́ | их | *their* |

The various forms of *our* are shown below.

|  | SINGULAR | | | PLURAL |
|---|---|---|---|---|
|  | Masc. | Fem. | Neut. | All genders |
| Nom. | наш | на́ша | на́ше | на́ши |
| Gen. | на́ш-его | на́ш-ей | на́ш-его | на́ш-их |
| Dat. | на́ш-ему | на́ш-ей | на́ш-ему | на́ш-им |
| Acc. | same as nom. or gen. | на́ш-у | на́ше | same as nom. or gen. |
| Inst. | на́ш-им | на́ш-ей(-ею) | на́ш-им | на́ш-ими |
| Prep. | о на́ш-ем | о на́ш-ей | о на́ш-ем | о на́ш-их |

Ваш (*pl.* or *form., your*) is declined in the same way.

*All* is shown in its various forms below.

|  | SINGULAR | | | PLURAL |
|---|---|---|---|---|
|  | Masc. | Fem. | Neut. | All genders |
| Nom. | весь | вся | всё | все |
| Gen. | вс-его́ | вс-ей | вс-его́ | вс-ех |
| Dat. | вс-ему́ | вс-ей | вс-ему́ | вс-ем |
| Acc. | same as nom. or gen. | вс-ю | всё | same as nom. or gen. |
| Inst. | вс-ем | вс-ей(-ею) | вс-ем | вс-еми |
| Prep. | обо вс-ём | обо вс-ей | обо вс-ём | обо вс-ех |

The forms of the demonstratives *this/these* are shown below.

|  | SINGULAR | | | PLURAL |
|---|---|---|---|---|
|  | Masc. | Fem. | Neut. | All genders |
| Nom. | э́тот | э́та | э́то | э́ти |
| Gen. | э́т-ого | э́т-ой | э́т-ого | э́т-их |
| Dat. | э́т-ому | э́т-ой | э́т-ому | э́т-им |
| Acc. | same as nom. or gen. | э́т-у | э́то | same as nom. or gen. |
| Inst. | э́т-им | э́т-ой | э́т-им | э́т-ими |
| Prep. | об э́т-ом | об э́т-ой | об э́т-ом | об э́т-их |

The forms of the demonstratives *that/those* are shown below.

|  | SINGULAR | | | PLURAL |
|---|---|---|---|---|
|  | Masc. | Fem. | Neut. | All genders |
| Nom. | тот | та | то | те |
| Gen. | т-ого́ | т-ой | т-ого́ | т-ех |

|  | SINGULAR | | | PLURAL |
|---|---|---|---|---|
|  | Masc. | Fem. | Neut. | All genders |
| Dat. | т-омý | т-ой | т-омý | т-ем |
| Acc. | same as nom. or gen. | т-у | т-о | same as nom. or gen. |
| Inst. | т-ем | т-ой | т-ем | т-еми |
| Prep. | о т-ом | о т-ой | о т-ом | о т-ех |

The forms of *oneself/themselves* are shown below.

|  | SINGULAR | | | PLURAL |
|---|---|---|---|---|
|  | Masc. | Fem. | Neut. | All genders |
| Nom. | сам | самá | самó | сáми |
| Gen. | сам-огó | сам-óй | сам-огó | сам-и́х |
| Dat. | сам-омý | сам-óй | сам-омý | сам-и́м |
| Acc. | same as nom. or gen. | сам-ý | сам-о | same as nom. or gen. |
| Inst. | сам-и́м | сам-óй | сам-и́м | сам-и́ми |
| Prep. | о сам-óм | о сам-óй | о сам-óм | о сам-и́х |

The forms of *whose* are shown below.

|  | SINGULAR | | | PLURAL |
|---|---|---|---|---|
|  | Masc. | Fem. | Neut. | All genders |
| Nom. | чей | чья | чьё | чьи |
| Gen. | чьегó | чьей | чьегó | чьих |
| Dat. | чьемý | чьей | чьемý | чьим |
| Acc. | same as nom. or gen. | чью | чьё | same as nom. or gen. |
| Inst. | чьим | чьей | чьим | чьи́ми |
| Prep. | о чьём | о чьей | о чьём | о чьих |

## 8. THE COMPARATIVE OF ADJECTIVES

To form most comparatives of adjectives, drop the gender ending and add –ee for all genders and the plural. The adjective does not decline in the comparative.

| | |
|---|---|
| краси́вый | *pretty* |
| краси́в-ее | *prettier* |
| тёплый | *warm* |
| тепл-е́е | *warmer* |
| весёлый | *merry* |
| весел-е́е | *merrier* |

Comparative forms with one –е in the ending:

| | |
|---|---|
| хоро́ший | *good* |
| лу́чше | *better* |
| большо́й | *big* |
| бо́льше | *bigger* |
| ма́ленький | *small* |
| ме́ньше | *smaller* |
| широ́кий | *wide* |
| ши́ре | *wider* |
| у́зкий | *narrow* |
| у́же | *narrower* |
| плохо́й | *bad* |
| ху́же | *worse* |
| высо́кий | *tall, high* |
| вы́ше | *taller, higher* |
| ти́хий | *quiet* |
| ти́ше | *quieter* |
| дорого́й | *dear, expensive* |

| доро́же | *dearer, more expensive* |
| простóй | *simple* |
| прóще | *simpler* |
| тóлстый | *fat, thick* |
| тóлще | *fatter, thicker* |

## 9. THE SUPERLATIVE OF ADJECTIVES

The superlative of adjectives has two forms. The simpler form—the one we will discuss here—makes use of the word сáмый, сáмая, сáмое, сáмые (*the most*).

| сáмый большóй | *the biggest* |
| сáмая красѝвая | *the prettiest* |
| сáмый ýмный | *the most clever* |

The word сáмый declines with the adjective:

в сáмом большóм доме

*in the largest house*

Он пришёл с сáмой красѝвой женщиной.

*He came with the prettiest woman.*

## 10. CASES USED WITH CARDINAL NUMBERS ОДИ́Н (*M.*), ОДНА́ (*F.*), ОДНО́ (*N.*), ОДНИ́ (*PL.*) AND ДВА (*M.*), ДВЕ (*F.*), ДВА (*N.*).

A. When the number is used in the nominative case or accusative inanimate:

after оди́н, однá, однó—use the nominative singular;

after одни́—use the nominative plural;

after два, две, три, четы́ре—use the genitive singular;

after пять, шесть, семь, etc.—use the genitive plural.

B. When the number is compound, the case of the noun depends on the last digit (excluding the zero):

два́дцать оди́н каранда́ш (*nominative singular*)
*twenty-one pencils*

два́дцать два карандаша́ (*genitive singular*)
*twenty-two pencils*

два́дцать пять карандаше́й (*genitive plural*)
*twenty-five pencils*

## 11. DECLENSION OF CARDINAL NUMERALS

All cardinal numerals decline, agreeing in case with the noun they modify (with the exception of the nominative and the accusative inanimate cases, discussed above).

Я оста́лся без одно́й копе́йки. (*genitive singular*)
*I was left without one kopeck.*

Он был там оди́н ме́сяц без двух дней. (*genitive plural*)
*He was there one month less two days.*

Мы пришли́ к пяти́ часа́м. (*dative plural*)
*We arrived by five o'clock.*

Они́ говоря́т о семи́ кни́гах. (*prepositional plural*)
*They are talking about seven books.*

## Declension of *One/Only*

|       | SINGULAR |          |          | PLURAL |
|-------|----------|----------|----------|--------|
|       | Masc.    | Fem.     | Neut.    | All genders |
| Nom.  | оди́н    | одна́    | одно́    | одни́  |
| Gen.  | одного́  | одно́й   | одного́  | одни́х |
| Dat.  | одному́  | одно́й   | одному́  | одни́м |
| Acc.  | same as nom. or gen. | одну́ | одно́ | same as nom. or gen. |
| Inst. | одни́м   | одно́й(-о́ю) | одни́м | одни́ми |
| Prep. | об одно́м | об одно́й | об одно́м | об одних |

## Declension of other numerals

|       | *TWO*    | *THREE*  | *FOUR*   | *FIVE* |
|-------|----------|----------|----------|--------|
| Nom.  | два/две  | три      | четы́ре  | пять   |
| Gen.  | двух     | трёх     | четырёх  | пяти́  |
| Dat.  | двум     | трём     | четырём  | пяти́  |
| Acc.  | same as nom. or gen. | same as nom. or gen. | same as nom. or gen. | пять |
| Inst. | двумя́   | тремя́   | четырьмя́ | пятью́ |
| Prep. | о двух   | о трёх   | о четырёх | о пяти́ |

Note: All numbers from 6 to 20 follow the same declension pattern as 5.

The numerals 40 (со́рок), 90 (девяно́сто), and 100 (сто) end in –a in all cases except for the nominative: сорока́, девяно́ста, and ста.

## 12. ORDINAL NUMERALS

All ordinal numerals are like adjectives, and decline in the same way as adjectives.

| MASC.    | FEM.     | NEUT.    | PLURAL (ALL GENDERS) |
|----------|----------|----------|----------------------|
| пе́рвый  | пе́рвая  | пе́рвое  | пе́рвые              |

| MASC. | FEM. | NEUT. | PLURAL (ALL GENDERS) |
|---|---|---|---|
| второ́й | втора́я | второ́е | вторы́е |

When they are compound, only the last digit changes its form, and only that digit is declined.

| двадца́тый век | twentieth century |
|---|---|
| Э́то бы́ло три́дцать пе́рвого декабря́. | That was on December 31. |
| тре́тий раз | third time |
| Втора́я мирова́я война́ зако́нчилась в ты́сяча девятьсо́т со́рок пя́том году́. | World War II ended in 1945 (lit., one thousand, nine hundred, forty-fifth year). |
| в пя́том году́ (prep., sing.) | in the fifth year |

## 13. DOUBLE NEGATIVES

With negative ни–words such as:

| ничего́ | nothing |
|---|---|
| никто́ | nobody |
| никогда́ | never |
| никуда́ | nowhere |

a second negative не must be used before the verb:

| Я ничего́ | не | хочу́, зна́ю |
|---|---|---|
| I nothing | not (don't) | want, know |
| Никто́ | не | ви́дит, говори́т |
| Nobody | not (don't) | see, speak |
| Он никогда́ | не | был в Москве́ |
| He never | not (don't) | was in Moscow |
| Мы никогда́ | не | говори́м по-ру́сски |

| We never | not (don't) | speak Russian |
|---|---|---|

## 14. VERBS

Regular Russian verbs have two conjugation types, Conjugation I and Conjugation II. Only three types of verbal stems belong to Conjugation II—е–types (e.g., ви́деть), и–types (e.g., говори́ть), and а2–types (e.g., слы́шать). All other regular verbs belong to Conjugation Type I (e.g., рабо́тать, жить, etc.). There are also irregular verbs (e.g., есть, хоте́ть). In addition, all Russian verbs are either imperfective or perfective.

### A. Typical conjugations of imperfective verbs

First conjugation

| ЧИТА́ТЬ<br>*TO READ* | |
|---|---|
| **Present tense:** | я чита́ю<br>ты чита́ешь<br>он чита́ет<br>мы чита́ем<br>вы чита́ете<br>они́ чита́ют |
| **Past tense:** | чита́л (*m.*)<br>чита́ла (*f.*)<br>чита́ло (*n.*)<br>чита́ли (*pl.*) |
| **Future tense:** | я бу́ду чита́ть<br>ты бу́дешь чита́ть<br>он бу́дет чита́ть<br>мы бу́дем чита́ть<br>вы бу́дете чита́ть<br>они́ бу́дут чита́ть |

| ЧИТА́ТЬ TO READ | |
|---|---|
| Imperative: | чита́й |
| | чита́йте |

## Participles

| ACTIVE | |
|---|---|
| Present tense: | чита́ющий |
| Past tense: | чита́вший |

| PASSIVE | |
|---|---|
| Present tense: | чита́емый |

| GERUND | |
|---|---|
| Imperfective gerund: | чита́я |

## Second conjugation

| ГОВОРИ́ТЬ TO SPEAK | |
|---|---|
| Present tense: | я говорю́ |
| | ты говори́шь |
| | он говори́т |
| | мы говори́м |
| | вы говори́те |
| | они́ говоря́т |
| Past tense: | говори́л (*m.*) |
| | говори́ла (*f.*) |
| | говори́ло (*n.*) |
| | говори́ли (*pl.*) |

| ГОВОРИ́ТЬ<br>*TO SPEAK* | |
|---|---|
| Future tense: | я бу́ду говори́ть |
| | ты бу́дешь говори́ть |
| | он бу́дет говори́ть |
| | мы бу́дем говори́ть |
| | вы бу́дете говори́ть |
| | они́ бу́дут говори́ть |
| Imperative: | говори́ |
| | говори́те |

| PARTICIPLES | |
|---|---|
| Present tense: | говоря́щий |
| Past tense: | говори́вший |

| GERUND | |
|---|---|
| Imperfective gerund: | говоря́ |

## B. Mixed conjugation

| PRESENT TENSE | |
|---|---|
| ХОТЕ́ТЬ<br>*TO WANT* | |
| я хочу́ | мы хоти́м |
| ты хо́чешь | вы хоти́те |
| он хо́чет | они́ хотя́т |

Note: This verb in the singular has first conjugation endings with the т changing to ч (т/ч mutation). In the plural it has second conjugation endings. The past tense is regular.

## C. Reflexive verbs

Verbs ending with –ся or –сь are reflexive. These verbs follow the general form of conjugation, retaining the endings –ся after consonants and –сь after vowels.

| ЗАНИМА́ТЬСЯ<br>*TO STUDY* | |
|---|---|
| я занима́юсь | мы занима́емся |
| ты занима́ешься | вы занима́етесь |
| он занима́ется | они́ занима́ются |

## D. The verb быть (*to be*)

The verb быть (*to be*) is usually omitted in the present tense, but is used in the past tense:

был (*m.*)
была́ (*f.*)
бы́ло (*n.*)
бы́ли (*pl.*)

and in the future tense:

| я бу́ду | мы бу́дем |
|---|---|
| ты бу́дешь | вы бу́дете |
| он бу́дет | они́ бу́дут |

It is also used as an auxiliary verb in the imperfective future tense.

## E. Conjugations of other verbs in the present tense

| БРАТЬ (NON-SYLLABIC A–TYPE, CONJUGATION I)<br>*TO TAKE* | |
|---|---|
| я беру́ | мы берём |
| ты берёшь | вы берёте |

## БРАТЬ (NON-SYLLABIC A–TYPE, CONJUGATION I)
*TO TAKE*

| он берёт | они́ беру́т |
|---|---|

## ВЕСТИ́ (Д–TYPE, CONJUGATION I)
*TO LEAD*

| я веду́ | мы ведём |
|---|---|
| ты ведёшь | вы ведёте |
| он ведёт | они́ веду́т |

## ЖИТЬ (В–TYPE, CONJUGATION I)
*TO LIVE*

| я живу́ | мы живём |
|---|---|
| ты живёшь | вы живёте |
| он живёт | они́ живу́т |

## ЗВАТЬ (NON-SYLLABIC A–TYPE, CONJUGATION I)
*TO CALL*

| я зову́ | мы зовём |
|---|---|
| ты зовёшь | вы зовёте |
| он зовёт | они́ зову́т |

## НЕСТИ́ (С–TYPE, CONJUGATION I)
*TO CARRY*

| я несу́ | мы несём |
|---|---|
| ты несёшь | вы несёте |
| он несёт | они́ несу́т |

## ДАВА́ТЬ (АВАЙ–TYPE, CONJUGATION I)
*TO GIVE*

| я даю́ | мы даём |
|---|---|
| ты даёшь | вы даёте |
| он даёт | они́ даю́т |

F. Conjugations of irregular perfective verbs (perfective future)

| ДАТЬ **(IRREGULAR)** TO GIVE | |
|---|---|
| я дам | мы дади́м |
| ты дашь | вы дади́те |
| он даст | они́ даду́т |

| СЕСТЬ **(И–TYPE, CONJUGATION II)** TO SIT DOWN | |
|---|---|
| я ся́ду | мы ся́дем |
| ты ся́дешь | вы ся́дете |
| он ся́дет | они́ ся́дут |

G. Perfective and imperfective aspects of Russian verbs

Russian verbs are either perfective or imperfective. Imperfective verbs express continuous actions, durations, or single actions taken out of immediate contexts, so called "statements of fact." They have three tenses—past, present, and future. Perfective verbs indicate complete and completed singular actions, changes of state relative to the existing context, and multiple actions in quick succession; all perfective verbs presuppose the interlocutor's awareness of their context. They have only two tenses—past and future.

Some perfective verbs are formed by adding the prefixes с–, на–, вы–, в–, по–, etc. to imperfective verbs; some others add suffixes such as –и– or –ну–. When an imperfective verb is turned into a perfective one, its meaning changes dramatically so it becomes a different verb.

| IMPERFECTIVE | PERFECTIVE |
|---|---|
| писа́ть to write | напи́сать to write down, to complete a written assignment |

| IMPERFECTIVE | PERFECTIVE |
| --- | --- |
| | переписа́ть<br>*to copy, to re-write* |

When you need to use the new prefixed verb переписа́ть (*to copy, to re-write*) in the imperfective aspect without losing the meaning of the prefix (e.g., if you *copy* something every day), you form a so-called "secondary imperfective form" by adding new imperfective suffixes to the perfective (prefixed) stem. The most common secondary imperfective suffix is –ыва–, but suffixes –ва– or –a– are also possible.

| IMPERFECTIVE | PERFECTIVE | IMPERFECTIVE |
| --- | --- | --- |
| писа́ть<br>*to write* | переписа́ть<br>*to copy* | перепи́сывать |
| чита́ть<br>*to read* | прочита́ть<br>*to finish reading or to read through*<br>перечита́ть<br>*to read over* | прочи́тывать<br>перечи́тывать |
| знать<br>*to know* | узна́ть<br>*to find out or to recognize* | узнава́ть |
| дава́ть<br>*to give* | дать<br>отда́ть<br>*to give out or away*<br>переда́ть<br>*to pass*<br>зада́ть<br>*to assign*<br>сдать<br>*to deal cards* | отдава́ть<br>передава́ть<br>задава́ть<br>сдава́ть |

Some perfective verbs have different roots.

| IMPERFECTIVE | PERFECTIVE |
|---|---|
| брать<br>*to take* | взять<br>*to take* |
| сади́ться<br>*to sit* | сесть<br>*to sit* |
| говори́ть<br>*to speak* | сказа́ть<br>*to say* |

Prefixes can be added to either говори́ть or сказа́ть, and each addition makes a new verb, e.g.:

| заговори́ть | *to begin talking* |
|---|---|
| заказа́ть | *to order something* |
| отговори́ть (отгова́ривать) | *to talk someone out of something* |
| рассказа́ть | *to tell a story* |

The past tense of the perfective verb is formed in the same way as the past tense of the imperfective verb.

## H. Future tense

The future tense has two forms: imperfective future and perfective future. As has already been pointed out, the imperfective future is formed by using the auxiliary verb быть with the infinitive of the imperfective verb.

| я бу́ду | говори́ть,<br>чита́ть,<br>рабо́тать, etc. | *I will* | *speak, read, work, etc.* |
|---|---|---|---|
| ты бу́дешь | | *you will* | |
| он бу́дет | | *he will* | |
| мы бу́дем | | *we will* | |
| вы бу́дете | | *you will* | |

| они бу́дут | | they will | |
|---|---|---|---|

The perfective future is formed without the use of the auxiliary verb быть. Since perfective verbs don't have the present tense, their present tense endings signify future. You can tell the difference between present and future by looking at the stem, not the endings.

| PRESENT | | PERFECTIVE FUTURE | |
|---|---|---|---|
| я пишу́ | I write | я напишу́ | I will write |
| ты говори́шь | you speak | ты ска́жешь | you will say |
| мы чита́ем | we read | мы прочита́ем | we will read (it) |
| вы смо́трите | you look | вы посмо́трите | you will look |
| они е́дут | they go (by vehicle) | они прие́дут | they will come (by vehicle) |

Note: The perfective verb is conjugated in the same way as the imperfective verb.

I. Verbs of motion

Verbs of motion have many variations of meaning. A different verb is used to express movement by vehicle than the one used to express movement on foot.

Each of these verbs (i.e., indicating movement on foot or movement by vehicle) has two forms: one describes a continuing or background action in one direction (unidirectional verb of motion), and the other, a single action in the past or a repeated/general action (multidirectional verb of motion). All of these forms are imperfective. The perfective is formed by adding a prefix to a unidirectional verb. But bear in mind that the addition of the prefix changes the meaning of the verb. The same prefix (with the exception of the prefix по–) added to multidirectional verbs of motion forms the imperfective of a new verb.

| IMPERFECTIVE | MULTIDIRECTIONAL | | UNIDIRECTIONAL | PERFECTIVE |
|---|---|---|---|---|
| | ходи́ть | to go on foot | идти́ | |

| IMPERFECTIVE | MULTIDIRECTIONAL | | UNIDIRECTIONAL | PERFECTIVE |
|---|---|---|---|---|
| | е́здить | to go by vehicle | е́хать | |
| выходи́ть | | to exit on foot | | вы́йти |
| выезжа́ть | | to drive out | | вы́ехать |
| приходи́ть | | to come on foot/arrive | | прийти́ |
| приезжа́ть | | to come by vehicle/ arrive | | прие́хать |
| заходить | | to drop in/ visit on foot | | зайти́ |
| заезжа́ть | | to drop in/ visit by vehicle | | зае́хать |
| | носи́ть | to carry on foot | нести́ | |
| | вози́ть | to carry by vehicle | везти́ | |
| приноси́ть | | to bring on foot | | принести́ |
| привози́ть | | to bring by vehicle | | привезти́ |

| ИДТИ́ | |
|---|---|
| *TO WALK* **(UNIDIRECTIONAL)** | |
| **PRESENT TENSE** | **PAST TENSE** |
| я иду́ | шёл (*m.*) |
| ты идёшь | шла (*f.*) |
| он идёт | шло (*n.*) |
| мы идём | шли́ (*pl.*) |
| вы идёте | |
| они́ иду́т | |

| ХОДИ́ТЬ | |
|---|---|
| *TO WALK* **(MULTIDIRECTIONAL)** | |
| **PRESENT TENSE** | **PAST TENSE** |
| я хожу́ | regular |
| ты хо́дишь | |
| он хо́дит | |
| мы хо́дим | |
| вы хо́дите | |
| они́ хо́дят | |

| Е́ХАТЬ | |
|---|---|
| *TO GO BY VEHICLE* **(SINGLE ACTION IN ONE DIRECTION)** | |
| **PRESENT TENSE** | **PAST TENSE** |
| я е́ду | regular |
| ты е́дешь | |
| он е́дет | |
| мы е́дем | |
| вы е́дете | |
| они́ е́дут | |

| ЕЗДИТЬ | |
|---|---|
| _TO GO BY VEHICLE_ **(MULTIDIRECTIONAL)** | |
| **PRESENT TENSE** | **PAST TENSE** |
| я е́зжу | regular |
| ты е́здишь | |
| он е́здит | |
| мы е́здим | |
| вы е́здите | |
| они́ е́здят | |

| НЕСТИ́ | |
|---|---|
| _TO CARRY ON FOOT_ **(UNIDIRECTIONAL)** | |
| **PRESENT TENSE** | **PAST TENSE** |
| я несу́ | нёс (_m._) |
| ты несёшь | несла́ (_f._) |
| он несёт | несло́ (_n._) |
| мы несём | несли́ (_pl._) |
| вы несёте | |
| они́ несу́т | |

| НОСИ́ТЬ | |
|---|---|
| _TO CARRY ON FOOT_ **(MULTIDIRECTIONAL)** | |
| **PRESENT TENSE** | **PAST TENSE** |
| я ношу́ | regular |
| ты но́сишь | |
| он но́сит | |
| мы но́сим | |
| вы но́сите | |
| они́ но́сят | |

| ВЕЗТИ | |
|---|---|
| *TO CARRY BY VEHICLE* (UNIDIRECTIONAL) | |
| **PRESENT TENSE** | **PAST TENSE** |
| я везу́ | вёз (*m.*) |
| ты везёшь | везла́ (*f.*) |
| он везёт | везло́ (*n.*) |
| мы везём | везли́ (*pl.*) |
| вы везёте | |
| они́ везу́т | |

| ВОЗИТЬ | |
|---|---|
| *TO CARRY BY VEHICLE* (MULTIDIRECTIONAL) | |
| **PRESENT TENSE** | **PAST TENSE** |
| я вожу́ | regular |
| ты во́зишь | |
| он во́зит | |
| мы во́зим | |
| вы во́зите | |
| они́ во́зят | |

## J. Subjunctive and conditional moods

The subjunctive and conditional in many languages constitute one of the most difficult grammatical constructions. However, in Russian they are easy and much less common. To form the subjunctive or conditional, the past tense of the verb is used together with the particle бы. Note that this form denotes the unrealizable condition only. For all real conditions, use the future tense.

| если бы | *if* |
|---|---|
| е́сли бы я знал | *if I had known* |
| я пошёл бы | *I would have gone* |
| Я позвони́л бы, е́сли бы у меня́ был ваш но́мер. | *I would have called you, had I had your telephone number.* |

## K. Imperatives

The imperative form of a verb is derived from its third person plural present tense form. If the conjugated form has an –й– in its stem (which often "hides" in the vowels я, ю, е, or ё after vowels), use this glide and cut off the rest of the ending. If the verbal stem doesn't have an й, check the stress in the first person singular. If the stress falls on the ending, replace this ending with –и, if the stress is on the stem, with a –ь. If the ending has two consonants, always add an –и regardless of the stress pattern. For the plural imperative, simply add –те to the singular imperative form.

| INFINITIVE | THIRD PERSON SINGULAR | FAMILIAR, SINGULAR | POLITE, PLURAL |
|---|---|---|---|
| писа́ть *to write* | пи́ш-ут пишу́ | пиши́ | пиши́те |
| повторя́ть *to repeat* | повторя[й-у]-т | повторя́й | повторя́йте |
| броса́ть *to throw* | броса[й-у]-т | броса́й | броса́йте |
| рабо́тать *to work* | работа[й-у]-т | рабо́тай | рабо́тайте |
| говори́ть *to speak* | говор-ят говорю́ | говори́ | говори́те |
| быть *to be* | бу́д-ут бу́ду | будь | бу́дьте |
| по́мнить *to remember* | по́мнишь | по́мни | по́мните |

When forming imperatives, the reflexive verb retains its ending -ся after a consonant or -й, and -сь after a vowel.

| мы́ться *to wash oneself* | мо[й-у]-тся | мо́йся | мо́йтесь |
|---|---|---|---|

| занима́ться *to study* | занима́[й-у]-тся | занима́йся | занима́йтесь |
|---|---|---|---|
| учи́ться *to study* | у́ч-атся учу́сь | учи́сь | учи́тесь |

In giving an order indirectly to a third person or persons, the forms пусть and пуска́й (*coll.*) are used with the conjugated non-past form of the verb. The following verb is future perfective if the speaker assigns the task (change of state); if the speaker consents to the other party's intention, use the imperfective present verb (no change of state in the existing context).

| Пусть он прочита́ет. | *Have him read (I want him to).* | Пусть он чита́ет | *Let him read (if he wants to).* |
|---|---|---|---|
| Пуска́й она́ ска́жет. | *Have her say (I want her to).* | Пусть она́ говори́т. | *Let her speak (if she wants to).* |

L. Participles and gerunds

Participles and gerunds are very important parts of the Russian language, so it is necessary to know how to recognize and understand them. However, it should be made clear that they are rarely used in simple conversation, but rather in literature and more formal discourse.

Participles are verbal adjectives; gerunds are adverbials. Participles are adjectives made out of verbs. The difference between an adjective and a participle is that a participle retains the verbal qualities of tense, aspect and voice. In every other respect they are adjectives. They have three genders: masculine, feminine, and neuter. They decline the same way as adjectives and agree with the words they modify in gender, case, and number.

| | **PRESENT** | **PAST** |
|---|---|---|
| говори́ть *to speak* | говоря́щий, –ая, –ее, –ие | говори́вший, –ая, –ее, –ие |

Here's an example in the prepositional plural.

Мы говори́м о говоря́щих по-англи́йски ученика́х.

or

Мы говори́м об ученика́х, говоря́щих по-англи́йски.

*We are talking about students who speak English (lit., speaking English students).*

Notice that, when the entire participial phrase follows the noun it modifies, it should be surrounded by commas; no commas are needed if it precedes the noun.

Gerunds are adverbials and as such do not change, but can be imperfective and perfective. The imperfective gerunds are characterized by a simultaneous action in any tense. The perfective gerunds are used when there are two actions, one following the other; when the first action is completed, the second one starts.

| IMPERFECTIVE | |
|---|---|
| чита́ть | Чита́я, он улыба́лся. |
| | *While reading, he was smiling.* (two simultaneous actions) |

| PERFECTIVE | |
|---|---|
| прочита́ть | Прочита́в газе́ту, он встал и ушёл. |
| | *Having finished reading the paper, he got up and left.* (one action following the other) |